PLANTS & FUNGI!

DK SMITHSONIAN
PLANTS & FUNGI!

Contributors Professor Lynne Boddy MBE, Dr. Chris Clennett,
Wendy Horobin, Dr. Sarah Jose, Jo Locke

Consultants Professor Lynne Boddy MBE, Cardiff University;
Professor Beverley Glover, Cambridge University Botanic Garden

Illustrators Andrew Beckett, Peter Bull, Arran Lewis,
Sofian Moumene, and KJA Artists

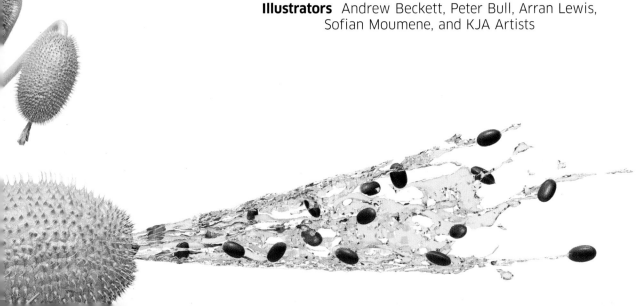

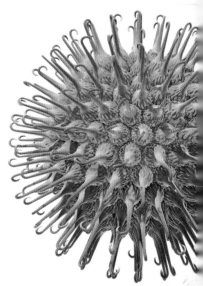

DK LONDON
Senior editor Ben Morgan
Senior art editor Emma Clayton
Editors Jolyon Goddard, Sarah MacLeod, Jane Simmonds
Designers Tannishtha Chakraborty, Laura Gardner, Tory Gordon-Harris, Clare Joyce, Lynne Moulding, Samantha Richiardi, Smiljka Surla
US Senior editor Kayla Dugger
US Executive editor Lori Cates Hand
Managing editor Rachel Fox
Managing art editor Owen Peyton Jones
Senior production editor Andy Hilliard
Production controller Laura Andrews
Jacket design development manager Sophia MTT
Publisher Andrew Macintyre
Associate publishing director Liz Wheeler
Art director Karen Self
Publishing director Jonathan Metcalf

DK DELHI
Senior editor Rupa Rao
Senior art editor Ragini Rawat
Project art editor Revati Anand
Editor Bipasha Roy
Assistant editor Arpit Aggarwal
Illustrators Aparajita Sen, Diya Varma
Assistant picture researcher Geetam Biswas
Picture research manager Taiyaba Khatoon
Managing editor Kingshuk Ghoshal
Managing art editor Govind Mittal
DTP designers Rakesh Kumar, Mohammad Rizwan, Anita Yadav
Pre-production manager Balwant Singh
Production manager Pankaj Sharma
Senior jacket designer Suhita Dharamjit
Senior jackets coordinator Priyanka Sharma Saddi
DK India Creative head Malavika Talukder

First American Edition, 2023
Published in the United States by DK Publishing
1745 Broadway, 20th Floor, New York, NY 10019

For the curious
www.dk.com

Smithsonian

Established in 1846, the Smithsonian is the world's largest museum and research complex, dedicated to public education, national service, and scholarship in the arts, sciences, and history. It includes 21 museums and galleries and the National Zoological Park. The total number of artifacts, works of art, and specimens in the Smithsonian's collection is estimated at 155.5 million.

MIX
Paper | Supporting responsible forestry
FSC™ C018179

This book was made with Forest Stewardship Council™ certified paper—one small step in DK's commitment to a sustainable future.
For more information go to www.dk.com/our-green-pledge

CONTENTS

Warning
Many of the plants and mushrooms found in the wild contain substances that may be poisonous or cause allergic reactions. You shouldn't pick wild plants or mushrooms to eat and should take care if handling them. If a double-page topic in this book has a warning symbol, you should take extra care not to touch the plants or fungi shown. This book aims to give general information on plants and mushrooms and every effort has been made to ensure the accuracy of the information. However, in no circumstances can the publisher or the authors accept any liability for any loss, injury, or damage arising from the use of any information contained in this book.

6   why plants and fungi matter

Oxygen from plants helps screen Earth's surface from **harmful ultraviolet rays** from the Sun.

Why plants and fungi matter

Plants and fungi make our planet what it is. Without them, we would not be here.

About 500 million years ago, plants began to colonize land. Fungi were already there. Plants and fungi teamed up and transformed the planet. Forests had spread across the continents by 380 million years ago, providing food and habitats for animals. Along with algae in the seas, plants pumped oxygen into the atmosphere and removed carbon dioxide. The air became breathable and life flourished. Today, we rely on plants and fungi as much as ever.

Habitats
Plants provide homes for all sorts of animals, large and small. Fungi help make homes for them too by rotting wood and creating hollows in trees.

Renewable materials
Plants and fungi provide us with many renewable materials. We use timber to build houses and furniture and cotton to make clothes. Fungi are used to make biodegradable packaging and to manufacture industrial chemicals.

Digestion
Plant-eating animals need help from fungi and other microbes to digest food. Herbivores such as deer have fungi in their stomachs to break down leaves, and some termites and ants have "fungus gardens" to turn leaves into food.

Soil
Fungi help turn dead organic matter into soil. As well as breaking down leaves and wood, they help bind soil together, preventing it from being blown away by wind or washed away in the rain.

Recycling
Every year, Earth's plants make more than 55 billion tons of organic matter. To keep things in balance, fungi break down and recycle a similar amount, releasing mineral nutrients that plants can use.

Making food
Through photosynthesis, plants and algae capture the energy in sunlight and use it to make the food that all other organisms rely on. So plants provide the power to run every ecosystem.

Every year, a mature tree releases as much oxygen as **10 people** breathe in.

The first organisms to photosynthesize appeared 3.4 billion years ago in the oceans.

7

Clean air
Trees clean the air by trapping dust and pollutants. They also reduce noise, provide shade, help prevent floods, and can cool our cities by several degrees.

Climate
Plants and algae help regulate the climate. When they photosynthesize, they absorb carbon dioxide from the atmosphere, which helps reduce the greenhouse effect.

Medicines
Plants and fungi are the source of many medicines. The painkiller aspirin originally came from the bark of willow trees, and the antibiotics that fight all sorts of infections were first discovered in fungi.

Oxygen
The process of photosynthesis releases oxygen into the air, which humans and other animals breathe.

Biodiversity
There are millions of different plant and fungus species. This great diversity helps keep ecosystems healthy, providing food to millions of animal species and ensuring that nutrient cycles keep working efficiently.

Food from fungi
Many small animals rely on fungi for food. Humans have used fungi for centuries to make bread, cheese, and wine.

Mycorrhizas
Fungi are essential for plant growth. Soil-dwelling fungi form partnerships called mycorrhizas with the roots of plants. The fungi provide water and minerals to plants, and plants provide sugars from photosynthesis in exchange.

THE PLANT KINGDOM

Wherever there is water, light, and air, plants are almost sure to grow. Scientists have identified and named around 400,000 different types of plants. These range from tiny, simple plants no bigger than grains of rice to the largest organisms to ever live on Earth.

10   the plant kingdom · **WHAT IS A PLANT?**

We share about **60 percent of our genes** with the average plant.

What is a plant?

The plant kingdom is made up of hundreds of thousands of very different species, from tiny mosses to towering redwood trees. Despite their diversity, all plants have certain key features in common.

It's easy to tell plants apart from animals. Plants are usually green, grow rooted to one spot, and make food using sunlight (photosynthesis). However, some organisms look like plants but aren't—such as seaweeds. The scientific definition of a plant is any member of a group of related organisms called embryophytes. Embryophytes either live on land or evolved from ancestors that lived on land. They make food in leaves by photosynthesis, and they grow from embryos that form inside or attached to their parents.

DEFINING FEATURES

When you think of a plant, you might picture broad leaves and colorful flowers, but not all plants are like that. To identify the features that all plants share, we have to look closer and examine their cells and the way they reproduce.

Sexual reproduction
Not all plants make flowers or seeds. However, sexual reproduction always produces an embryo that starts life protected inside or attached to the parent plant. This is very different from the way seaweeds reproduce.

Photosynthesis
Plants use light energy to make food molecules in a chemical process called photosynthesis.

Growth
Plants don't stop growing when they become mature. They keep adding new branches and roots from stem cells—cells that can divide and form any other kind of cell.

Immobility
Plants grow fixed to one spot and can't move around as animals can. However, not all plants have roots. Some have simpler, hairlike structures called rhizoids merely to anchor them to the ground.

Leaves
All plants have leaves of some kind, though they may not be obvious. In mosses, they are very tiny, and in cacti, they have become defensive spines.

Cell wall
Plant cells have certain features not found in other organisms. One is a tough cell wall made of a fibrous substance called cellulose.

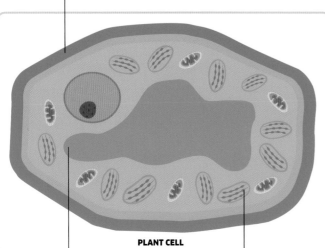

PLANT CELL

Vacuole
Plant cells have a water-storage area called a vacuole. Vacuoles keep cells plump to stop a plant from wilting.

Chloroplast
Plant cells contain tiny green bodies called chloroplasts. Photosynthesis takes place inside these bodies.

400,000 —the approximate **number of plant species** known to science.

11

PLANT OR NOT?

The wonderful diversity of the natural world can be confusing. Some organisms look, grow, and feed like plants but belong to other kingdoms of life. And a few true plants have lost some of their defining features.

Plant: living stone
Living stones are found in deserts and look more like stones than plants. The camouflage protects their precious store of water from thirsty animals.

Not plant: coral
Colorful corals are sometimes mistaken for aquatic plants, but they are actually colonies of tiny brainless animals. Many have photosynthesizing algae living inside them, so like plants, they can obtain food by photosynthesis.

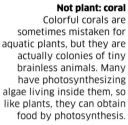

Not plant: algae
Seaweeds and the slimy green stuff in ponds are not plants but algae. Algae use chlorophyll to photosynthesize, but they can't live out of water and they reproduce in a different way from plants.

Plant: ghost plant
This ghostly white plant has no chlorophyll because it has given up photosynthesizing and steals food from other organisms. However, it has all the other defining features of a true plant.

Plant: watermeal
This may look like algae, but watermeal (duckweed) is actually the smallest flowering plant in the world. It grows floating on water.

Not plant: mushrooms
Although mushrooms are immobile and have rigid cell walls, they do not photosynthesize. They are more closely related to humans than to plants.

PHOTOSYNTHESIS

With just a handful of exceptions, all plants make food by photosynthesis. In this process, plants capture energy from the Sun and use it to convert carbon dioxide (from air) and water (usually from soil) into sugar molecules. The sugar can then be used as a kind of fuel to power other chemical processes. Or it can be used as a building block to make larger molecules needed for growth.

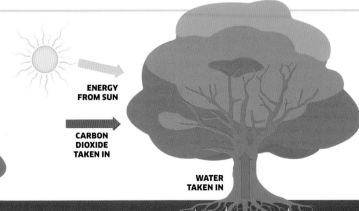

ENERGY FROM SUN

CARBON DIOXIDE TAKEN IN

OXYGEN RELEASED AS WASTE

WATER TAKEN IN

Classifying plants

Since ancient times, people have tried to make sense of the natural world by naming each type of animal and plant and grouping them in families. The process of classifying plants continues to this day and is now based on how plants evolved.

A distinct type of plant that can breed with other individuals of the same type—such as an apple tree or a buttercup—is called a species. There are hundreds of thousands of different plant species, but anyone who studies plants soon notices patterns among them. For example, apple trees have similar flowers to wild roses, peaches, and plums, so all these are grouped together in the rose family. In the past, people used the features of flowers to classify plants, but today scientists study every part of a plant, including its DNA. These studies have helped them build a family tree of the entire plant kingdom.

THE PLANT KINGDOM

The plant kingdom is one of the major kingdoms of life, along with the animal kingdom, fungus kingdom, and several kingdoms of mostly microscopic organisms. The first members of the plant kingdom appeared about 500 million years ago when aquatic organisms called algae began to live in the margins between land and water. As plants gradually evolved to live outside water, their descendants split into the major groups of plants that we know today.

CORD MOSS

SCAPANIA, A LIVERWORT

Mosses, liverworts, and hornworts
The first true plants were close relatives of today's mosses, liverworts, and hornworts. These plants are restricted to damp habitats because they reproduce using sperm cells that swim through water. They spread by making spores rather than seeds, and they have no roots or veins.

480 MILLION YEARS AGO: FIRST LAND PLANTS

Gymnosperms
The evolution of seeds and pollen, which replaced free-swimming sperm, finally freed plants from damp habitats. The first seed plants were gymnosperms, which produce seeds in cones like those of today's conifers.

FIR CONE

SEEDS

FIR TREE

320 MILLION YEARS AGO: SEEDS EVOLVE

NOT PLANTS

PLANTS

ONE BILLION YEARS AGO: GREEN ALGAE EVOLVE

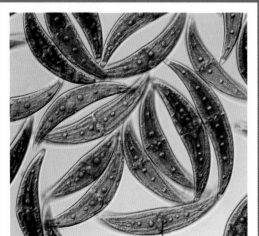

Green algae
Plants evolved from aquatic organisms called green algae. These very simple life forms use chlorophyll to photosynthesize, but they do not have roots, leaves, seeds, or flowers.

The single-celled green alga *Closterium* is a close relative of the first land plants.

450 MILLION YEARS AGO: VEINS AND ROOTS EVOLVE

COMMON CLUB MOSS, A LYCOPHYTE

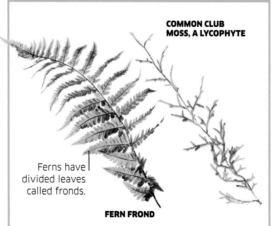

Ferns have divided leaves called fronds.

FERN FROND

Ferns and lycophytes
Ferns and their lycophyte relatives are vascular plants, which means they have veins to carry water and nutrients around the plant and to provide structural support. This allows them to grow much larger than nonvascular plants and survive in drier conditions. However, like nonvascular plants, ferns and lycophytes need damp habitats for their sexual reproduction, which relies on swimming sperm cells.

250-150 MILLION YEARS AGO: FLOWERS EVOLVE

Flowering plants
While gymnosperms rely on wind to pollinate cones, flowering plants evolved partnerships with pollinating animals such as insects. Sexual reproduction became much more efficient as the shapes, colors, and scents of different flowers adapted to suit specific pollinators. Thanks partly to this breakthrough, flowering plants became the dominant group of plants in the world.

MAGNOLIA FLOWER

The first tree, a close relative of ferns, lived **385 million years ago**.

432 million years—the age of the **oldest** known plant fossil, *Cooksonia barrandei*.

13

SCIENTIFIC NAMES

Just like animals, every plant species has a scientific name with two parts as well as its more familiar common name. The peach tree, for instance, is *Prunus persica*. The second word is unique to the species, while the first is its genus—a group that includes closely related species, such as apricots, nectarines, and plums. Similar genera (the plural of genus) are grouped together to form a family, similar families are grouped to form an order, and so on.

Domain
Eukaryota (organisms with a cell nucleus)

Kingdom
Plantae (the plant kingdom)

Division
Angiosperms (flowering plants)

Class
Eudicots (flowering plants whose seeds contain two baby leaves)

Order
Rosales (rose family and related families)

Family
Rosaceae (rose family)

Genus
Prunus (peaches, plums, cherries, and relatives)

Species
Prunus persica
(peach tree)

PEACH TREE

OTHER PLANT CATEGORIES

While scientists base plant classification on evolution, gardeners often use other systems, such as the shapes of plants or how long they live. Many of the terms they use for these features work in pairs.

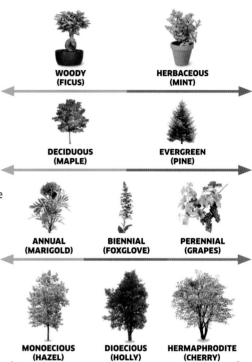

Woody plants, such as trees, have stems strengthened by woody tissue, while herbaceous plants do not.

WOODY (FICUS) **HERBACEOUS (MINT)**

Deciduous plants shed their leaves, usually in fall and winter, while evergreen trees keep them.

DECIDUOUS (MAPLE) **EVERGREEN (PINE)**

Annual plants complete their life cycle in one year. Biennials live for two years and perennials live for many years.

ANNUAL (MARIGOLD) **BIENNIAL (FOXGLOVE)** **PERENNIAL (GRAPES)**

Monoecious plants have separate male and female flowers on the same plant, while dioecious plants are either wholly male or female. Hermaphrodites have male and female parts on the same flower.

MONOECIOUS (HAZEL) **DIOECIOUS (HOLLY)** **HERMAPHRODITE (CHERRY)**

MAJOR FAMILIES

There are more than 600 plant families, most of which are families of flowering plants. The top five are shown here.

Asteraceae (daisies)
Members of this family have composite flowers made of small individual flowers (florets). Many garden flowers belong to this family.

CHRYSANTHEMUM

Rubiaceae (coffees and bedstraws)
These tropical and subtropical plants include trees, lianas (vines), herbs, and coffee plants.

COFFEE FLOWERS

PEA FLOWERS

Orchidaceae (orchids)
Orchid flowers are symmetrical and produce extremely tiny seeds. Many orchids are epiphytes (plants that grow on other plants).

CATTLEYA ORCHID

Fabaceae (legumes)
The legumes include important food crops such as peas, beans, and lentils. Their roots contain microorganisms that convert nitrogen from air into nitrate minerals used for growth.

Poaceae (grasses)
Grasses include grain crops such as wheat, rice, and maize, and the largest grasses of all—bamboos. Wheat is grown for its nutritious seeds, which are ground to make flour for making bread and other foods.

WHEAT

14 the plant kingdom ∘ **ALGAE AND SEAWEEDS**

Giant kelp, the **world's largest seaweed,** can grow to more than 196 ft (60 m) tall.

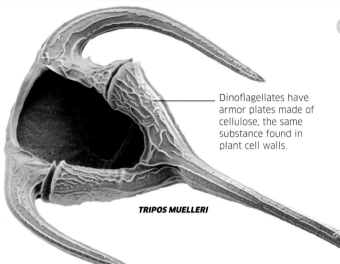

Dinoflagellates have armor plates made of cellulose, the same substance found in plant cell walls.

TRIPOS MUELLERI

DINOFLAGELLATES

Type: Phytoplankton
Habitat: Fresh and marine water
Size: Up to 0.08 in (2 mm)

These single-celled algae are so named because they have a pair of microscopic whips (flagella) used for swimming. Some dinoflagellates emit light, making the sea glow blue-green at night. Occasionally, dinoflagellates multiply in such numbers that they cause "red tides," turning patches of sea red and poisoning fish.

DIATOMS

Type: Phytoplankton
Habitat: Fresh and marine water, as well as soils, damp surfaces, and ice
Size: 0.001–0.01 in (0.02–0.2 mm)

Diatoms produce almost half the oxygen in Earth's atmosphere. Their cell walls are hardened by silica—the main ingredient in glass—and take many different shapes, some resembling tiny jewels. Most diatoms live floating in the sea, but some live inside other organisms and provide them with food.

Algae and seaweeds

You may have heard that plants make the oxygen we breathe, but most of our oxygen doesn't come from plants. Instead, it comes from aquatic organisms called algae.

Scientists use the word "algae" for all sorts of organisms that live in water and can make food through photosynthesis. Algae are very different from land plants, so they are not classed as members of the plant kingdom. Most are microscopic single cells that live floating in water. Leave a glass of water on a sunny windowsill for a few days and algae will soon appear, creating a greenish haze. Microscopic floating algae are called phytoplankton and form the base of marine and freshwater food chains. Other algae, such as seaweeds, grow as large as plants.

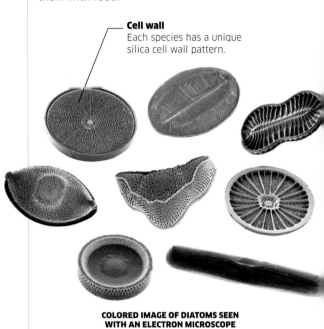

Cell wall
Each species has a unique silica cell wall pattern.

COLORED IMAGE OF DIATOMS SEEN WITH AN ELECTRON MICROSCOPE

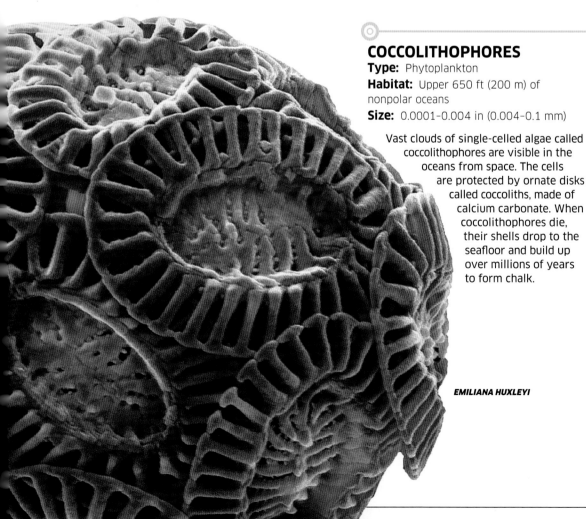

EMILIANA HUXLEYI

COCCOLITHOPHORES

Type: Phytoplankton
Habitat: Upper 650 ft (200 m) of nonpolar oceans
Size: 0.0001–0.004 in (0.004–0.1 mm)

Vast clouds of single-celled algae called coccolithophores are visible in the oceans from space. The cells are protected by ornate disks called coccoliths, made of calcium carbonate. When coccolithophores die, their shells drop to the seafloor and build up over millions of years to form chalk.

SPIROGYRA

Type: Phytoplankton
Habitat: Freshwater habitats and stagnant water
Size: Up to 0.004 in (0.1 mm) wide and several centimeters long

This alga is visible to the naked eye as a slimy green scum floating in standing water. However, a close look through a microscope reveals its intricate structure. It grows in long threads a single cell wide, with each cell containing a spiral-shaped green chloroplast.

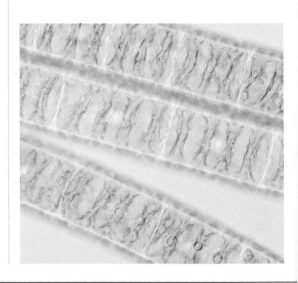

There are about **1 billion billion billion phytoplankton** in the world's oceans.

Cyanobacteria have been living on Earth for **2.9 billion years**.

15

CYANOBACTERIA

Type: Phytoplankton
Habitat: Every kind of aquatic habitat and on wet ground and damp rocks
Size: 0.00004–0.0004 in (0.001–0.01 mm)

Cyanobacteria are the smallest known photosynthesizing organisms. Although sometimes called blue-green algae, they are not algae and belong to a very different domain of life: the bacteria. Despite this, they are considered to be phytoplankton and form a very important part of marine food chains.

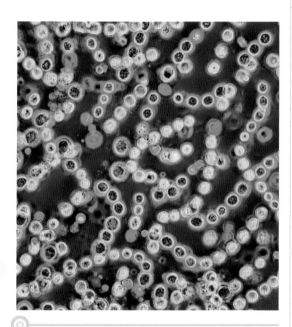

PYROPIA

Type: Red algae (seaweed)
Habitat: Temperate ocean shoreline
Size: Up to 19 in (50 cm)

The thin, delicate fronds of this seaweed are used to make the nori sheets used to wrap sushi. It looks similar to sea lettuce but is red because its chloroplasts use red pigments as well as chlorophyll to capture sunlight for photosynthesis.

Sushi is wrapped with *Pyropia*.

PYROPIA LEUCOSTICTA

EUGLENA

Type: Phytoplankton
Habitat: Ponds, lakes, damp soil, and saltwater
Size: Up to 0.02 in (0.5 mm)

This single-celled alga baffled early biologists, as it seemed to be halfway between animal and plant. *Euglena* contains chloroplasts and can photosynthesize, but it can also swim around by beating its flagellum and it can survive in dark water by taking in food.

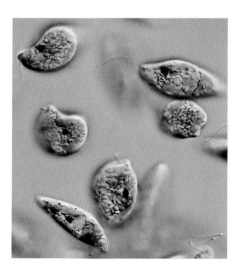

BLADDERWRACK

Type: Brown algae (seaweed)
Habitat: Temperate and polar shorelines
Size: Up to 5 ft (1.5 m)

Air-filled "bladders" keep the fronds of this floppy seaweed upright when submerged at high tide, helping them absorb sunlight. At the base of the seaweed is a rootlike structure that anchors it to rock so that waves won't wash it away. Brown algae such as bladderwrack are very common on rocky beaches in cooler parts of the world.

Bladder

FUCUS VESICULOSUS

The leaflike sheets are just two cells thick, giving sea lettuce a translucent appearance.

ULVA LACTUCA

SEA LETTUCE

Type: Green algae (seaweed)
Habitat: Ocean shoreline
Size: Up to 23 in (60 cm)

A bright green, edible seaweed, the sea lettuce clings to rocks with a tiny, disklike holdfast. Green algae such as sea lettuce use the same kinds of chlorophyll as plants to capture light for photosynthesis.

NODDING THREAD-MOSS
Pohlia nutans

Location: All seven continents

Size: Up to 3 in (8 cm) tall

This common moss grows in boggy soil, on rocks, and on rotting logs—habitats where there is little soil for larger plants to thrive. Its green spore capsules grow on bright red stems, shedding their microscopic spores into the wind like tiny pepper pots.

Club-shaped spore capsule

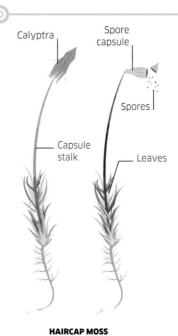

Calyptra

Spore capsule

Spores

Capsule stalk

Leaves

HAIRCAP MOSS

Reddish-brown spore capsules

HAIRCAP MOSS
Polytrichum

Location: Asia, Europe, and North America

Size: Up to 12 in (30 cm) tall

This common moss forms large cushions packed with dark, spiky leaves. The leaves fold back against the stem when dry but spread out when moist. The reddish spore capsules develop at the tips of tall stalks. Each is protected by a structure called a calyptra; on these mosses, it looks like a shower cap, or haircap.

Moss life cycle

The life cycle of mosses and liverworts alternates between two distinct kinds of plants: one that makes sex cells and another that makes spores. This is known as alternation of generations and is a feature of all plants, though not always obvious. In mosses and liverworts, one generation grows out of the other, giving the appearance of a single plant.

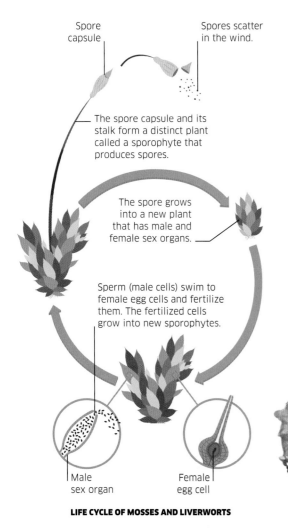

Spore capsule

Spores scatter in the wind.

The spore capsule and its stalk form a distinct plant called a sporophyte that produces spores.

The spore grows into a new plant that has male and female sex organs.

Sperm (male cells) swim to female egg cells and fertilize them. The fertilized cells grow into new sporophytes.

Male sex organ

Female egg cell

LIFE CYCLE OF MOSSES AND LIVERWORTS

Mosses and liverworts

The simplest and most ancient types of plant to live on land, mosses and liverworts first appeared about 480 million years ago. These small plants have changed relatively little since then.

Mosses and liverworts have no true roots and no veins to carry water, so most are restricted to damp habitats and are small, forming clumps or cushions. Even so, they can be remarkably tough. They don't produce flowers or spread by making seeds. Instead, they spread to new habitats by releasing tiny, single-celled particles called spores.

LIVERWORT
Marchantia polymorpha

Location: Europe

Size: Up to 4 in (10 cm) across, with spore-bearing structures up to 1 in (2 cm) tall

Liverworts are so named because many types have a flat shape with leaflike lobes, which resemble lobes of the human liver. Other liverwort species look very similar to mosses, though they are only distantly related.

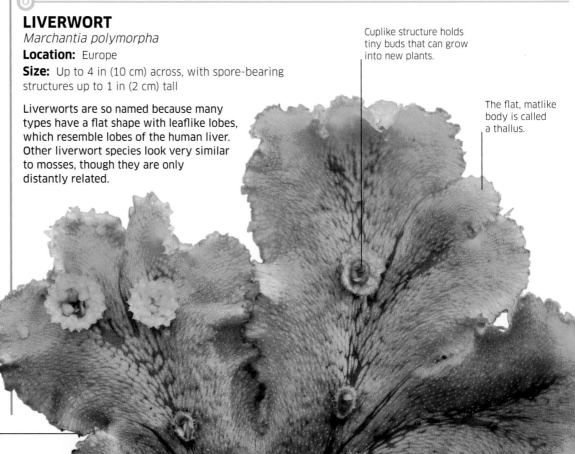

Cuplike structure holds tiny buds that can grow into new plants.

The flat, matlike body is called a thallus.

Ferns

Like mosses and liverworts, ferns spread by making spores and never produce flowers or seeds. However, they have features that mosses and liverworts lack, such as roots and veins, allowing them to grow bigger, with large, often divided leaves (fronds).

Ferns are an ancient group of plants that first appeared around 400 million years ago. Some grow to tree size, while others remain tiny and hidden in shady places. Ferns can survive in drier places than mosses and liverworts, but the reproductive stage of their life cycle needs damp conditions because, like mosses and liverworts, ferns also release sperm cells that swim through water to find female cells.

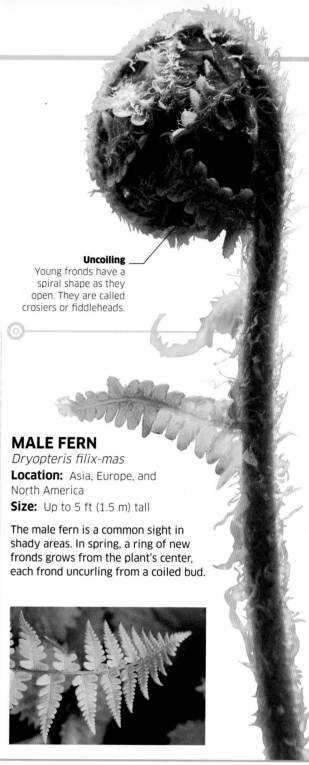

Uncoiling
Young fronds have a spiral shape as they open. They are called crosiers or fiddleheads.

NORTHERN MAIDENHAIR FERN
Adiantum pedatum
Location: South America
Size: Up to 20 in (50 cm) tall

This small fern is called maidenhair because its thin black stalks look like hair. The fronds are divided into lobes, creating a cascade of what looks like hundreds of tiny leaves. It grows well indoors and is a very popular houseplant.

SOFT TREE FERN
Dicksonia antarctica
Location: New Zealand
Size: Up to 10 ft (3 m) tall

Tree ferns were common in the age of the dinosaurs but today are found only in damp tropical or subtropical forests. The soft tree fern develops a kind of trunk made up of roots. It grows slowly, increasing in height by only about 1–3 in (2–6 cm) a year. Because the trunk consists of roots, it can be cut and the top part will regrow again if planted.

MALE FERN
Dryopteris filix-mas
Location: Asia, Europe, and North America
Size: Up to 5 ft (1.5 m) tall

The male fern is a common sight in shady areas. In spring, a ring of new fronds grows from the plant's center, each frond uncurling from a coiled bud.

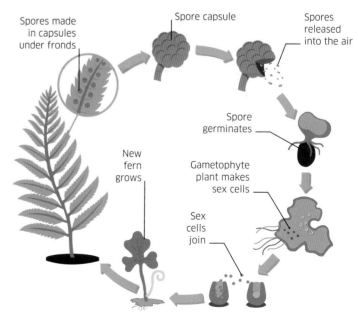

STAGHORN FERN
Platycerium bifurcatum
Location: Australia
Size: Fronds up to 3 ft (1 m) long

Staghorn ferns grow up in the trees. They are epiphytes, which means they use trees for support. They have two types of fronds: heart-shaped ones that photosynthesize, and longer ones that make spores and are shaped like deer antlers.

Fern life cycle

Ferns have a life cycle that involves two distinct plants. Spores are made by the main plant. When a spore germinates, it grows into a tiny plant (a gametophyte) that looks like a liverwort. This plant produces male and female sex cells. The male cells swim through surface water to reach the female cells. After the two join, the first frond of a new fern plant grows and the cycle continues.

Spores made in capsules under fronds

Spore capsule

Spores released into the air

Spore germinates

New fern grows

Gametophyte plant makes sex cells

Sex cells join

Spore capsules

In late summer, neat rows of brown bumps appear on the underside of fern leaves. Each bump is a cluster of tiny round spore capsules.

Ferns spread by catapulting single-celled particles called spores into the air. These develop inside capsules called sporangia, each of which contains 64 spores. Wrapping around every sporangium is a chain of cells (orange in this image) that acts as a kind of spring mechanism. As spores ripen, the spring gradually dries out, which makes it uncurl and tear open the capsule. Finally, when completely dry, it flicks back suddenly into its curved shape and hurls the spores away.

Conifers are found on **every continent except Antarctica.**

Earth's northern hemisphere has **2.3 million sq miles (6 million sq km)** of conifer forest.

Conifers

Conifers are plants that produce seeds inside cones— hence their name, which means "cone-bearing" in Latin. They have no flowers or fruits, and most are evergreen trees with needle-shaped leaves.

Conifer trees cover huge swathes of the cold lands in the northern hemisphere, forming a continuous belt of forest around the globe from Alaska to Canada, Scandinavia, and Russia. Conifers also flourish on mountains and in deserts. They are tough plants, with many features that help them endure harsh conditions— from natural antifreeze in their cells to a waterproof covering on their needles to preserve water.

GIANT REDWOOD
Sequoiadendron giganteum

Location: Sierra Nevada mountains, California, USA

Height: Up to 278 ft (85 m)

The giant redwood is among the tallest and most long-lived trees in the world and can reach an age of more than 3,000 years. As a young tree, it has a triangular shape. As it ages, the lower branches are shed and a tall trunk covered with reddish, fire-resistant bark develops.

Oval cones
Egg-shaped female cones grow up to 2.7 in (7 cm) long.

MEDITERRANEAN CYPRESS
Cupressus sempervirens

Location: Mediterranean countries and western Asia

Height: Up to 115 ft (35 m)

This very slender conifer is a familiar sight in Mediterranean countries such as Greece, where the trees stand out on hillsides. Its scented timber was once used to make church doors and musical instruments.

Cone clusters
Small, round cones grow in clusters among dense evergreen foliage.

Life cycle of a conifer

Conifers reproduce by making seeds, but they have cones instead of flowers. Cones are either male or female. Male cones release pollen, a dustlike substance that is dispersed by the wind onto female cones. It fertilizes female cells inside ovules, which then turn into seeds.

Mature conifer

Female cone produces ovules

Male cone releases pollen

Male cone

Seeds released from mature cone

Ovules pollinated by pollen

Seeds develop inside cone

380 ft (116 m)—the height of the **world's tallest living tree,** a coast redwood in California.

21

SCOTS PINE
Pinus sylvestris

Location: Asia and Europe
Height: Up to 115 ft (35 m)

Britain's only native conifer gets its name from Scotland, but this species is found across Europe and Asia. It typically has orange-red bark and bluish-green needles arranged in pairs. Its cones take up to three years to mature, changing from green to brown as they ripen.

Inside a needle
Pine needles are covered in a layer of waterproof wax to conserve water. Transport vessels for water and sugar run down the middle. Smaller vessels carry pine resin, a sticky substance that seals wounds and repels insects.

Layer of waterproof wax

Resin canal

Central cylinder containing transport vessels

Stoma (pore)

Seed

Inside a pine cone
The female cones are made up of scales arranged in a spiral. On the top of each scale is a naked seed (a seed without a seed coat).

Pine cones
Female cones produce seeds after fertilization.

Pine needles
Like most conifers, the Scots pine has needlelike leaves. Their narrow shape helps reduce water loss and keeps snow from building up.

Thick bark
The mature bark is gray-green, while younger branches at the top of the tree are more reddish.

MONKEY PUZZLE
Araucaria araucana

Location: Lower slopes of the Andes mountains
Height: Up to 98 ft (30 m)

This South American conifer clings to life amid volcanic lava flows in Argentina and Chile. Its unusual name comes from an English lawyer who in 1850 saw the spiky leaves and declared that "even a monkey would puzzle how to climb this tree."

Spiky leaves grow directly from the trunk and branches.

KAURI
Agathis australis

Location: New Zealand's North Island
Height: Up to 164 ft (50 m)

The kauri of New Zealand is one of the world's largest conifers, with a trunk that can reach 16 ft (5 m) wide. It looks very different from most conifers, with flat leaves and round cones that break apart when seeds are shed.

Leathery leaves
Flat and thick, the leathery leaves can grow to 2.7 in (7 cm) long.

Round cones
The distinctive cones take up to 20 months to mature and then release winged seeds.

FEMALE KAURI CONE

WOLLEMI PINE
Wollemia nobilis

Location: Wollemi National Park, Australia
Height: Up to 131 ft (40 m)

Confined to only a few valleys in Australia, the Wollemi pine was discovered by scientists in 1994. It is almost identical to fossils of conifers that lived in the Cretaceous Period, around 100 million years ago.

Dangling cones
The male cones dangle from the tree like catkins.

ROSE FAMILY
Rosaceae

Location: Worldwide, especially northern hemisphere

Number of species: Almost 5,000

The rose family includes a wealth of apparently different plants, from apple and peach trees to strawberries and many garden flowers. Linking them all are regular, five-petaled flowers. Their seedheads can vary a great deal, from the glossy red hips of the dog rose to edible fruits, nuts, and dry hooked seeds.

DOG ROSE

Stamens
Flowers typically have a central mass of stamens arranged in a spiral.

Five petals
Flowers are usually radially symmetrical with five petals each.

MINT FAMILY
Lamiaceae

Location: Worldwide

Number of species: Around 7,000

Cooking herbs such as mint, basil, rosemary, thyme, oregano, and sage all come from this family. Their aromatic flavors come from oils secreted by hairs on the leaves to ward off plant eaters.

Fused petals
Flowers of plants in the mint family have fused petals with lips to support large insects such as bees.

COMMON SAGE

Flowering plants

More than three-quarters of all the world's plant species are flowering plants. These plants reproduce sexually by making flowers, seeds, and fruits.

Flowering plants first appeared while dinosaurs still roamed our planet. The earliest flowers were a bit like the cones of conifers, but with bright colors to attract beetles. Using insects to carry pollen from flower to flower was a huge step forward in the evolution of plants and led to an explosion in the number of species. Today, there are around 370,000 known flowering plant species divided into more than 400 families. The biggest families are shown here.

PEA FAMILY
Fabaceae

Location: Worldwide

Number of species: Around 20,000

The flowers of plants in this family develop into distinctive seed pods. They usually have five petals, with one large, upright petal and the others forming a landing platform for insect pollinators. Visiting insects get dusted with pollen from below as their weight pushes down on the platform.

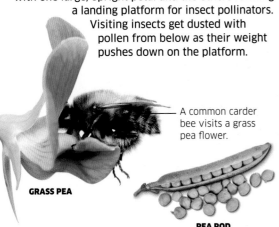

A common carder bee visits a grass pea flower.

GRASS PEA

PEA POD

CABBAGE FAMILY
Brassicaceae

Location: Worldwide

Number of species: Around 4,000

This family contains many of the plants we eat as vegetables, including cabbage, cauliflower, and broccoli. The flowers often develop into pods containing oil-rich seeds, some of which are crops, such as canola and mustard.

The four petals make flowers of plants in this family look like a cross.

WILD CABBAGE

CELERY FAMILY
Apiaceae

Location: Worldwide

Number of species: More than 3,500

Most members of the celery family are small, nonwoody plants with large, umbrella-shaped flower heads (umbels). The family contains edible plants, such as celery and carrots, but also very poisonous ones, such as hemlock.

Umbrella-shaped flower head with many florets (small flowers)

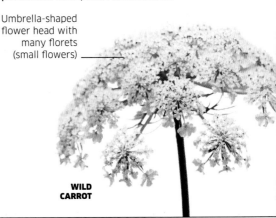

WILD CARROT

Little bigger than a **grain of sand**, watermeal is the smallest flowering plant in the world.

23

DAISY FAMILY
Asteraceae

Location: Worldwide
Number of species: More than 32,000

Starlike flowers make the members of the daisy family easy to recognize. All have a composite flower head made up of hundreds or thousands of tiny individual florets. Together, they appear like one huge flower, which attracts pollinators from afar. Many are small annual plants, but others are long-lived, and a few species are trees.

The outer parts look like petals but are actually whole tiny flowers (florets).

COMMON DAISY

Central florets are packed in a disk.

ORCHID FAMILY
Orchidaceae

Location: Worldwide
Number of species: Around 28,000

The orchids make up one of the largest families of flowering plants. Many are epiphytic, which means they grow on trees, but a large number are ground dwellers with a bulb to store nutrients. Their flowers are complex and often attract only one specific pollinator.

Wasp mimic
The mirror orchid mimics a kind of female wasp, which attracts male wasps.

MIRROR ORCHID

Landing platform
Pollinators land on the bottom part of an orchid flower, which is called a labellum.

LILY FAMILY
Liliaceae

Location: Worldwide
Number of species: Around 600

Plants in the lily family have underground bulbs that store food during cold winters or hot, dry summers. Lilies have what look like six petals, but in fact only three are petals and the other three are sepals that look just like the petals. Lilies and tulips have been cultivated for thousands of years for their flowers.

Long, prominent stamens

Only the inner three petals are true petals.

Leaves with nonbranching, parallel veins

PINK LILY

GRASS FAMILY
Poaceae

Location: Worldwide
Number of species: Around 12,000

Flowers of grasses have no petals and use the wind to carry pollen to other plants. In many grasses, the growing points (meristems) are at the base of the plant, so the leaves keep growing even when the tips are chewed off by animals. This gives grasses an advantage over other plants in habitats with grazing animals.

Tiller
New branches (tillers) grow from the base.

YORKSHIRE FOG

BEDSTRAW FAMILY
Rubiaceae

Location: Mostly tropical or subtropical
Number of species: Around 13,500

Members of the bedstraw family typically have leaves in opposite pairs and flower heads with many tiny flowers. The family includes many tropical species, including coffee. Temperate species include bedstraws and cleavers, whose sticky leaves and seeds often cling to walkers' boots and, like coffee beans, contain caffeine.

LADY'S BEDSTRAW

SILVER BIRCH
Betula pendula

Location: Europe, North America, and western Asia

Size: Height of 98 ft (30 m) with a spread of 33 ft (10 m)

These tough, fast-growing trees can withstand bitterly cold winters and thrive in colder countries and on mountains. Their name comes from the distinctive pale bark. Strong and flexible, the bark can be peeled off in strips and was traditionally used to make canoes in North America.

LEAF

White bark
The bark is smooth and white with black markings.

HORSE CHESTNUT
Aesculus hippocastanum

Location: Originally from the Balkan Peninsula, introduced and naturalized in Europe and parts of North America

Size: Height of 98 ft (30 m) with a spread of 49 ft (15 m)

This large tree is often grown in parks, as it forms a majestic, rounded shape and produces clusters of large, pinkish-white flowers in spring. In fall, the flowers turn into spiky fruits containing conkers. The leaves are palmate (hand shaped), with 5–7 large leaflets.

CONKER **PALMATE LEAF**

Broadleaved trees

Broadleaved trees have leaves that are wide and flat, unlike the needles of conifers. These trees dominate many of the world's forests, from rainforests in the tropics to deciduous woodlands in cooler countries.

Broadleaved trees don't make up a single branch of the plant family tree. Instead, species from many different plant families grow large enough to be described as trees. All these diverse species have several things in common: wide leaves to capture lots of sunlight and a woody trunk to support a canopy of leaves high above the ground.

EUROPEAN BEECH
Fagus sylvatica

Location: Europe

Size: Height of 131 ft (40 m) with a spread of 65 ft (20 m)

Like oak, to which it is related, the beech tree flowers in spring before the leaves open, with male and female flowers growing on separate catkins. The trunk is smooth and grayish, and the leaves are a distinctive oval shape with toothed edges. Few wildflowers grow beneath the beech tree, as its dense canopy of leaves does not let much sunlight reach the ground.

Hard, dry fruits called beech mast are a source of food for animals in fall.

BEECH MAST

BANYAN
Ficus benghalensis

Location: South Asia

Size: Height of 98 ft (30 m) with a spread of 330 ft (100 m)

The banyan is a tropical fig tree from Asia. It starts life as a seed that germinates high up in another tree. Aerial roots grow down to the ground, then become woody trunks, supporting the banyan as it smothers its host. Banyans widen as their hanging roots form ever more trunks. In terms of canopy size, they are the largest trees in the world.

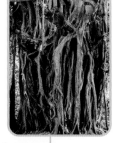

Aerial roots
Roots hang down from the branches and grow into the ground to support the wide canopy.

A cork oak tree can be harvested more than 15 times in its life.

The largest forest of broadleaved trees is the **Amazon Rainforest** in South America.

25

Acorns
The fruits of oak trees are called acorns and change color from green to brown as they ripen. Each consists of a scaly cup containing a single large seed.

RED RIVER GUM
Eucalyptus camaldulensis

Location: Inland Australia and places with a similar climate

Size: Height of 164 ft (50 m) with a spread of 115 ft (35 m)

The most common broadleaved trees in Australia are eucalyptus trees. Their narrow, silvery leaves contain strong-smelling oils that make them inedible to most herbivores. The evergreen red river gum grows on riversides, providing shelter and nesting sites for birds such as the superb parrot.

Antiseptic oils
The oils in the leaves have antiseptic properties and are used to make soap and other cleaning products.

LEAVES

CORK OAK
Quercus suber

Location: Southwestern Europe around the Mediterranean Sea

Size: Height of 65 ft (20 m) with a spread of 65 ft (20 m)

This evergreen oak grows in hot, dry countries. It has thick, fire-resistant bark that has been used for centuries to make bottle corks. The bark is harvested sustainably by removing thin strips once a decade, then letting it regrow.

Knobby bark
The fire-resistant bark gets thicker and spongier as the tree grows.

SAGUARO
Carnegiea gigantea

Location: Southwestern USA and Sonora in Mexico

Height: Up to 52 ft (16 m)

Saguaros grow as tall as trees and have ribbed stems that can expand to store water. Their flowers grow in clusters right at the top, where pollinating bats can reach them easily. Like most cacti, they are pollinated at night.

Slow growers
Saguaro cacti don't grow branches until around 75 years old.

GOLDEN BARREL CACTUS
Echinocactus grusonii

Location: Central Mexico

Height: Up to 3 ft (1 m)

Barrel cacti get their name from their round shape. Dense spines protect the flesh from herbivores and trap still air around the plant to reduce evaporation. When times are good, vibrant yellow flowers sprout around the top.

Vertical ribs
Vertical ribs allow the cactus to expand and contract as water is absorbed or used up.

Cacti and succulents

Plants that store water to survive in deserts are known as succulents. The most famous succulents are the cacti, which make up a single botanical family native to the Americas.

In places with little rain, plants must catch and store as much water as they can. They might do this with a swollen stem, a large root, or fleshy leaves. Cacti store water in swollen stems and have prickly spines instead of leaves for protection. Many desert plants also have large root systems to reach water and special features to preserve it so they can survive until it rains again.

CANDELABRA SPURGE
Euphorbia abyssinica

Location: Northeastern Africa

Height: Up to 33 ft (10 m)

In African deserts, plants of the spurge family have evolved similar features to the cacti of American deserts. The candelabra spurge resembles a saguaro cactus when young, though it matures into a treelike shape as it ages. Its thick stems store water and produce a poisonous white sap to deter animals.

Flowers
Small, yellowish flowers grow along the edges of stems.

PEANUT CACTUS
Echinopsis chamaecereus

Location: Argentina

Height: Up to 12 in (30 cm)

Not all cacti live in deserts. Some grow on the boughs of rainforest trees, while others, such as the peanut cactus, flourish on rocky mountain slopes. The succulent stems of this species sprawl across the ground, forming a mat. They are covered in spines as sharp as needles.

A saguaro cactus can hold **up to 1,000 gallons (3,800 liters)** of water.

Up to **2,000 cactus species** are known, all of them native to North, Central, or South America.

27

CENTURY PLANT
Agave americana
Location: Mexico and southern USA
Height: Up to 10 ft (3 m)

This plant gets its name from the mistaken belief that it flowers once a century. In fact, the tall flower spike rises from the rosette of thick, spine-edged leaves when the plant is 10–30 years old. After setting seed, the century plant dies.

GOLDMOSS STONECROP
Sedum acre
Location: Europe
Height: Up to 1 in (2 cm)

Instead of growing in deserts, this succulent has adapted to life on old stone walls, pebbly beaches, and other places with dry, rocky soil. It stores water in small, fleshy leaves that cover its creeping stems. It is also called wallpepper because the leaves have a peppery taste.

Flower clusters
The five-petaled flowers grow in small clusters.

LIVING STONE
Lithops pseudotruncatella
Location: Southern Africa
Height: Up to 1 in (2 cm)

Also called a pebble plant, this succulent stores water in a pair of thick leaves camouflaged as stones so animals won't see them. Beautiful yellow flowers appear in spring to attract pollinators across open stony plains.

Single flower
A flower emerges from the slit between the leaves when the plant has matured.

WINDOW PLANT
Fenestraria rhopalophylla
Location: Southern Africa
Length: Leaves up to 1.5 in (4 cm) tall

When growing wild, the window plant is almost entirely buried in sandy ground, with only the tops of its fleshy leaves visible. A transparent window at the top of each leaf lets light reach the green cells deep below, where photosynthesis takes place.

CARRION PLANT
Stapelia gigantea
Location: Southern Africa
Height: Up to 8 in (20 cm)

This African succulent stores water in cactuslike stems. In fall, enormous, star-shaped flowers appear. They stink of rotting meat to attract blowflies, which pollinate them. The flowers then develop into long pods full of silky seeds that catch the wind and blow away.

Flesh mimic
The purplish pattern on the carrion plant's flowers resembles flesh.

Bamboo plants can grow
35 in (91 cm) taller each day.

RYE GRASS
Lolium perenne

Location: Asia, Europe, North Africa, now widely planted worldwide

Height: Up to 3 ft (1 m), leaves around 4 in (10 cm) long

A typical grass, rye grass grows back after being cut. Its flat leaves grow from the base and contain sharp silica particles called phytoliths to stop grazing animals from eating them.

Flower cluster
Clusters of 4–14 small flowers (florets) are grouped together to form a spikelet.

Grasses and sedges

Grasses and their close relatives the sedges are flowering plants, but they have no need for showy flowers, as they are pollinated by the wind.

Grasses appeared around the time the dinosaurs died out. They evolved to survive being grazed by the large herbivorous mammals that took the dinosaurs' place. Their blade-shaped leaves grow from fast-dividing cells at the base of the plant, allowing grasses to keep growing back strongly after being half eaten. Today, grasses cover around a third of the world's land and produce more than half of our food. Sedges look similar to grasses but form a separate family and are mostly found in wetter habitats.

BLACK BAMBOO
Phyllostachys nigra

Location: China

Height: Up to 82 ft (25 m), leaves up to 5 in (13 cm) long

The tall, fast-growing black bamboo is one of the giant panda's favorite foods. The bamboo stems are hollow and contain few nutrients, so pandas have to consume up to 77 lb (35 kg) of it a day. Unlike most grasses, bamboos flower only once in their life, after which the entire plant dies.

PAPYRUS
Cyperus papyrus

Location: Africa, Asia

Height: Up to 16 ft (5 m)

This sedge is a tropical plant that needs warm conditions and lots of water to grow well. It can be seen growing in marshes or on riverbanks, with rounded clusters of shoots and flowers growing on top of tall stems. Ancient Egyptians used its fiber to make boat sails and other items of daily use. The most important of these was a thick type of paper that could be used to write on and keep records. As a result, papyrus was widely cultivated in ancient Egypt.

SUGAR CANE
Saccharum officinarum

Location: India, Southeast Asia, now planted worldwide, especially in the Caribbean

Height: Up to 20 ft (6 m), leaves up to 5 ft (1.5 m) long

Sugar cane is a large, bamboolike grass that stores sugar in its solid and juicy stems. The plant is widely cultivated, as it is the main source of the white sugar we eat. Sugar is made by crushing the stems to extract the juice, which is then boiled down into a syrup and cooled so crystals form.

Palms

Most palms are evergreen, tropical plants with divided leaves called fronds. While many palms are trees, they are actually closely related to grasses.

Palms are so named because their leaves often grow in the shape of a spread hand. However, in many palms, the leaves are shaped more like a feather, with leaflets along either side of a central rib. Unlike woody plants, palms have stems that don't widen with age, so palm trees tend to be tall and thin, with a bare trunk topped by a crown of fronds. Other types of palms grow as shrubs or as climbers in forests.

DATE PALM
Phoenix dactylifera

Location: North Africa, Middle East, now cultivated in Asia and America

Height: Up to 98 ft (30 m), leaves up to 20 ft (6 m) long

The tough, fibrous leaf bases of this desert plant remain stuck to it as it grows, giving the trunk a knobby appearance like a pineapple. One of the first plants to be cultivated, the date palm has been grown in desert oases in the Middle East for thousands of years. The sweet, sticky dates that it produces helped sustain travelers crossing the desert by camel.

Waterproof leaves
The leaves have a waxy, waterproof layer to conserve water.

COCONUT PALM
Cocos nucifera

Location: Origin probably Southeast Asia and Australasia, now worldwide in tropical regions

Height: Up to 98 ft (30 m), leaves up to 20 ft (6 m) long

The coconut palm grows on tropical beaches. Its fruit floats in the sea and has a thick, fibrous husk that stops saltwater from reaching the single seed (a coconut) within. Coconuts can drift on currents from one beach to another, so they have colonized many tropical islands.

OIL PALM
Elaeis guineensis

Location: Africa, Southeast Asia

Height: Up to 65 ft (20 m), leaves up to 16 ft (5 m) long

The plum-sized fruits of this palm tree are rich in oil that can be used to make everything from foods and cosmetics to fuel. Oil palms are grown in huge plantations in Southeast Asia where rainforests once stood. The crop's spread has caused the decline of many rainforest species, such as the orangutan.

OIL PALM FRUIT

OIL PALM PLANTATION

CHINESE WINDMILL PALM
Trachycarpus fortunei

Location: China, Japan, and Southeast Asia, now widely planted

Height: Up to 98 ft (30 m), leaves up to 6 ft (1.8 m) long

Not all palms are tropical. One of the hardiest (most cold-tolerant) species is the windmill palm, which can endure temperatures as low as −4°F (−20°C). It is a popular garden plant in Europe and has spread into the wild in Switzerland.

Climbers and creepers

Climbers and creepers include many unrelated plants. They all have one thing in common, though—they clamber up and over other objects to reach the light.

All climbing plants have the same aim: to get as much sunlight as possible without wasting time or energy growing a thick, woody stem for support. They scramble over other plants or creep across the ground, holding on with hooks, suckers, and twining stems. Their shoots use the sense of touch to explore their surroundings and grow rapidly, often smothering other plants.

WILD PEA
Pisum sativum

Location: Native to the Mediterranean, now cultivated worldwide

Length: Up to 5 ft (1.5 m)

The wild pea uses threadlike leaf extensions called tendrils to grasp other plants. The tendrils grow from the outermost leaves and swing slowly through the air until they touch a stem. Then they circle around it and tighten. Wild peas have been bred over centuries into the pea crop we eat today.

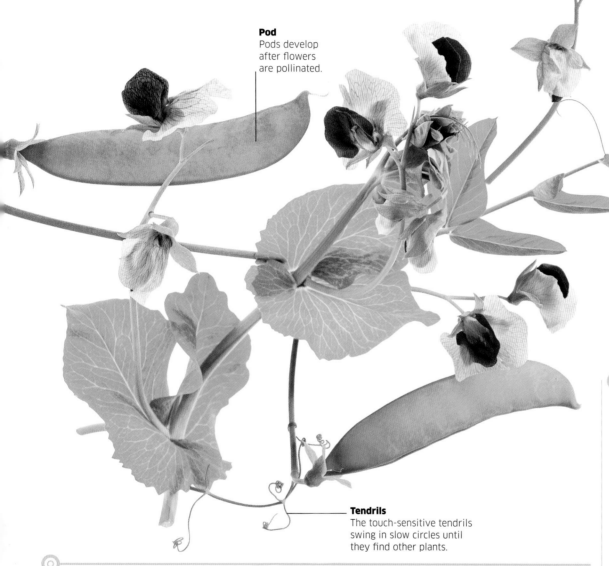

Pod
Pods develop after flowers are pollinated.

Tendrils
The touch-sensitive tendrils swing in slow circles until they find other plants.

Holding on
After making contact, a tendril coils tightly around its support.

VIRGINIA CREEPER
Parthenocissus quinquefolia

Location: Native to North America, planted worldwide as an ornamental

Length: Up to 98 ft (30 m)

Virginia creeper uses tendrils tipped with adhesive pads to climb tree trunks, rocks, and walls. It is sometimes planted by buildings, which it smothers in dense foliage. The leaves turn a spectacular red in fall before falling.

RATTAN PALM
Calamus

Location: Tropical Asia and Africa

Length: Up to 656 ft (200 m)

Rattan palms scramble through rainforests using rings of razor-sharp spines to anchor themselves to other plants. There are hundreds of different species, and some have spines so sharp, they can pierce the sole of a shoe. The flexible stems of rattans are used for making furniture.

At least five different climbing plant species are nicknamed **mile-a-minute** because they grow so fast.

BOUGAINVILLEA
Bougainvillea spectabilis

Location: Native to South America, planted worldwide

Length: Up to 39 ft (12 m)

This spectacular plant has large, hooked thorns that catch on other plants or rocks to help it climb its way to sunlight, where tiny white flowers appear, each surrounded by three bright pink bracts (modified leaves).

Hooked thorns
The sharp thorns hook into various surfaces, allowing the stems to grow up to 39 ft (12 m) long.

WISTERIA
Wisteria sinensis

Location: Native to China, widely planted in temperate countries as an ornamental

Length: Up to 98 ft (30 m)

Wisteria's long, woody vines twine around other plants, allowing it to climb trees and reach great heights. A popular garden plant, it is often trained along wires fixed to walls to create a dazzling display of cascading flowers in spring.

Hanging garden
Wisteria's scented flowers hang from the vines in dense clusters.

Petal-like bracts
Colorful bracts surround and protect the small tubular flowers within.

CAT'S CLAW
Dolichandra unguis-cati

Location: Native to South and Central America, invasive in Australia, southern Africa, and Asia

Length: Up to 98 ft (30 m)

The cat's claw has tendrils like small hooks to latch onto anything they touch, while its aerial roots hold the stems in place. This combination helps the plant grow aggressively over other shrubs and trees to reach sunlight.

LOOFAH
Luffa aegyptiaca

Location: South Asia, now widely cultivated in tropical climates

Length: Up to 10 ft (3 m)

A relative of cucumbers and zucchini, the loofah is a vigorous climber. Its coiling tendrils move at speed to help the plant reach sunlight, where its flowers and fruit develop. Its fruits can be eaten when young.

Natural sponge
The loofah's fruit can be dried out to make a kind of sponge for scrubbing the skin.

LOOFAH FRUIT

32 the plant kingdom ○ **AQUATIC PLANTS**

The earliest-known aquatic flowering plant was *Montsechia*, which lived **130 million years** ago.

YELLOW WATER LILY
Nuphar lutea

Location: Parts of Europe, parts of North America, and western Asia

Size: Leaves up to 16 in (40 cm) wide

The leaves and stalks of the yellow water lily contain air spaces that not only help them float but also transport oxygen to roots buried deep in mud. Most of the plant dies back in winter, but rhizomes (underground stems) survive until spring, unless they are eaten by moose or beavers. Flowers appear when the plant is three years old, and seeds are dispersed on the water surface.

Floating leaves
The large, oval leaves float at the surface to capture as much sunlight as possible.

EEL GRASS
Vallisneria spiralis

Location: Freshwater habitats in warm tropical and subtropical climates

Size: Leaves up to 3 ft (1 m) long

The wavy, ribbon-shaped leaves of eel grass form lush underwater meadows in ponds and lakes. Male and female flowers grow on separate plants. The male flowers detach and float to the surface to release pollen. The female flowers rise on long, spiral stems that pull them back down after pollination.

Aquatic plants

While most plants live on land, some have adapted to spend their lives partly or entirely submerged in water.

Aquatic plants face different challenges from plants that live on land. Sunlight is weaker underwater, so aquatic plants often have floating leaves to make sure they get enough light. Water provides support, so woody stems aren't needed. However, strong currents can wash plants away if they aren't firmly anchored, and stems need extra flexibility to bend with the moving water. Many aquatic plants rely on flying insects to pollinate them, so their flowers need to be raised above the water level.

GIANT WATER LILIES
Victoria amazonica and *Victoria boliviana*

Location: South America

Size: Leaves up to 10 ft (3 m) wide, stems up to 23 ft (7 m) long

The world's largest water lilies have giant, floating leaves that can support a person's weight. The leaves grow very quickly from buds, getting 20 in (50 cm) wider a day and pushing competing plants out of the way. Equally spectacular are the huge, pineapple-scented flowers. These are white when they open. They close to trap pollinating beetles and turn pink before opening again.

Ribbed underside
Air bubbles rising in the water get trapped in a network of ribs on the leaf's underside. This makes it float.

Although they live in water, **seaweeds are classed as algae** rather than aquatic plants.

The waterwheel plant is a **carnivorous aquatic plant** that uses snapping traps like the Venus flytrap.

33

WATER CROWFOOT
Ranunculus peltatus

Location: Asia, Europe, and North Africa

Size: Shoots up to 6.5 ft (2 m) long

This close relative of the buttercup grows in streams and ponds. It has two different kinds of leaves: underwater leaves that are feathery to let water flow through them, and rounded leaves that float on the surface.

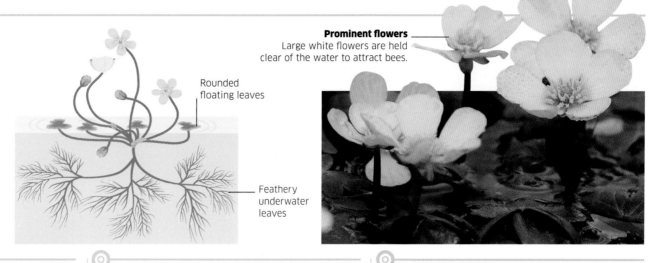

Rounded floating leaves

Prominent flowers — Large white flowers are held clear of the water to attract bees.

Feathery underwater leaves

WATERMOSS
Salvinia auriculata

Location: Mexico and tropical South America, introduced in Africa and Europe

Size: Leaves 1–2 in (3–5 cm) long

Watermoss is a floating fern. Its leaves grow in groups of three, with one dangling like a root in the water and the other two using water-repelling hairs to stay above the surface. Like many tropical aquatic plants, it spreads quickly and can choke waterways.

FROGBIT
Hydrocharis morsus-ranae

Location: Parts of Europe and western Asia, invasive in North America

Size: Leaves 1–2 in (3–5 cm) wide

Frogbit is like a small water lily. It rests over winter as a bud on the bottom of a pond before floating up in spring to the surface, where the round leaves open. The roots dangle below without touching the bottom. Frogbit reproduces asexually by making clones of itself. It spreads rapidly across the water and is considered an invasive pest in North America's Great Lakes.

White, three-petaled flowers appear in summer.

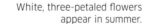

SEAGRASS
Posidonia oceanica

Location: North Africa and Southern Europe

Size: Narrow leaves up to 3 ft (1 m) long

Seagrasses are the only flowering plants that grow in the sea. They live entirely submerged in coastal shallows, where they form rich meadows. Seagrass ecosystems provide food and shelter to many animals, from fish, shrimp, and crabs to turtles and manatees. However, they are easily damaged by human activity. About 1.5 percent of the world's seagrass area is lost each year.

WATER HYACINTH
Pontederia crassipes

Location: Native to South America, but invasive in many tropical waterways

Size: Leaves 4–8 in (10–20 cm) wide

Water hyacinth uses air-filled stems to float on the surface of ponds, lakes, and rivers, its roots dangling freely. It spreads rapidly by cloning itself and can choke rivers and cover huge areas of lakes. Once grown ornamentally for its mauve flowers, it has been introduced to many countries and become a major nuisance.

Giant water lily

The world's largest undivided leaves belong to the giant water lilies of South America. The secret to their size and strength lies in their veins.

On the underside of a giant water lily leaf is a network of riblike veins that are covered in spines to ward off animals. They radiate out from the center and are linked by cross-ribs that trap air in pockets. The result is an air-filled framework that can support an adult's weight, but only if it is spread out—the leaf tissue between the ribs is thin and easily pierced.

GROWING AND FEEDING

All organisms need food. Food provides the energy that living cells need to stay alive, as well as the raw materials for growth. While animals get food by eating other organisms, plants create their own food using just three ingredients: water, air, and the energy of sunlight.

How plants work

Plants use the process of photosynthesis to transform the energy of sunlight into the chemical energy of food.

Most plants have simple needs: air, water, sunlight, and a handful of essential elements. Equipped with these, plants can synthesize thousands of different organic molecules and build the cells they need to grow. Like all living things, plants face continual challenges in their struggle to survive and reproduce. They must grow and adapt to their surroundings; change with the seasons; endure droughts, heatwaves, and freezing weather; and defend themselves against hungry animals. Yet they do all this without appearing to move or make an effort.

FOOD AND ENERGY

All living organisms need food. Like fuel in a car, food molecules provide energy to power chemical reactions inside cells. Food also provides the raw materials needed to make new cells as an organism grows. Animals and fungi get food by consuming other organisms or decaying matter, but plants make their food through photosynthesis. They also release energy from food in the same way animals do—through respiration.

Photosynthesis

In photosynthesis, plants use the energy in sunlight to make the sugar glucose from carbon dioxide and water. Oxygen is released as a waste product. Photosynthesis takes place only during daylight and requires a constant supply of water and carbon dioxide.

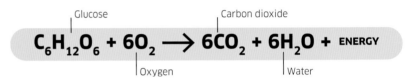

$$6H_2O + 6CO_2 + \text{SUNLIGHT} \longrightarrow C_6H_{12}O_6 + 6O_2$$

Water — $6H_2O$ Carbon dioxide — $6CO_2$ Glucose — $C_6H_{12}O_6$ Oxygen — $6O_2$

Respiration

The opposite of photosynthesis, respiration breaks down glucose molecules to release energy, producing carbon dioxide and water as wastes. Respiration takes place in all animals and plants and requires a constant supply of oxygen.

$$C_6H_{12}O_6 + 6O_2 \longrightarrow 6CO_2 + 6H_2O + \text{ENERGY}$$

Glucose — $C_6H_{12}O_6$ Oxygen — $6O_2$ Carbon dioxide — $6CO_2$ Water — $6H_2O$

USING SUGAR

The glucose made by photosynthesis can be used in many ways. Some of it is used right away to power chemical reactions that need energy, but most of it is converted into other substances.

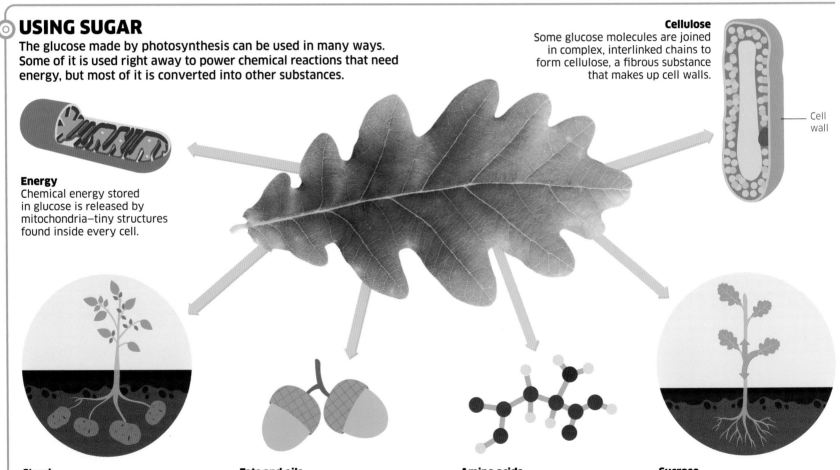

Cellulose
Some glucose molecules are joined in complex, interlinked chains to form cellulose, a fibrous substance that makes up cell walls.

Cell wall

Energy
Chemical energy stored in glucose is released by mitochondria—tiny structures found inside every cell.

Starch
Surplus glucose is used to make starch. Starch is made up of chains of glucose molecules and is stored in leaves, roots, and storage organs such as potatoes.

Fats and oils
Glucose can also be used to make fats and oils, which take up less space than starch and are used to store energy in seeds.

Amino acids
Plants combine glucose with nitrogen from minerals in the soil to create amino acids—the building blocks of all proteins.

Sucrose
Some of the glucose is used to make the sugar sucrose, which is then carried in phloem vessels to other parts of the plant that need energy.

Plants can use their sugar
levels to **tell the time** of day.

An average plant cell
has **10-100 chloroplasts.**

39

HOW PLANTS GROW

Unlike animals, which reach a certain size and become adults, plants grow continually. They grow by adding repeating units, each of which has a bud that can form a new repeating unit. If a part breaks off or is eaten, it can regrow. Special cells (stem cells) found throughout plants can regenerate new roots, shoots, leaves, or flowers according to need. Many plants let everything above the ground die off in winter, then regrow in spring.

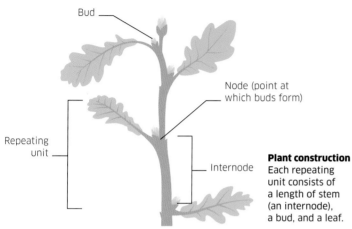

Bud

Node (point at which buds form)

Repeating unit

Internode

Plant construction
Each repeating unit consists of a length of stem (an internode), a bud, and a leaf.

Growth rate

The speed at which plants grow varies enormously and depends on the season, climate, and type of plant. In very dry or cold places, plants may grow incredibly slowly but can survive for hundreds or even thousands of years. Other plants grow very quickly but lead shorter lives.

Cactus
In deserts, cacti grow as little as 0.4 in (1 cm) a year, mainly due to a lack of water and nutrients.

Giant bromeliad
The slowest plant to flower is the giant bromeliad plant of Bolivia, South America. It flowers at around 80 years of age, but then dies.

Asparagus
It can take an asparagus plant up to six years to grow from a seed.

Kudzu
The kudzu vine of East Asia grows at a rate of 12 in (30 cm) a day.

Bamboo
The fastest-growing plant is a type of bamboo. It can grow 1.5 in (4 cm) taller in a single hour.

ESSENTIAL ELEMENTS

As well as needing water and carbon dioxide, plants need small amounts of some elements to make proteins and other essential organic substances. They get these elements from the soil.

Pure potassium in an airless glass case

Potassium
This element helps plants transport food and water. It also strengthens cell walls and helps plants retain water in times of drought.

Sulfur crystals

Sulfur
This element is used to make proteins. It helps with seed formation and resistance to disease and improves survival through the winter.

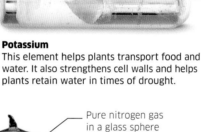

Pure nitrogen gas in a glass sphere

Purple crystals of apatite, a mineral rich in phosphorus

Natural copper

Copper
Copper is needed to help plants make proteins and grow. A lack of copper can lead to crop failure and plant diseases.

Nitrogen
Nitrogen is vital for growth. Plants use nitrogen to make proteins, DNA, and chlorophyll.

Iron
This metal is used to make chlorophyll and help enzymes function and cells divide. A lack of iron makes leaves turn yellow and reduces fruiting.

Phosphorus
Phosphorus is important in the early growth of plants. It promotes root development, flowering, and ripening of fruits.

Magnesium
Plants need magnesium to make chlorophyll. Without it, they can't photosynthesize.

40 growing and feeding ○ **A PLANT IS BORN**

Lettuce seeds will germinate in two days,
but arum lilies can take up to six months.

A plant is born

To become a new plant, a seed has to go through many changes. Conditions also need to be just right if it is to stand any chance of developing into a seedling.

Each seed is packed with everything a new plant needs to start its life. It has an outer seed coat to stop it from drying out, an embryo that is the beginnings of a new plant, and a food store to sustain the growth of the embryo. Even with these, the seed still needs water and oxygen to germinate, then light and warmth to help it grow. Until then, it remains alive but dormant (inactive).

Inside a seed

In each seed is a food store to power its growth before it reaches the light. In some, there is a food storage area called an endosperm; in others, the food is stored in one or two large lobes known as cotyledons, which grow into simple, rounded leaves ("seed leaves"). The larger the food store, the faster a young plant develops. A seed also contains a radicle (primary root), a hypocotyl (stem), and a plumule (a shoot bearing the first true leaves).

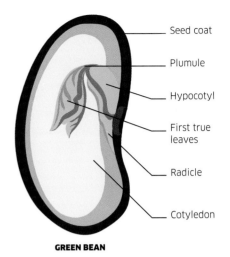

Seed coat

Plumule

Hypocotyl

First true leaves

Radicle

Cotyledon

GREEN BEAN

The seed coat swells and splits as the seed takes in water, which penetrates the food stores.

The embryo's cells multiply and enlarge as oxygen enters the seed.

The radicle (primary root) emerges from the embryo.

The hypocotyl forms a hook shape that pushes upward, raising the cotyledons out of the soil.

Rootlets on the radicle grow into new roots that take up water and nutrients to help the plant grow faster.

Cotyledons

Water enters the seed.

1 Embryo develops
As water starts to seep through the seed coat, it stimulates the embryo inside to start to develop. It activates chemical processes that turn the stored carbohydrates, proteins, and oils into forms that can be used for growth.

2 First roots
The radicle pushes down into the soil and anchors the new plant into place. At the same time, the plumule (shoot) breaks out of the seed coat and pushes its way out of the soil.

The radicle grows away from the light and toward gravity, driving the young root deeper into the soil.

Australian snottygobble seeds will germinate more easily if they have been **eaten and expelled in droppings** by emus.

41

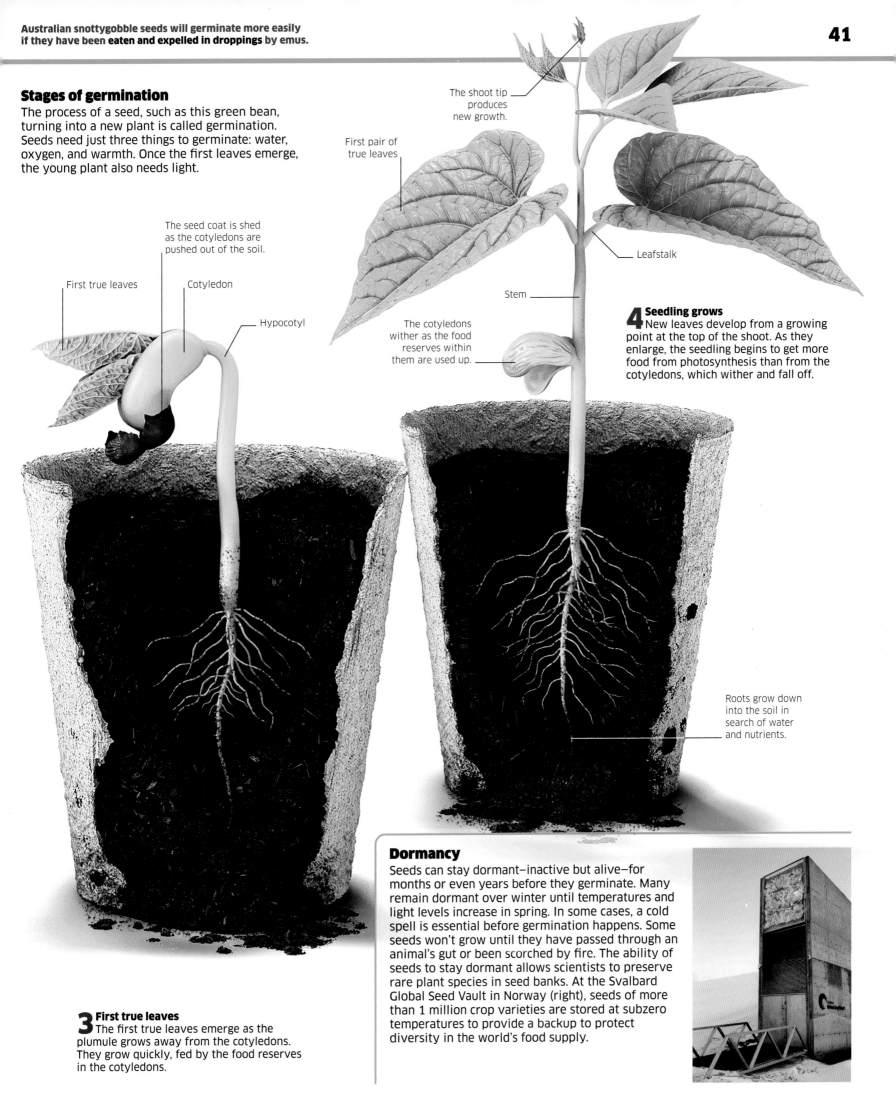

Stages of germination

The process of a seed, such as this green bean, turning into a new plant is called germination. Seeds need just three things to germinate: water, oxygen, and warmth. Once the first leaves emerge, the young plant also needs light.

The shoot tip produces new growth.

First pair of true leaves

The seed coat is shed as the cotyledons are pushed out of the soil.

First true leaves

Cotyledon

Hypocotyl

Leafstalk

Stem

The cotyledons wither as the food reserves within them are used up.

4 Seedling grows
New leaves develop from a growing point at the top of the shoot. As they enlarge, the seedling begins to get more food from photosynthesis than from the cotyledons, which wither and fall off.

Roots grow down into the soil in search of water and nutrients.

3 First true leaves
The first true leaves emerge as the plumule grows away from the cotyledons. They grow quickly, fed by the food reserves in the cotyledons.

Dormancy

Seeds can stay dormant—inactive but alive—for months or even years before they germinate. Many remain dormant over winter until temperatures and light levels increase in spring. In some cases, a cold spell is essential before germination happens. Some seeds won't grow until they have passed through an animal's gut or been scorched by fire. The ability of seeds to stay dormant allows scientists to preserve rare plant species in seed banks. At the Svalbard Global Seed Vault in Norway (right), seeds of more than 1 million crop varieties are stored at subzero temperatures to provide a backup to protect diversity in the world's food supply.

Growing points

We stop growing around the age of 18, but plants never stop growing. A plant can produce new tissues, organs, and even whole clones of itself at any age.

New parts of a plant grow from stem cells—unspecialized cells that have the potential to divide and produce any kind of specialized cell, such as those of stems, leaves, roots, or flowers. Animals have stem cells, too, but plants have far more. They occur in regions called meristems, which are found inside buds, at the tips of shoots and roots, and in growing areas of stems. A meristem has the ability to grow into a whole new plant, which is why gardeners can create plants by making cuttings.

Inside a bud

In fall, deciduous trees such as sycamores stop growing and their leaves fall off. At the tip of every twig, a bud forms around the meristem. Inside the bud, tiny leaves and flowers develop, wrapped tightly around each other. When spring arrives, the bud opens and the leaves spread out and start growing quickly.

Pinching out

In many plants, the meristem at the top releases chemicals called hormones that suppress meristems in side buds, stopping them from growing into branches. Gardeners sometimes "pinch out" the top bud to trigger the growth of side buds, which makes a plant bushier.

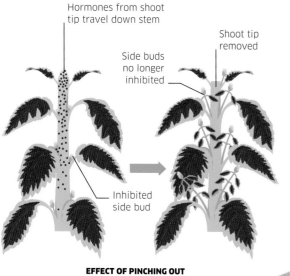

Hormones from shoot tip travel down stem

Side buds no longer inhibited

Shoot tip removed

Inhibited side bud

EFFECT OF PINCHING OUT

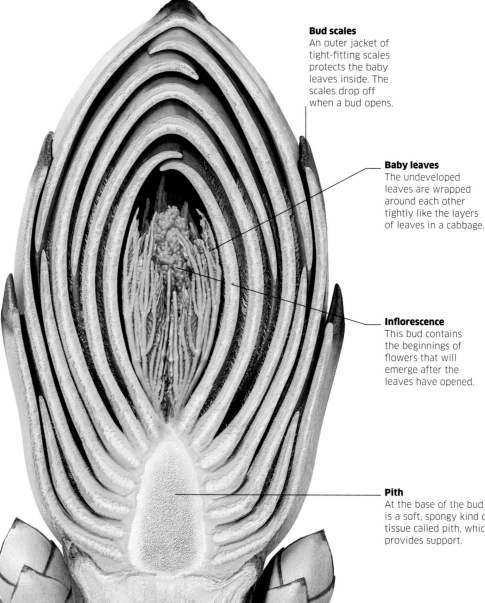

Bud scales
An outer jacket of tight-fitting scales protects the baby leaves inside. The scales drop off when a bud opens.

Baby leaves
The undeveloped leaves are wrapped around each other tightly like the layers of leaves in a cabbage.

Inflorescence
This bud contains the beginnings of flowers that will emerge after the leaves have opened.

Pith
At the base of the bud is a soft, spongy kind of tissue called pith, which provides support.

Tree trunks **grow a new outer ring** of wood every year thanks to meristem tissue under the bark.

Cabbages and Brussels sprouts are **giant leaf buds.**

43

1 Bud opens
Warmer weather and longer days trigger the opening of buds in spring. The leaves inside swell with water, pushing the scales apart.

2 Leaves emerge
The expanding leaves push their way out of the bud and emerge into full sunlight. They begin to photosynthesize, which helps them grow faster.

Flower head

3 Flowers emerge
Flower heads bearing hundreds of tiny, yellow-green flowers emerge soon after the leaves. The nectar-rich flowers will be pollinated by insects.

4 Spreading out
The growing leaves spread out to capture more sunlight, speeding the tree's growth.

Meristem locations
Most plants have meristems at the tips of shoots and roots and in the stem. In the microscope images below, meristem cells are stained with colored dyes to make them easier to see.

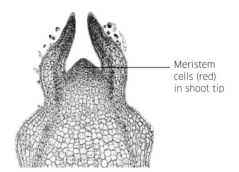

Meristem cells (red) in shoot tip

Shoot tips
Meristems at the tips of shoots and inside buds are called shoot apical meristems. They are packed with tiny round cells that divide repeatedly. The cells can develop into leaves, buds, branches, and flowers.

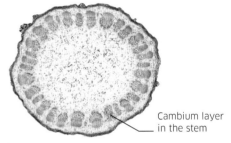

Cambium layer in the stem

In the stem
Plant stems and tree trunks grow wider with age thanks to a ring of meristematic tissue called cambium.

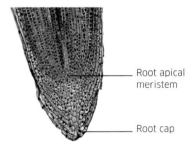

Root apical meristem

Root cap

Root tips
Just behind the tips of roots are growing zones called root apical meristems. Rapidly dividing cells here make the root elongate and push into the soil. The root meristem is protected by a zone of tough cells called the root cap.

How phototropism works

The way plants respond to light is controlled by growth hormones known as auxins. Auxins make cells grow faster by making their walls stretchier. They are produced in the growing tips of plants and spread back down the shoot, but they move away from the light and become more concentrated on the dark side.

1. Growing straight
When the light is directly overhead, auxins spread out evenly. Both sides of a shoot grow at the same speed, so the shoot grows upward.

2. Response to light
When the light comes from the side, auxins move to the opposite side of the shoot.

3. Shoot bends
The cells on the darker side of the shoot grow faster, making the shoot bend toward the light.

Second bend
Here, the light is stronger overhead. The lower side of the stem grows faster, making the stem bend upward.

First bend
Here, the light is stronger on the right. As a result, the left side of the stem grows faster, bending the stem.

Leaves develop
Once the shoot reaches sunlight, the stem stops elongating and leaves develop.

Responding to gravity
Roots can detect the pull of gravity. The main root responds to gravity by growing straight down.

Upward growth
After germinating, the seedling grows directly upward toward the faint source of light above.

The flower heads of **young sunflowers follow the Sun** from east to west over the course of a day.

In the low gravity of the Space Station, plants grow with their **roots toward Earth** and their shoots growing up.

45

Responding to change

Plants don't just sit in the ground. They are moving, growing, changing, and reacting to things all the time, but often so slowly that we fail to notice.

Watch a pea or a bean growing over several months and you'll notice how it reacts to its environment. After racing upward to find light, it grows branches, spreads its leaves in the sunlight, extends tendrils to climb, and makes flowers and fruits at just the right times of year before sinking into dormancy as winter comes. These changes are triggered by many different environmental cues, including light, gravity, temperature, water, and touch.

Responding to light

Seeds often germinate in dark, shady places. Fueled by their on-board food reserves, they grow quickly in search of sunlight so they can start to photosynthesize. Plants use a simple trick to grow toward the light: If one side of a stem is darker than the other, the dark side grows faster. This makes the stem bend away from shade and toward light. A change of growth in response to light is called phototropism. Shoots are positively phototropic, growing toward light, while roots are negatively phototropic, growing away from light.

Tropisms

Responses to physical triggers like light, gravity, touch, and water are called tropisms. All of these things can change the direction of growth.

Geotropism
Reacting to gravity is called geotropism (or gravitropism). Roots grow toward the pull of gravity (positive geotropism), but shoots grow away from it (negative geotropism).

Hydrotropism
Reacting to water is called hydrotropism. Roots grow toward areas with higher moisture (positive hydrotropism).

Thigmotropism
Reacting to touch is called thigmotropism. Many climbing plants have touch-sensitive tendrils that reach out for solid objects, then wrap around whatever they touch.

Plant hormones

Like animals, plants make hormones—powerful chemicals that change and control the way plants grow and develop.

Gibberellins
These hormones break dormancy in seeds, triggering germination.

Cytokinins
Cytokinins encourage cell division and the development of new shoots and roots.

Ethylene
This gas is released by ripening fruit, causing surrounding fruits to ripen more quickly.

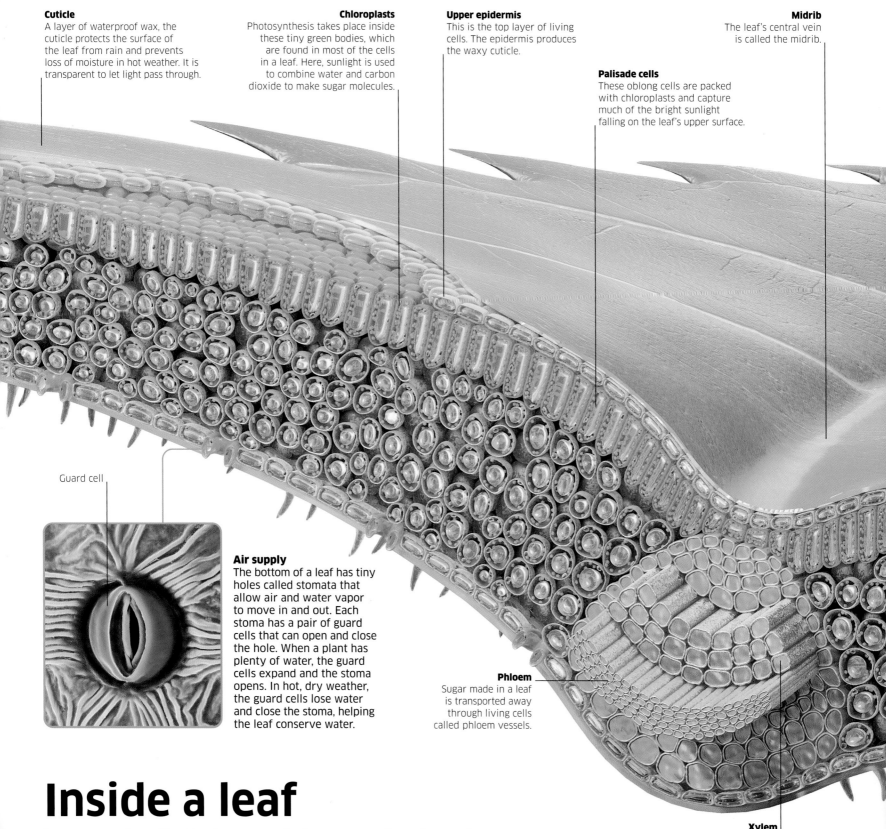

Cuticle
A layer of waterproof wax, the cuticle protects the surface of the leaf from rain and prevents loss of moisture in hot weather. It is transparent to let light pass through.

Chloroplasts
Photosynthesis takes place inside these tiny green bodies, which are found in most of the cells in a leaf. Here, sunlight is used to combine water and carbon dioxide to make sugar molecules.

Upper epidermis
This is the top layer of living cells. The epidermis produces the waxy cuticle.

Palisade cells
These oblong cells are packed with chloroplasts and capture much of the bright sunlight falling on the leaf's upper surface.

Midrib
The leaf's central vein is called the midrib.

Guard cell

Air supply
The bottom of a leaf has tiny holes called stomata that allow air and water vapor to move in and out. Each stoma has a pair of guard cells that can open and close the hole. When a plant has plenty of water, the guard cells expand and the stoma opens. In hot, dry weather, the guard cells lose water and close the stoma, helping the leaf conserve water.

Phloem
Sugar made in a leaf is transported away through living cells called phloem vessels.

Xylem
Water from the roots is carried to leaves by dead, tube-shaped cells called xylem vessels.

Inside a leaf

Leaves capture the Sun's energy but are more than just solar panels. They use light to make a plant's food out of air and water through the process of photosynthesis.

Leaves come in many shapes and sizes to suit different environments. They can be broad and flat, needle-thin, thick and fleshy, or hard and scaly. The vast majority are green, but some leaves are yellow, white, red, bronze, or a mix of colors (variegated). Nearly all leaves have the same basic parts. A stalk called a petiole connects a leaf to the plant. The broadest part of a leaf is its blade, and running centrally down the length of the blade is the midrib. Sprouting from the midrib are veins that supply the leaf with water.

Structure of a leaf

A typical leaf has protective upper and lower layers of what are called epidermal cells. Sandwiched between them are two layers of cells whose main job is photosynthesis. All the cells in a leaf can photosynthesize, but the upper layers do it best as they get the brightest light.

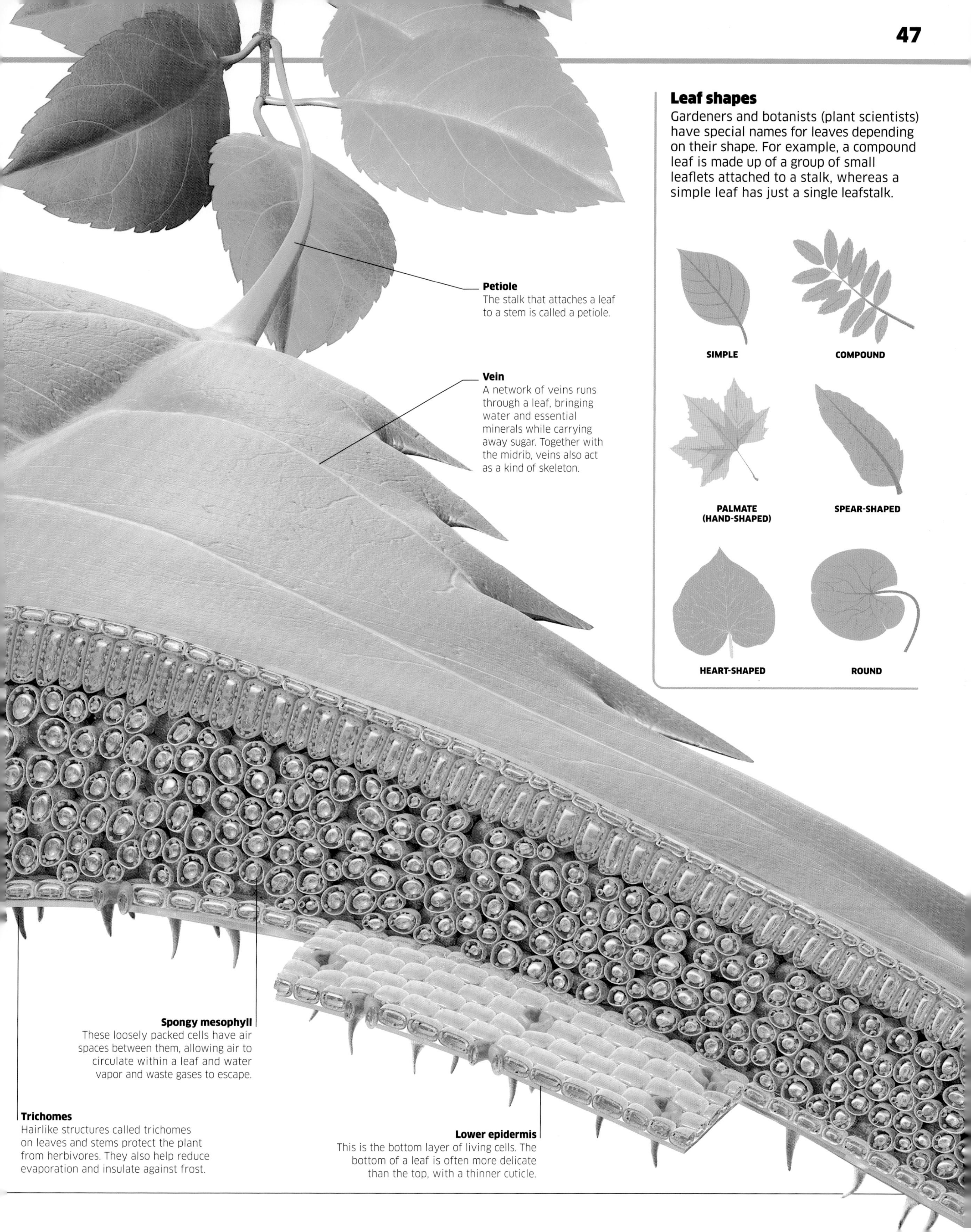

Petiole
The stalk that attaches a leaf to a stem is called a petiole.

Vein
A network of veins runs through a leaf, bringing water and essential minerals while carrying away sugar. Together with the midrib, veins also act as a kind of skeleton.

Leaf shapes
Gardeners and botanists (plant scientists) have special names for leaves depending on their shape. For example, a compound leaf is made up of a group of small leaflets attached to a stalk, whereas a simple leaf has just a single leafstalk.

SIMPLE

COMPOUND

PALMATE (HAND-SHAPED)

SPEAR-SHAPED

HEART-SHAPED

ROUND

Spongy mesophyll
These loosely packed cells have air spaces between them, allowing air to circulate within a leaf and water vapor and waste gases to escape.

Trichomes
Hairlike structures called trichomes on leaves and stems protect the plant from herbivores. They also help reduce evaporation and insulate against frost.

Lower epidermis
This is the bottom layer of living cells. The bottom of a leaf is often more delicate than the top, with a thinner cuticle.

Plant cells

Plant cells are similar to those of animals but have some extra features, such as a thick cell wall, a fluid store, and chloroplasts to carry out photosynthesis.

Plants get much of their structural strength from the way their cells are built. Each cell has a large central vacuole to store fluid and keep the cell plump. Meanwhile, a rigid outer wall maintains the cell's shape and prevents it from bursting as the vacuole expands. Like all living cells, plant cells contain numerous tiny structures called organelles that each do a particular job—from storing genes or manufacturing proteins to capturing sunlight. Cells in different parts of a plant vary in shape, size, and function. Leaf cells are packed with chloroplasts for photosynthesis, for example, while other cells are specialized to transmit vital resources around a plant or to store energy reserves.

Cell wall ——————

Cellulose

Plant cell walls are made of cellulose—the most abundant organic substance on Earth. Cellulose is a polymer, which means that its molecules are long chains of repeating units—in this case, sugar molecules. Cellulose is tough and incredibly difficult to digest. Animals can't digest it without the help of cellulose-eating microorganisms in their intestines. In humans, undigested cellulose forms dietary fiber, which is good for health.

Cell membrane
Under the cell wall is a thin membrane that controls which substances can enter or leave the cell.

Endoplasmic reticulum
This system of tubes and sheets of membrane forms a network throughout the cell. It transports large substances, such as proteins made by ribosomes.

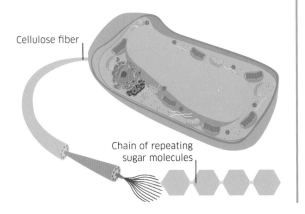
Cellulose fiber

Chain of repeating sugar molecules

Nucleus
This large organelle is the cell's control center. It stores a complete copy of all the plant's genes as molecules of DNA. Genes control how each cell works.

Water pressure

Plant cell vacuoles contain a solution of sugars and salts that draw in water by a process called osmosis. In dry weather, cells don't get enough water and their vacuoles shrink. As a result, cells soften and shrink slightly, causing the whole plant to wilt.

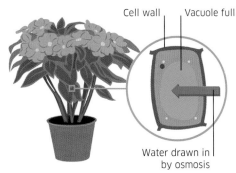

Cell wall   Vacuole full

Water drawn in by osmosis

Healthy plant
When a plant has enough water, cell vacuoles absorb water by osmosis. They expand and push against the cell walls, making the cells plump and firm (turgid).

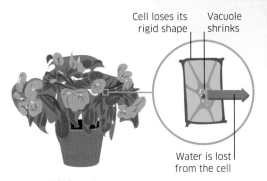

Cell loses its rigid shape   Vacuole shrinks

Water is lost from the cell

Wilting plant
If the vacuoles lose water, they shrink and stop pushing outward on the cell walls. The cells become soft (flaccid), losing their rigidity, and the plant wilts.

Golgi apparatus
This stack of folded membranes helps manufacture complex substances, such as the parts needed to build the cell wall. Small bubbles of material break off it to be transported elsewhere.

95 percent of the cells in a tree are **dead**.

99 percent of the weight of purified cotton is **cellulose**.

Chloroplasts and mitochondria both have their **own DNA and genes**.

49

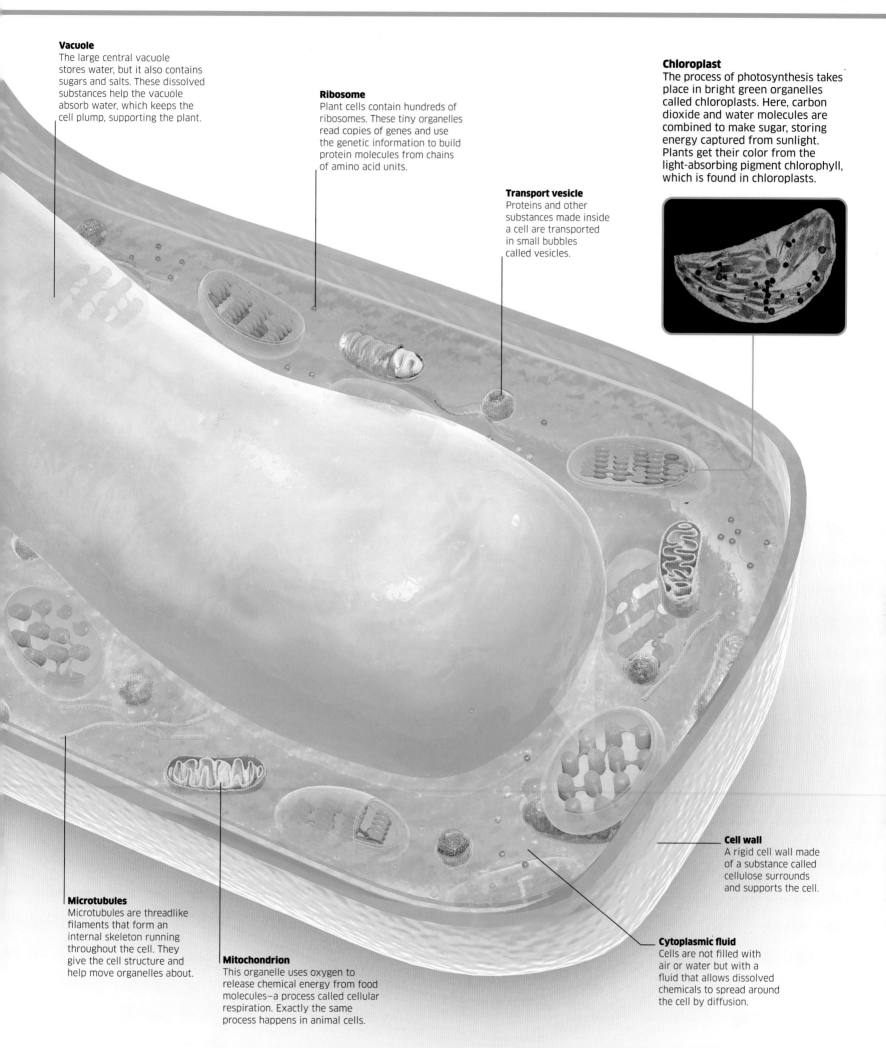

Vacuole
The large central vacuole stores water, but it also contains sugars and salts. These dissolved substances help the vacuole absorb water, which keeps the cell plump, supporting the plant.

Ribosome
Plant cells contain hundreds of ribosomes. These tiny organelles read copies of genes and use the genetic information to build protein molecules from chains of amino acid units.

Transport vesicle
Proteins and other substances made inside a cell are transported in small bubbles called vesicles.

Chloroplast
The process of photosynthesis takes place in bright green organelles called chloroplasts. Here, carbon dioxide and water molecules are combined to make sugar, storing energy captured from sunlight. Plants get their color from the light-absorbing pigment chlorophyll, which is found in chloroplasts.

Microtubules
Microtubules are threadlike filaments that form an internal skeleton running throughout the cell. They give the cell structure and help move organelles about.

Mitochondrion
This organelle uses oxygen to release chemical energy from food molecules—a process called cellular respiration. Exactly the same process happens in animal cells.

Cell wall
A rigid cell wall made of a substance called cellulose surrounds and supports the cell.

Cytoplasmic fluid
Cells are not filled with air or water but with a fluid that allows dissolved chemicals to spread around the cell by diffusion.

Photosynthesis

Plants use the energy in sunlight to make food in a process called photosynthesis. This process is vital to life on Earth, as it provides the energy that nearly every food web depends on.

Photosynthesis takes place mainly in leaves. Only three ingredients are needed: water from the ground, carbon dioxide from air, and sunlight. The energy in sunlight is used to combine water and carbon dioxide molecules into more complex, energy-rich sugar molecules, such as glucose. These are used as building blocks for every part of a plant.

Inside a chloroplast

The chemical reactions of photosynthesis happen in chloroplasts—tiny green bodies within plant cells. Inside a chloroplast are stacks of bright green disks called thylakoids. They are green because they are surrounded by the light-capturing pigment chlorophyll. In the first stage of photosynthesis, the thylakoids use sunlight to split water molecules (H_2O) into oxygen and hydrogen atoms. In the second stage, captured energy is used to combine hydrogen atoms with carbon dioxide (CO_2) and make sugar ($C_6H_{12}O_6$).

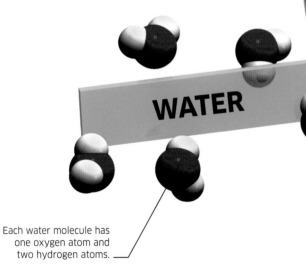

CARBON DIOXIDE

Each carbon dioxide molecule has one carbon atom and two oxygen atoms.

LIGHT

WATER

Each water molecule has one oxygen atom and two hydrogen atoms.

Chemical process

This chemical equation summarizes what happens during photosynthesis. Water and carbon dioxide combine to make glucose (a kind of sugar), and oxygen gas is produced as waste.

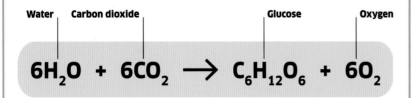

Water	Carbon dioxide		Glucose	Oxygen

$$6H_2O + 6CO_2 \rightarrow C_6H_{12}O_6 + 6O_2$$

Photosynthesis versus respiration

Photosynthesis stores chemical energy by building sugar molecules. Respiration, which takes place in animals as well as plants, does the opposite—it breaks down sugar molecules to release energy, producing carbon dioxide and water as waste. Photosynthesis and respiration both take place in daylight. At night, only respiration takes place.

▶ Photosynthesis   ▶ Respiration

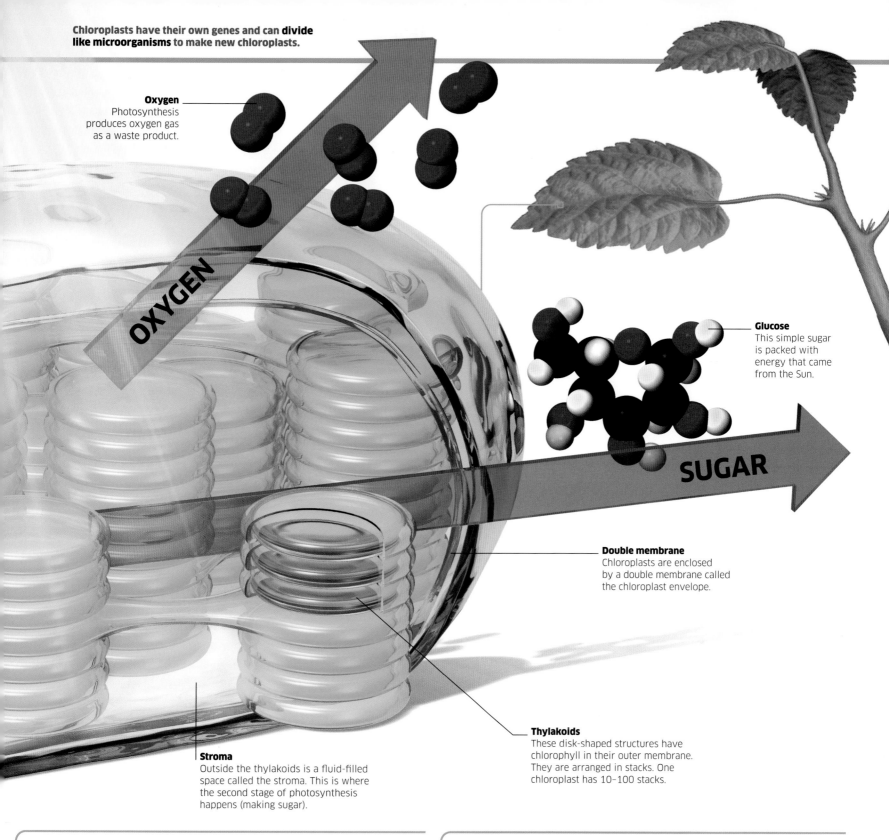

Chloroplasts have their own genes and can divide like microorganisms to make new chloroplasts.

Oxygen
Photosynthesis produces oxygen gas as a waste product.

OXYGEN

SUGAR

Glucose
This simple sugar is packed with energy that came from the Sun.

Double membrane
Chloroplasts are enclosed by a double membrane called the chloroplast envelope.

Thylakoids
These disk-shaped structures have chlorophyll in their outer membrane. They are arranged in stacks. One chloroplast has 10–100 stacks.

Stroma
Outside the thylakoids is a fluid-filled space called the stroma. This is where the second stage of photosynthesis happens (making sugar).

Factors affecting photosynthesis

A plant with bigger leaves and more chlorophyll can trap more energy, but the surroundings of a plant can speed up or slow down photosynthesis as well.

Light
Brighter light means more energy can be absorbed by the plant.

Temperature
Warm conditions make the reactions in photosynthesis happen faster.

CO₂
More carbon dioxide in the air speeds up photosynthesis.

Commercial greenhouses

By growing plants in a greenhouse, farmers can raise the temperature and carbon dioxide level, both of which increase the rate of photosynthesis. The plants grow faster, and crops can be grown all year round.

Inside a stem

Just as the human body has a system of veins and arteries to carry vital substances to organs, plants have a transport system to move water and nutrients to wherever they are needed.

Running along a plant's stem are two different sets of transport tubes. One set of tubes, called xylem, moves water and dissolved minerals up the stem from the roots to the leaves. The second set, called phloem, carries sugar and nutrients away from the leaves to be used elsewhere. Xylem and phloem are both made of elongated cells joined end to end. They are arranged alongside each other in structures called vascular bundles.

Xylem
In flowering plants, the xylem cells have no end walls, so they form continuous hollow tubes. Their walls are strengthened by a woody substance called lignin, sometimes in a spiral pattern. Xylem cells die after forming but continue transporting water.

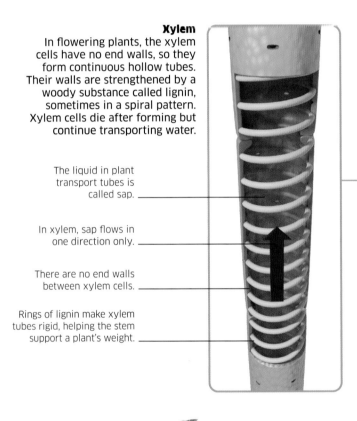

The liquid in plant transport tubes is called sap.

In xylem, sap flows in one direction only.

There are no end walls between xylem cells.

Rings of lignin make xylem tubes rigid, helping the stem support a plant's weight.

Cambium layer
Between the xylem and phloem is a layer of cambium cells. These cells constantly divide, creating new xylem on one side and new phloem on the other. In this way, the transport systems grow with the plant.

TOMATO PLANT

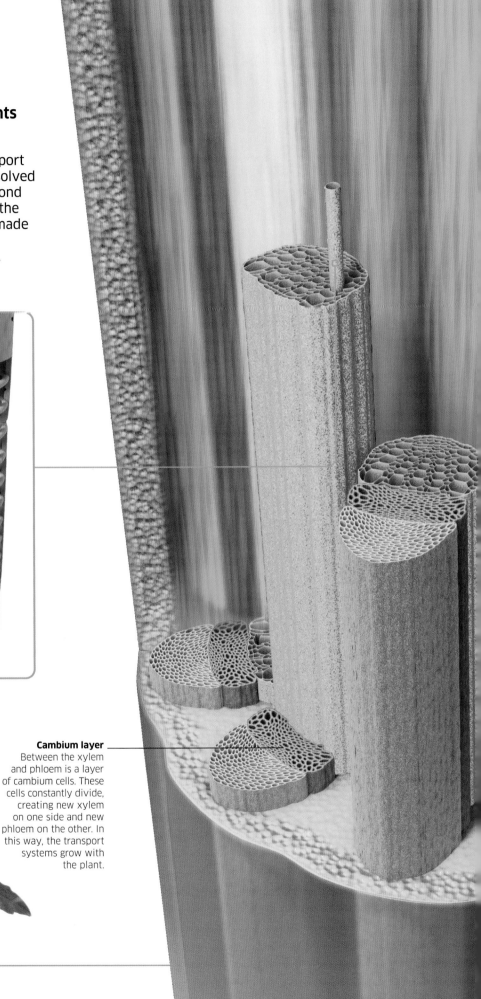

30,000 –the **number of cells** in a 3 ft (1 m) length of phloem.

More than **50 percent** of the weight of a tree is water.

53

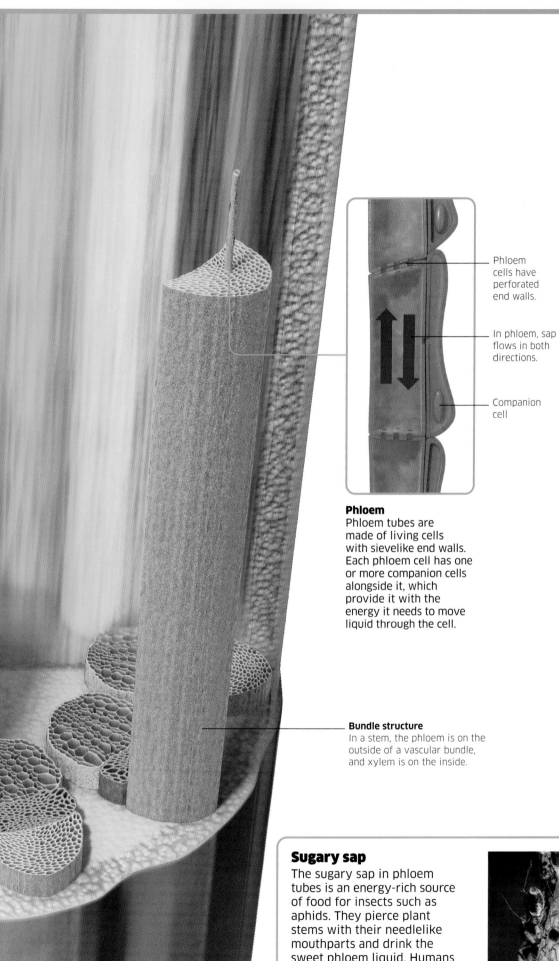

Vascular bundles

Vascular bundles in various parts of a plant are arranged in different ways. In leaves, they form veins, with xylem on top. In roots, they are in the center, strengthening the root's core and helping anchor it in the soil.

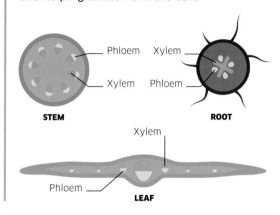

Phloem — Xylem

Xylem — Phloem

STEM   **ROOT**

Xylem

Phloem

LEAF

Phloem cells have perforated end walls.

In phloem, sap flows in both directions.

Companion cell

Phloem
Phloem tubes are made of living cells with sievelike end walls. Each phloem cell has one or more companion cells alongside it, which provide it with the energy it needs to move liquid through the cell.

Bundle structure
In a stem, the phloem is on the outside of a vascular bundle, and xylem is on the inside.

Transpiration

The movement of water through a plant is called transpiration. Tiny holes on the surface of leaves, called stomata, allow water to evaporate. The loss of water pulls a continuous column of water up the xylem. This, in turn, draws water from the soil into the roots.

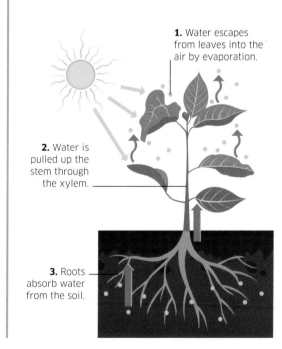

1. Water escapes from leaves into the air by evaporation.

2. Water is pulled up the stem through the xylem.

3. Roots absorb water from the soil.

Sugary sap

The sugary sap in phloem tubes is an energy-rich source of food for insects such as aphids. They pierce plant stems with their needlelike mouthparts and drink the sweet phloem liquid. Humans eat sap from phloem, too— the sweet sap of maple trees is used to make syrup.

APHIDS DRINKING PHLOEM SAP

SAP COLLECTED FROM MAPLE TREE

Root pressure

Some plants have tiny beads of water along their leaf edges in the early morning. This is not dew but water pushed all the way up from the roots.

To stay alive, plants must continually transport water from their roots to their leaves. The main force driving this flow is evaporation from leaves. However, another force, known as root pressure, also plays a role. At night, when the air is cool and humid, evaporation slows down but root pressure continues to drive water upward. So tiny pores at the end of leaf veins open to let the excess water escape.

56 growing and feeding ∘ **INSIDE A TREE TRUNK**

The world's **oldest wooden building** is Hōryū-ji, a 1,300-year-old Buddhist temple in Japan.

Tree rings

A tree trunk only grows near the bark, in a circle. This creates rings of growth, pale in spring and summer (when large xylem tubes are created to transport more water) and dark in fall (when growth slows and smaller tubes form). Each pair of rings represents a year's growth. Counting all the rings tells you the tree's age.

First year's growth

Tree rings are wider in warm, wet years, when trees grow more.

Most recent growth

TREE RINGS

Tree-ring dating

The study of tree rings can help archaeologists work out the age of ancient timber-containing buildings. Although the timbers in old buildings come from trees that died long ago, archaeologists can find matching patterns of tree rings in younger timbers or in living trees. This way, they can build up a timeline of tree rings that stretches back centuries.

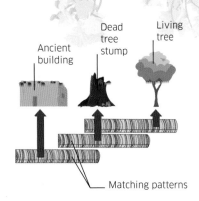

Ancient building

Dead tree stump

Living tree

Matching patterns

Hardwood and softwood

Fast-growing conifers such as pine have less dense, lighter wood, usually called softwood. Slow-growing broadleaved trees, such as mahogany, tend to have denser, darker wood, known as hardwood.

Mahogany is now a protected tree, but its hardwood was traditionally used to make ornaments, musical instruments, and fine furniture.

The light softwood pine is used to make mass-produced furniture.

The mighty oak

Oak trees are famous for the strength of the dense wood they produce. For centuries, oak beams were used to create the frameworks of ships and large buildings, such as churches. The wood is still used for buildings today and to make sturdy furniture.

Bark

A tree's bark is made up of two layers: a dead, outer layer called cork and an inner, living layer called phloem. Cork is very tough to protect the tree and contains a waterproof substance to keep out moisture. Tiny openings called lenticels let air enter to reach the living cells underneath.

Inside a tree trunk

The immense weight of a tree's canopy is supported by its woody trunk. As well as providing homes for birds, insects, and other animals, tree trunks supply us with timber for making things.

A tall trunk holds a tree's leaves high in the air, where they can photosynthesize in bright sunlight. To keep the leaves working, the trunk must also allow water and nutrients to move freely between the roots and the canopy, sometimes over distances of more than 330 ft (100 m). To do this, the trunk has a layered structure that expands year by year as the tree grows from a small seedling to a towering giant.

Phloem

Sugars travel up and down the trunk in phloem tubes. In fall, the phloem moves sugars and chemicals from the leaves to the roots, where they are stored until spring.

Sapwood

This layer transports water and minerals from the roots to the canopy. It consists of long, hollow cells called xylem tubes. These are alive at first but die after their cell walls thicken with lignin, the substance that gives wood its strength.

99 percent of the cells in a tree trunk are **dead**.

The timbers of Seahenge, an ancient monument on England's Norfolk coast, are **4,000 years old**.

57

Animal attack
As cork ages, weaknesses develop. These allow woodpeckers, beetles, and other animals to get at the soft, living wood inside and make hollows or tunnels to live in.

Knot
If the expanding trunk gradually grows over the remains of a dead branch, it leaves a rounded scar called a knot. Knots can be seen on wooden objects as rounded patterns with dark centers.

Medullary rays
Bands of cells that radiate out from the center are called medullary rays. These cells allow water and nutrients to move sideways across the tree trunk instead of just up and down.

Heartwood
At the center of the trunk is the heartwood, the hardest wood in a tree. It is made up of old xylem tubes now blocked by lignin. The lignin makes them strong enough to support the tree, but they can no longer transport water.

Vascular cambium
This narrow layer is made up of actively dividing cells that create new phloem and xylem tubes. This is where the tree trunk expands.

Inside a root

Roots are the underground parts of plants. Their main job is to absorb water and minerals, but they also provide anchorage and hold plants firmly in the ground.

Unlike animals, plants can't move around to find water or other resources. Instead, they must absorb everything they need from the ground and air. Roots grow continuously, pushing their way through soil and actively absorbing minerals via microscopic root hairs. All of this requires energy, so roots rely on a steady supply of sugar from the leaves above, as well as oxygen from the air so they can breathe. Because of the need for air, most of a plant's roots are usually near the soil surface.

Root systems

Most plants, including trees, have a large taproot (main root) that takes up water and keeps the plant securely upright. Other plants, such as grasses, produce a mass of shallow roots, which absorb water quickly from a wide area.

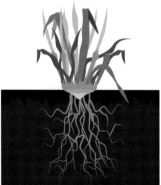
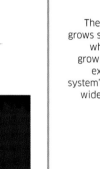

Taproot
A taproot grows straight down into the soil and has side branches to take up water.

Fibrous roots
These form a dense, shallow network of tiny, fibrous roots with no main root.

Absorbing water and minerals

Water is easier for roots to absorb than minerals. Water naturally travels from an area of high concentration (such as soil) to an area of lower concentration (inside roots). However, the opposite is true of minerals. They are less concentrated in soil than in roots, but plants still need more. They are taken in by a process called active transport, which uses energy.

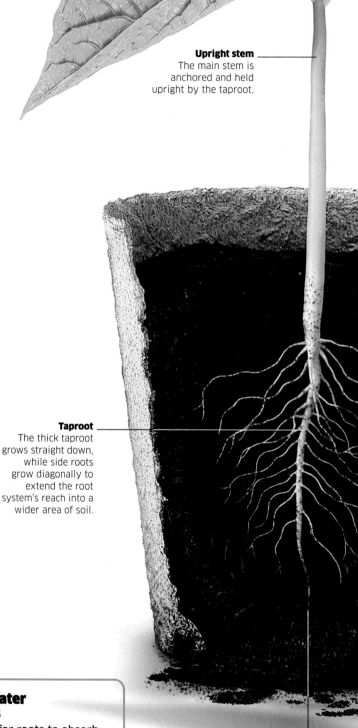

Upright stem
The main stem is anchored and held upright by the taproot.

Taproot
The thick taproot grows straight down, while side roots grow diagonally to extend the root system's reach into a wider area of soil.

Root growth
Only the ends of roots are actively growing and absorbing water and minerals.

OUTSIDE ROOT   **INSIDE ROOT**

Water

Minerals

Energy

387 miles (623 km)—the total length of the **longest known root system**, which belonged to a rye grass plant.

400 ft (122 m)—the **deepest known root**, of a fig tree at Echo Caves in South Africa.

59

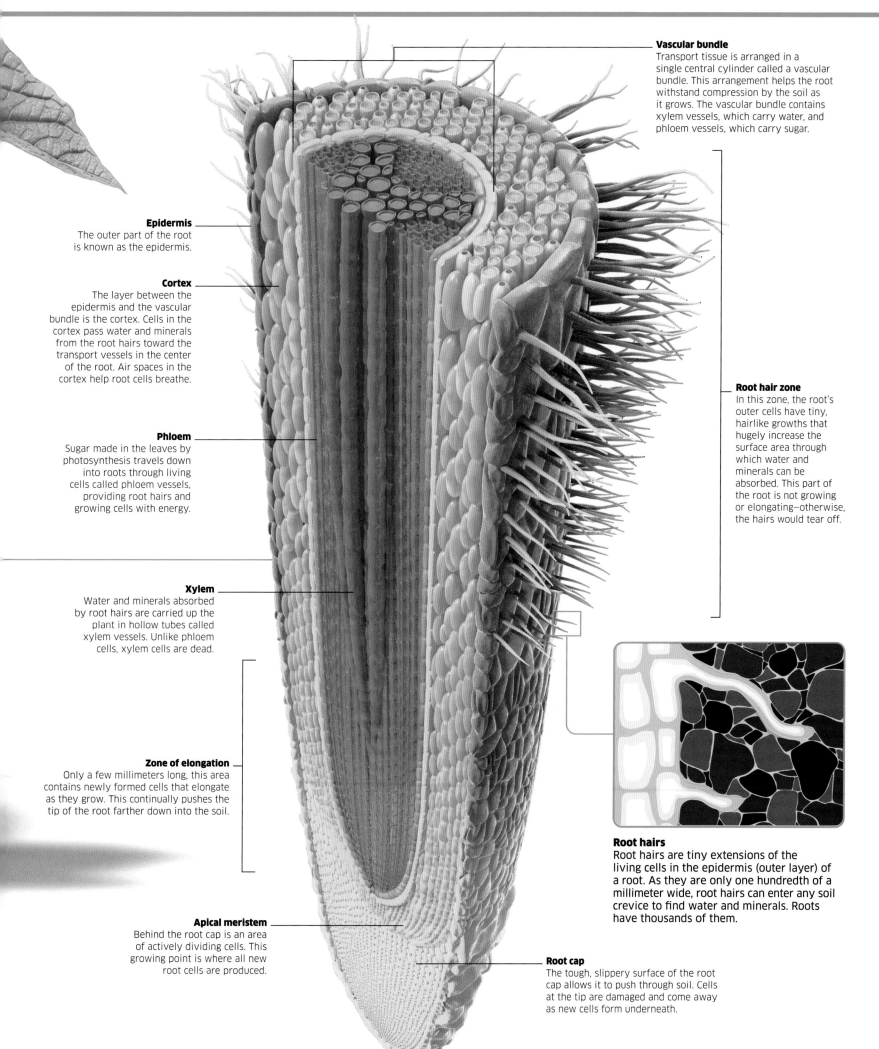

Vascular bundle
Transport tissue is arranged in a single central cylinder called a vascular bundle. This arrangement helps the root withstand compression by the soil as it grows. The vascular bundle contains xylem vessels, which carry water, and phloem vessels, which carry sugar.

Epidermis
The outer part of the root is known as the epidermis.

Cortex
The layer between the epidermis and the vascular bundle is the cortex. Cells in the cortex pass water and minerals from the root hairs toward the transport vessels in the center of the root. Air spaces in the cortex help root cells breathe.

Phloem
Sugar made in the leaves by photosynthesis travels down into roots through living cells called phloem vessels, providing root hairs and growing cells with energy.

Xylem
Water and minerals absorbed by root hairs are carried up the plant in hollow tubes called xylem vessels. Unlike phloem cells, xylem cells are dead.

Zone of elongation
Only a few millimeters long, this area contains newly formed cells that elongate as they grow. This continually pushes the tip of the root farther down into the soil.

Apical meristem
Behind the root cap is an area of actively dividing cells. This growing point is where all new root cells are produced.

Root hair zone
In this zone, the root's outer cells have tiny, hairlike growths that hugely increase the surface area through which water and minerals can be absorbed. This part of the root is not growing or elongating—otherwise, the hairs would tear off.

Root hairs
Root hairs are tiny extensions of the living cells in the epidermis (outer layer) of a root. As they are only one hundredth of a millimeter wide, root hairs can enter any soil crevice to find water and minerals. Roots have thousands of them.

Root cap
The tough, slippery surface of the root cap allows it to push through soil. Cells at the tip are damaged and come away as new cells form underneath.

Storage organs

Some plants endure long cold or dry seasons when they are unable to grow. They survive by storing food in organs hidden underground, safe from herbivores and harsh weather.

Bulbs, corms, tubers, rhizomes, and taproots are all different kinds of storage organs. They are made up of specialized leaves, roots, or stems that swell up with reserves of starch—a carbohydrate made by joining sugar molecules into long chains. These storage organs can stay dormant for months before springing to life when conditions are right for growth. The store of nutrients can power rapid development, giving plants a head start on their competitors when the growing season begins.

SWEET POTATO

IRIS

CROCUS

Root tuber
Sweet potatoes store food in swellings called root tubers. In the growing season, a new shoot grows from one end of a root tuber and roots develop from the opposite end. Dahlias also store food in root tubers.

Rhizome
A rhizome is a kind of stem that grows horizontally in the ground. As well as storing starch, rhizomes help plants reproduce, as broken fragments can grow into new plants. Plants with rhizomes include bamboos and irises.

Corm
A corm is a swollen stem, often with a protective "tunic" formed from the remains of leaves to keep out insects and water. Corms are very short, often wider than they are tall, but they are packed with stored nutrients. The base grows roots and side shoots that become new corms. Gladioli and freesias develop from corms.

Tulip mania

In the 17th century, tulips became extremely fashionable in the Netherlands in Europe, but the most popular striped varieties were hard to grow and the supply of bulbs was limited. Prices rose, making the rare varieties even more desirable, so demand increased, pushing prices higher still. The result was a dramatic rise in the price of tulips. At the height of "tulip mania," some bulbs sold for more than 10 times an average person's annual income.

Semper Augustus tulip
The most valuable bulb in history produced this striped tulip flower.

POTATO

CARROT

ONION

Starch store
The cells in a potato contain tiny grains called leucoplasts, which are filled with starch. A fresh potato is about 15 percent starch. Most of the rest of its weight is water.

Tunic
The tunic is the "skin" of the bulb, made of dried outer scales.

Scale
Each scale is a swollen leaf base.

Basal plate
This flat stem produces new growth.

Stem tuber
Potatoes may look like swollen roots, but they are in fact swollen stems. The "eyes" are buds that will grow into next season's shoots. Potatoes and yams both store food as stem tubers.

Taproot
A taproot is the main vertical root of a plant. Many plants that have taproots as storage organs are grown as vegetable crops, including carrots, radishes, turnips, parsnips, and beetroot.

Bulb
Concentric rings of swollen leaf bases make up a bulb. They grow from a basal plate, which is a shortened stem. The next season's leaves and even flowers develop within a bulb before it becomes dormant. Tulips, snowdrops, and daffodils grow from bulbs.

REPRODUCTION

Plants create new offspring in surprisingly varied ways. Some plants use flowers to reproduce sexually, then make fruits to disperse their seeds to new homes. Others spread by scattering millions of tiny particles called spores. And many plants have the ability to make clones of themselves.

Cycle of life

All living things go through a sequence of changes called a life cycle. They grow and develop until they are mature enough to reproduce, and eventually they die.

The life cycle of plants starts with a seed or a single-celled particle called a spore. It germinates and grows until it has enough energy and resources to reproduce. Most plants can reproduce in two different ways: sexually, which requires two parents, and asexually, which doesn't. In some plants, known as annuals, the life cycle lasts a single year. Plants with a two-year life cycle are called biennials, and plants that live for many years are perennials.

PLANT LIFESPANS

Plants can reach incredible ages thanks to their ability to regenerate damaged parts. Even so, plant lifespans vary enormously. Some species are genetically programmed to die after flowering, while others can live thousands of years. The world's oldest individual plant is a bristlecone pine tree in California that's about 4,900 years old. Plants that reproduce by making clones of themselves can survive longer as colonies. The oldest clonal colony is a group of aspen trees in Utah that started life as a seed possibly as long as 80,000 years ago.

SEEDLESS PLANTS

Ferns and mosses don't make flowers, fruits, or seeds. Instead, they grow from spores. Their life cycle alternates between two very different kinds of plants—a process called alternation of generations. One plant produces spores and is called a sporophyte. The other produces sex cells (gametes) and is called a gametophyte. The male sex cells (sperm) must swim through water to find female sex cells, so ferns and mosses are limited to damp habitats.

■ Gametophyte
■ Sporophyte

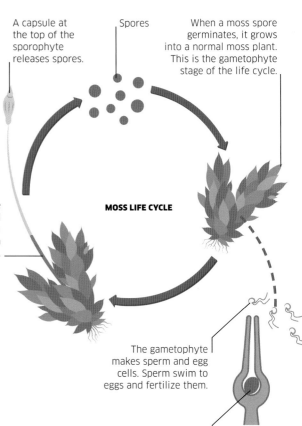

Spores

A fern spore grows into a small, flat plant called a gametophyte. It produces sperm and egg cells.

Egg cell

FERN LIFE CYCLE

The main leafy part of a fern plant is the sporophyte. It produces spores inside capsules on the underside of leaves.

The fertilized egg cell grows into a sporophyte.

Sperm cells swim from other gametophytes to fertilize egg cells.

A capsule at the top of the sporophyte releases spores.

Spores

When a moss spore germinates, it grows into a normal moss plant. This is the gametophyte stage of the life cycle.

MOSS LIFE CYCLE

The fertilized egg cell grows into a sporophyte.

The gametophyte makes sperm and egg cells. Sperm swim to eggs and fertilize them.

Egg

ASEXUAL REPRODUCTION

Plants are very good at reproducing asexually and can do so in many different ways. Throughout a plant are small clusters of unspecialized cells (stem cells). These cells can generate new roots, stems, leaves, or even whole new plants. Gardeners take advantage of this ability by using cuttings to grow clones of plants they like.

1 TAKING A CUTTING
To make a cutting, a gardener starts by using a sharp blade to cut a healthy shoot up to 4 in (10 cm) long.

2 ROOTING HORMONE
Some gardeners treat cuttings with a hormone that stimulates root development, but this isn't essential.

3 PLANT IN SOIL
Cuttings are planted in soil and left for a few weeks while new roots develop from the cut.

The so-called century plant lives for
10–30 years, then **dies after flowering.**

0.05 mm—the size of the world's
smallest seeds, made by orchids.

65

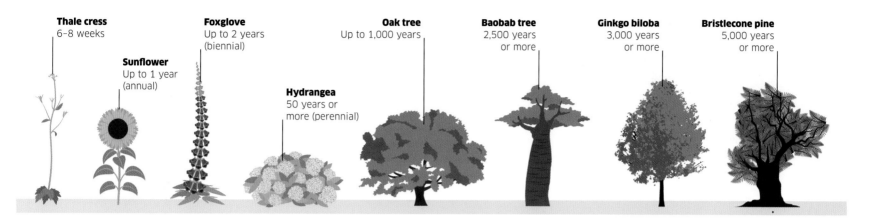

Thale cress
6–8 weeks

Sunflower
Up to 1 year
(annual)

Foxglove
Up to 2 years
(biennial)

Hydrangea
50 years or
more (perennial)

Oak tree
Up to 1,000 years

Baobab tree
2,500 years
or more

Ginkgo biloba
3,000 years
or more

Bristlecone pine
5,000 years
or more

FLOWERING PLANTS

Flowering plants start life as seeds. A seed contains an
embryo (a baby plant) and a food store to help the young
plant grow. Flowering plants reproduce sexually by making
flowers, which develop into fruits containing seeds.

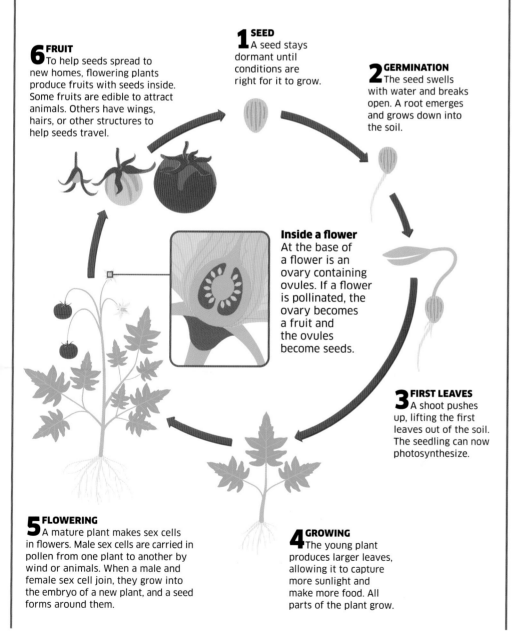

6 FRUIT
To help seeds spread to
new homes, flowering plants
produce fruits with seeds inside.
Some fruits are edible to attract
animals. Others have wings,
hairs, or other structures to
help seeds travel.

1 SEED
A seed stays
dormant until
conditions are
right for it to grow.

2 GERMINATION
The seed swells
with water and breaks
open. A root emerges
and grows down into
the soil.

Inside a flower
At the base of
a flower is an
ovary containing
ovules. If a flower
is pollinated, the
ovary becomes
a fruit and
the ovules
become seeds.

3 FIRST LEAVES
A shoot pushes
up, lifting the first
leaves out of the soil.
The seedling can now
photosynthesize.

5 FLOWERING
A mature plant makes sex cells
in flowers. Male sex cells are carried in
pollen from one plant to another by
wind or animals. When a male and
female sex cell join, they grow into
the embryo of a new plant, and a seed
forms around them.

4 GROWING
The young plant
produces larger leaves,
allowing it to capture
more sunlight and
make more food. All
parts of the plant grow.

ALTERNATION OF GENERATIONS

Alternation of generations doesn't just happen in
ferns and mosses. It takes place in all plants, including
flowering plants. However, it's less obvious in flowering
plants, as the gametophytes are microscopic and have
very short lives.

Flowering plants produce male and female gametophytes from spores
that form inside flowers. The male gametophytes are pollen grains.
When they pollinate a flower, they grow through it and deliver male
sex cells (sperm) to the ovary. The female gametophytes are even less
obvious. They are tiny sacs that form deep inside a flower's ovary.
These hidden plants within plants produce female sex cells (egg cells)
that are fertilized by sperm from pollen. After the two sex cells meet,
they form an embryo inside a seed. This embryo is a new sporophyte.

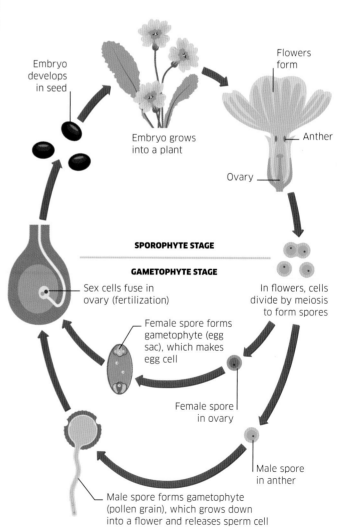

Embryo
develops
in seed

Embryo grows
into a plant

Flowers
form

Anther

Ovary

SPOROPHYTE STAGE

GAMETOPHYTE STAGE

Sex cells fuse in
ovary (fertilization)

In flowers, cells
divide by meiosis
to form spores

Female spore forms
gametophyte (egg
sac), which makes
egg cell

Female spore
in ovary

Male spore
in anther

Male spore forms gametophyte
(pollen grain), which grows down
into a flower and releases sperm cell

0.002 in (0.04 mm)—the width of a typical pollen grain.

Inside a flower

Flowers are often the most eye-catching parts of plants. There's a good reason for this: their job is to attract pollinators, which help flowering plants reproduce.

Look closely at a flower and you'll see its male and female sex organs hidden within the ring of brightly colored petals. The male organs release a powdery substance called pollen, which contains male sex cells. When pollen lands on the tip of a flower's female sex organ, the male cells join with female cells deep inside the flower, triggering the formation of seeds. Flowers come in many different varieties, but all flowers share the same underlying structure.

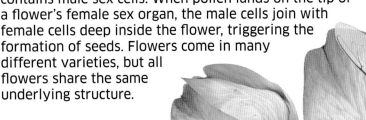

Pollen
Pollen grains form in the anthers and stick to pollinators such as bees and butterflies. Wind-pollinated grains are small and round. Animal-pollinated grains are larger, often with angles or spines, so that they catch on the body of an animal.

Cherry flower
Like most flowers, cherry flowers are hermaphrodites, which means that they contain both male and female sex organs. In the middle of the flower is a single female organ, the carpel. Its base is a chamber called an ovary. At the top of the carpel, a sticky tip called a stigma catches pollen. Surrounding the carpel are the flower's 20 male organs—stamens—which produce pollen.

How insects see flowers
Flowers pollinated by insects have colors that humans cannot see. Insect eyes can detect ultraviolet (UV) light, allowing them to see bold patterns that direct flying visitors to the flower's center.

WHAT HUMANS SEE

WHAT BEES SEE

Anther
At the tip of a stamen is an anther—a set of long sacs of pollen. Often yellow, they are easy to see.

Filament
This long stalk holds the anther in the right place for pollen dispersal.

Stamen
The filament and anther make up one male organ, which is called a stamen. Pollinators brush the stamen when feeding on nectar.

A pollen grain is a **microscopic organism** that produces sperm (male sex cells).

75 percent of food crops are **pollinated by insects.**

67

Stigma
A landing platform for pollen grains, the stigma is sticky to keep the grains in place.

Style
Pollen grains grow down through this long stalk so that the male sex cells reach the ovules.

Carpel
The female parts of the flower are collectively known as the carpel or pistil.

Ovary
The ovary protects the ovules. After pollination, the ovary develops into a fruit.

Ovules
These structures inside the ovary develop into seeds if the flower is pollinated.

Petals
The most colorful and obvious parts of a flower, petals attract pollinators such as insects.

Sepals
These modified leaves at the base of the flower protect the delicate inner parts of the flower while it is still a bud.

Nectar
A sugary liquid produced in the base of the flower attracts pollinating insects.

Receptacle
This is the base of the flower.

68 reproduction ○ ANIMAL POLLINATION

More than **70 percent** of plant
species rely on animal pollinators.

Self- and cross-pollination

Many flowers can pollinate themselves, but the offspring of self-pollinated plants have little genetic variation and are less able to adapt to changes in their environment. To avoid self-pollination, some plants have features to ensure they can only be pollinated by other plants. This is known as cross-pollination.

Separate sexes

Some plants are either wholly male or wholly female, making self-pollination impossible. Examples include willow trees and date palms.

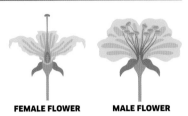

FEMALE FLOWER   **MALE FLOWER**

Different timing

In many flowers, the male parts ripen at a different time from female parts, ensuring cross-pollination.

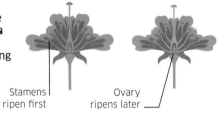

Stamens ripen first

Ovary ripens later

Pin and thrum

Primroses have two types of flowers to encourage cross-pollination. "Pin" flowers have a long style and a high stigma to collect pollen from insects. "Thrum" flowers have a short style but long stamens to deposit pollen on insects.

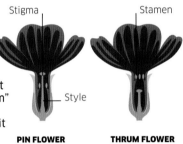

Stigma

Stamen

Style

PIN FLOWER   **THRUM FLOWER**

Chemical signals

In clover, cabbage, and some other plants, pollen grains don't germinate if they detect chemicals in the stigma that indicate they have landed on the plant that produced them.

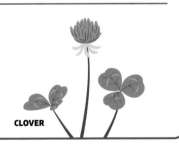

CLOVER

Animal pollination

Most flowering plants rely on animals to carry pollen from flower to flower. Flowers pollinated by animals are often large, colorful, and scented to attract pollinators. Many also reward visitors with an energy drink: nectar.

In order to reproduce sexually, a plant must exchange sex cells with a mate. Unlike animals, which can move around and search for mates, plants are rooted to the spot and may be a long distance from other members of their species. The solution is to produce pollen–tiny, powdery grains that contain male sex cells and can travel from plant to plant. Wind-pollinated flowers produce millions of powdery pollen grains and let the wind scatter them everywhere. Animal-pollinated flowers, however, produce a smaller number of sticky pollen grains that cling to visiting animals and rub off on other flowers, so they find the right target much more easily.

Fertilization

After a pollen grain lands on a flower's stigma (the tip of the female organ), it germinates like a seed and grows a long tube. The pollen tube extends deep into the flower, fed by nutritious fluids, to reach the ovary. Here, its tip opens to release two sperm cells (male sex cells). One fuses with a female sex cell inside an ovule, fertilizing it. The ovule will now develop into a seed. The second sperm cell fuses with other female cells in the ovule to form the seed's food store.

Pollen tube
After pollen lands on the stigma, a pollen tube grows deep into the flower until it reaches the ovary.

Long tongue
The tubular shape of the flower forces the bat to reach deep inside with its tongue to get nectar. As it does so, it unwittingly deposits pollen picked up in other flowers.

Ovary
At the base of the female part of the flower is an ovary. This contains ovules. The ovary wall usually develops into a fruit.

Ovule
The pollen tube has reached and fertilized an ovule inside the ovary. The ovule will now develop into a seed.

**IPOMOEA FLOWER
(IPOMOEA MARCELLIA)**

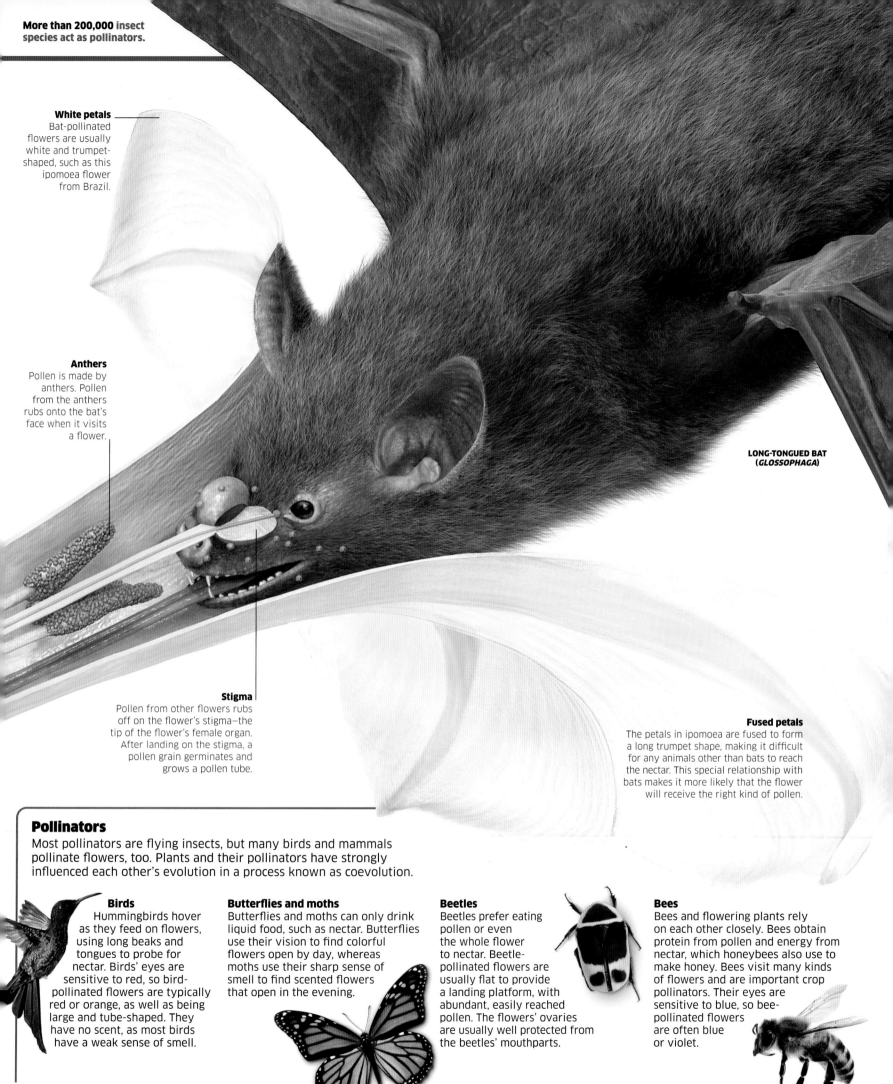

More than 200,000 insect species act as pollinators.

White petals
Bat-pollinated flowers are usually white and trumpet-shaped, such as this ipomoea flower from Brazil.

Anthers
Pollen is made by anthers. Pollen from the anthers rubs onto the bat's face when it visits a flower.

LONG-TONGUED BAT (*GLOSSOPHAGA*)

Stigma
Pollen from other flowers rubs off on the flower's stigma–the tip of the flower's female organ. After landing on the stigma, a pollen grain germinates and grows a pollen tube.

Fused petals
The petals in ipomoea are fused to form a long trumpet shape, making it difficult for any animals other than bats to reach the nectar. This special relationship with bats makes it more likely that the flower will receive the right kind of pollen.

Pollinators

Most pollinators are flying insects, but many birds and mammals pollinate flowers, too. Plants and their pollinators have strongly influenced each other's evolution in a process known as coevolution.

Birds
Hummingbirds hover as they feed on flowers, using long beaks and tongues to probe for nectar. Birds' eyes are sensitive to red, so bird-pollinated flowers are typically red or orange, as well as being large and tube-shaped. They have no scent, as most birds have a weak sense of smell.

Butterflies and moths
Butterflies and moths can only drink liquid food, such as nectar. Butterflies use their vision to find colorful flowers open by day, whereas moths use their sharp sense of smell to find scented flowers that open in the evening.

Beetles
Beetles prefer eating pollen or even the whole flower to nectar. Beetle-pollinated flowers are usually flat to provide a landing platform, with abundant, easily reached pollen. The flowers' ovaries are usually well protected from the beetles' mouthparts.

Bees
Bees and flowering plants rely on each other closely. Bees obtain protein from pollen and energy from nectar, which honeybees also use to make honey. Bees visit many kinds of flowers and are important crop pollinators. Their eyes are sensitive to blue, so bee-pollinated flowers are often blue or violet.

Pollen carrier

About 90 percent of flowering plant species rely on insects to pollinate their flowers and thereby help them reproduce.

Unlike most insects, the elephant hawkmoth doesn't land on flowers. Instead, it hovers by them like a hummingbird and unrolls its long, coiled proboscis (tongue) to suck nectar. As it does so, pollen sticks to its hairy body, attracted by static electricity—much like styrofoam peanuts stick to your hands when opening cardboard packaging. When the moth visits another flower, pollen grains brush off and pollinate it.

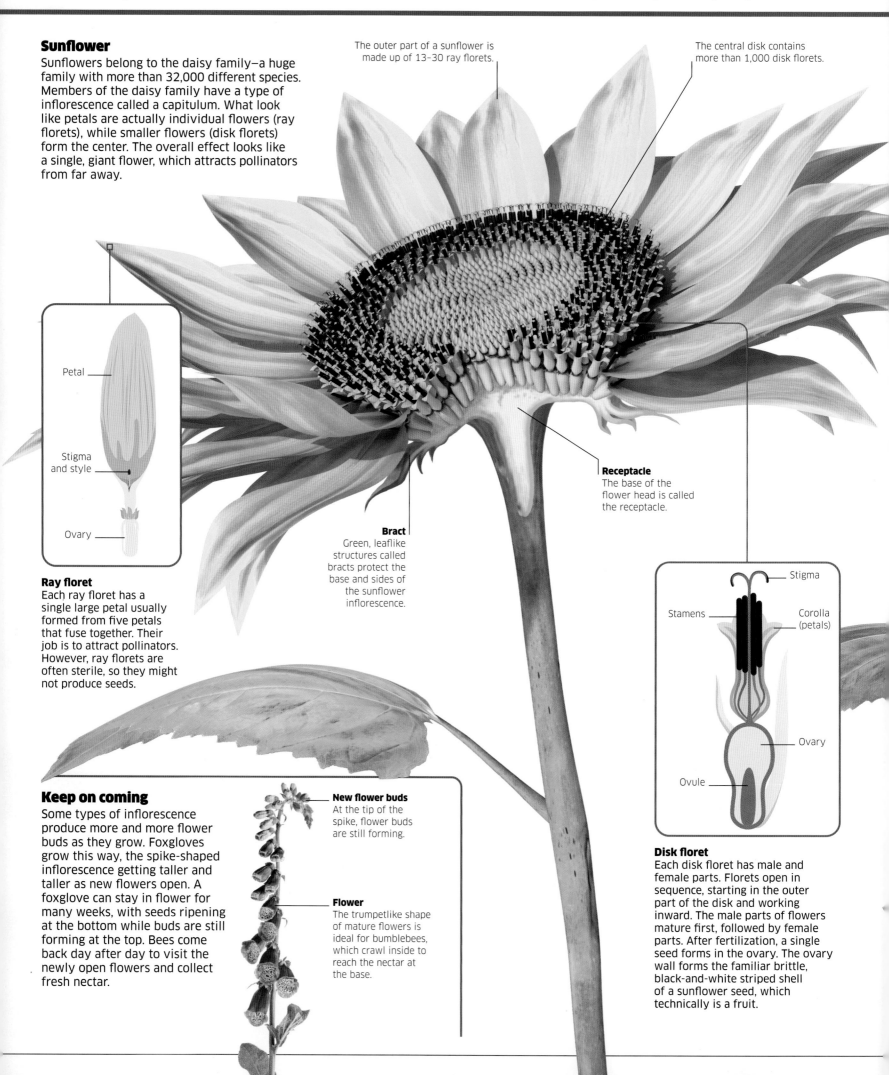

Sunflower

Sunflowers belong to the daisy family—a huge family with more than 32,000 different species. Members of the daisy family have a type of inflorescence called a capitulum. What look like petals are actually individual flowers (ray florets), while smaller flowers (disk florets) form the center. The overall effect looks like a single, giant flower, which attracts pollinators from far away.

The outer part of a sunflower is made up of 13–30 ray florets.

The central disk contains more than 1,000 disk florets.

Petal

Stigma and style

Ovary

Ray floret

Each ray floret has a single large petal usually formed from five petals that fuse together. Their job is to attract pollinators. However, ray florets are often sterile, so they might not produce seeds.

Receptacle
The base of the flower head is called the receptacle.

Bract
Green, leaflike structures called bracts protect the base and sides of the sunflower inflorescence.

Stigma

Stamens

Corolla (petals)

Ovary

Ovule

Keep on coming

Some types of inflorescence produce more and more flower buds as they grow. Foxgloves grow this way, the spike-shaped inflorescence getting taller and taller as new flowers open. A foxglove can stay in flower for many weeks, with seeds ripening at the bottom while buds are still forming at the top. Bees come back day after day to visit the newly open flowers and collect fresh nectar.

New flower buds
At the tip of the spike, flower buds are still forming.

Flower
The trumpetlike shape of mature flowers is ideal for bumblebees, which crawl inside to reach the nectar at the base.

Disk floret

Each disk floret has male and female parts. Florets open in sequence, starting in the outer part of the disk and working inward. The male parts of flowers mature first, followed by female parts. After fertilization, a single seed forms in the ovary. The ovary wall forms the familiar brittle, black-and-white striped shell of a sunflower seed, which technically is a fruit.

10 ft (3 m)—the **height of the world's tallest inflorescence,** which belongs to the foul-smelling corpse flower.

Broccoli and cauliflower are the inflorescences of the cabbage plant.

73

Flowers in flowers

Some flowers are not quite what they seem. The spectacular yellow bloom of a sunflower is not a single flower but a cluster of 1,000 tiny ones—florets—packed together. A cluster of flowers is called an inflorescence.

Inflorescences come in many shapes and sizes, from the neat round shapes of daisies and sunflowers to the tall spikes of foxgloves and the frothy, umbrella-shaped flower heads of parsley. Most inflorescences can be classified as one of two main types. In an indeterminate inflorescence, new flowers keep growing and forming at the top while lower ones mature. In a determinate inflorescence, the top flower opens first and lower ones open later.

Tracking the Sun
Young sunflower stalks bend during the day to keep the flower head facing the Sun. This keeps the tiny florets warm, helping bees pollinate them. Once mature, however, the flower head remains facing east.

Mathematical pattern
Flower heads of the daisy family have florets growing in interlocking spirals to pack in as many florets as possible. The numbers of these clockwise and counterclockwise spirals follow a famous mathematical pattern called the Fibonacci sequence.

Types of inflorescence

Plant scientists and gardeners have special names for the various different types of inflorescence. For instance, members of the daisy family have a flat, compact inflorescence called a "capitulum," while members of the parsley family have an "umbel," with florets on small stalks like the spokes in an umbrella.

Capitulum
The florets are packed together on a wide, flat base, forming what looks like a single flower.

Spike
The florets grow from a single stem and don't have separate stalks.

Raceme
The florets grow from a single tall stem and each floret has a short stalk (a pedicel).

Compound raceme
Lots of small racemes are arranged together in a single larger raceme.

Corymb
The florets are arranged like a raceme, but the outer florets have progressively longer pedicels.

Catkin
The inflorescence is similar to a spike or a raceme but hangs upside down.

Umbel
The florets are on short stalks (pedicels) that all come from the same point.

Compound umbel
Lots of small umbels are joined together in a single large umbel.

Spadix
A fleshy spike with many tiny florets is accompanied by a large, petal-like structure called a spathe.

Tricks and traps

Pollinators usually earn a reward such as nectar for their services, but some plants resort to tricks and traps to make sure that they are pollinated successfully.

Making nectar is expensive for plants, as this sugary substance contains a lot of energy. To minimize waste, some plants have evolved ways of luring pollinators to land on flowers without giving visitors anything in return. Orchids are masters of this sneaky strategy. Many orchids also have highly specialized relationships with a particular pollinator, ensuring the precious pollen is carried only to other flowers of the same species.

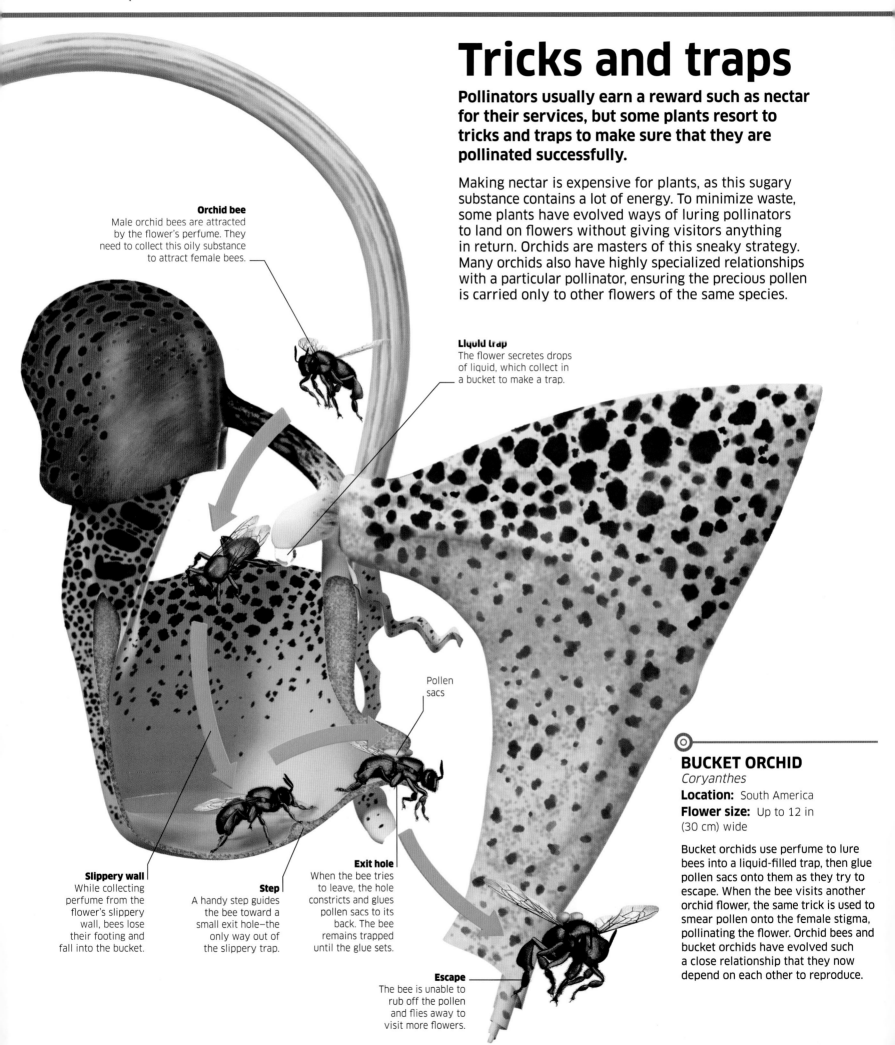

Orchid bee
Male orchid bees are attracted by the flower's perfume. They need to collect this oily substance to attract female bees.

Liquid trap
The flower secretes drops of liquid, which collect in a bucket to make a trap.

Pollen sacs

Slippery wall
While collecting perfume from the flower's slippery wall, bees lose their footing and fall into the bucket.

Step
A handy step guides the bee toward a small exit hole—the only way out of the slippery trap.

Exit hole
When the bee tries to leave, the hole constricts and glues pollen sacs to its back. The bee remains trapped until the glue sets.

Escape
The bee is unable to rub off the pollen and flies away to visit more flowers.

BUCKET ORCHID
Coryanthes
Location: South America
Flower size: Up to 12 in (30 cm) wide

Bucket orchids use perfume to lure bees into a liquid-filled trap, then glue pollen sacs onto them as they try to escape. When the bee visits another orchid flower, the same trick is used to smear pollen onto the female stigma, pollinating the flower. Orchid bees and bucket orchids have evolved such a close relationship that they now depend on each other to reproduce.

10,000 —the number of orchid species that use **deception** to attract pollinators.

The **foul odor** of the titan arum can attract insects from up to 0.6 miles (1 km) away.

75

FAKE FLIES
Gorteria diffusa
Location: South Africa
Flower size: 1-2 in (3-6 cm) wide

The black blobs on the beetle daisy plant look just like small insects, with tiny hairs and specks of white to complete the illusion. Male bee flies are fooled, too. They land on the flowers and pick up pollen as they fumble around trying to find the nonexistent females.

Fake fly

SACRED LOTUS
Nelumbo nucifera
Location: South and Southeast Asia
Flower size: Up to 12 in (30 cm) wide

The sacred lotus does give its pollinators a reward, but only when it's ready. The flower opens only a little on the first day, attracting beetles with its scent. It then closes tightly overnight, trapping the beetles and ensuring that any pollen they carry is deposited on the female stigmas. The next day, the stamens shed their pollen, dusting the beetles, and the flower opens to free them. Lotus flowers have the remarkable ability to maintain a constant warm temperature like warm-blooded animals, which helps keep the beetles active.

Carpel (female part)

BEE ORCHID
Ophrys
Location: Europe, North Africa
Flower size: 0.5-1 in (1-3 cm) long

Bee orchids so strongly resemble female bees that males land on them and try to mate with the flower, pollinating it as they do so. Scientists call this pseudocopulation. There are hundreds of different bee orchid species, many of which mimic a particular kind of bee. As well as fooling the crude vision of bees, the flowers produce a scent that mimics the scent of female bees.

DUCK ORCHID
Caleana
Location: Western Australia
Flower size: 1 in (0-25 mm) long

The duck-shaped flowers of this Australian orchid evolved to fool male sawflies, which are also attracted by the orchid's perfume—a perfect match for females. When a male sawfly tries to mate with the flower, the duck's "head" snaps down and presses him into the flower's base, trapping him. As he wriggles out, pollen sacs stick to his back.

The duck's "head" folds down to trap visiting flies.

TITAN ARUM
Amorphophallus titanum
Location: Sumatran rainforest
Flower size: Up to 10 ft (3 m) tall

The flower head of the titan arum plant is nearly twice as tall as an adult human, making it the largest unbranched flower head in the world. Also called the corpse flower, it produces a disgusting odor like rotting flesh to attract carrion flies, which normally lay their eggs on rotting flesh. The flower head normally opens in the evening, warming up as it does so to help spread its smell. Flies searching for flesh bump into a cluster of tiny flowers around the base of the giant spike. Female flowers are receptive to pollen first, and pollen is released later. The next day, the giant structure wilts and collapses.

The central spike is called a spadix. Small flowers are hidden at its base.

The flesh-colored outer part of the corpse flower is called a spathe. It looks like a giant petal but is a modified leaf.

The story of figs

Fig trees have an extraordinary relationship with tiny wasps that live and breed inside their hollow fruits. Neither could exist without the other.

Figs are soft, juicy fruits that develop in a very unusual way. They are inside out, with hundreds of tiny flowers pointing into the hollow center of each unripe fig. These flowers can only be pollinated by fig wasps, which spend their whole life inside figs. The male wasps are wingless and never leave. The females leave only to fly from one fig to another, pollinating the flowers as they do so.

Intricate pollination

Fig wasps and figs depend on each other to complete their life cycle. The female wasp lays its eggs inside the tiny fig flowers. It also pollinates the fig, enabling the fruit to ripen successfully.

Fig flower

Wasp deposits egg inside the flower

2 Pollination
Inside the fig, the wasp finds hundreds of male and female flowers. She pollinates some female flowers using pollen stored on her legs. This ensures the fig will ripen. Then she stabs other female flowers with the tip of her tail and lays eggs in them. She then dies.

Female flower

1 Female enters
Attracted by a fig's scent, a female wasp enters an unripe fig through a small opening called an ostiole. This is so tight that it tears off her wings as she enters. She will never fly again.

Fig wasps are **tiny**, measuring about 0.06 in (1.5 mm) long.

Fig wasps that **die inside figs** are digested and absorbed by enzymes in the plant.

77

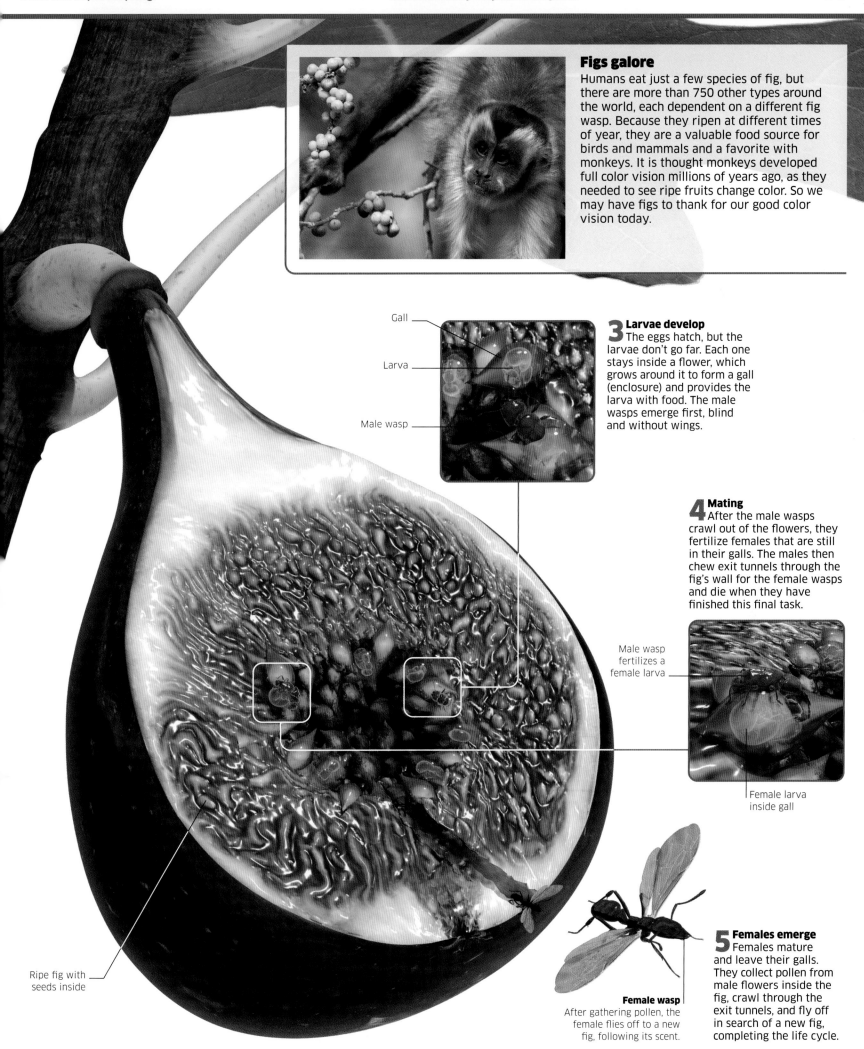

Figs galore
Humans eat just a few species of fig, but there are more than 750 other types around the world, each dependent on a different fig wasp. Because they ripen at different times of year, they are a valuable food source for birds and mammals and a favorite with monkeys. It is thought monkeys developed full color vision millions of years ago, as they needed to see ripe fruits change color. So we may have figs to thank for our good color vision today.

Gall

Larva

Male wasp

3 Larvae develop
The eggs hatch, but the larvae don't go far. Each one stays inside a flower, which grows around it to form a gall (enclosure) and provides the larva with food. The male wasps emerge first, blind and without wings.

4 Mating
After the male wasps crawl out of the flowers, they fertilize females that are still in their galls. The males then chew exit tunnels through the fig's wall for the female wasps and die when they have finished this final task.

Male wasp fertilizes a female larva

Female larva inside gall

Ripe fig with seeds inside

Female wasp
After gathering pollen, the female flies off to a new fig, following its scent.

5 Females emerge
Females mature and leave their galls. They collect pollen from male flowers inside the fig, crawl through the exit tunnels, and fly off in search of a new fig, completing the life cycle.

Wind pollination

Many plants produce small flowers we barely notice. That's because they are pollinated by wind and don't need bright colors or large petals to attract the attention of animals.

Wind-pollinated plants include all the world's grasses; all types of conifer trees (such as pines and firs); and many broadleaved trees, including oak, ash, birch, elm, and hazel. Unlike a pollen grain carried by a bee, a pollen grain blown randomly by wind has only the tiniest chance of landing on its target: another flower of the right species. To make up for this, wind-pollinated plants produce billions of minute pollen grains that float on air and can travel great distances. Even so, the vast majority go to waste.

Awn
Some grass flowers have a long bristle called an awn. The awn stays attached to the seed when it is released. Tiny, one-way bristles on the awn help dig the seed into the ground.

Spikelet
A small cluster of grass florets is called a spikelet. Each grass flower head has lots of spikelets.

Pollen
The flower head of a grass plant can produce 10 million pollen grains. Each one is less than a twentieth of a millimeter wide.

About **12 percent** of the world's flowering plants are pollinated by wind, including grasses, grain crops, and many trees.

A single annual mercury plant can produce **1.25 billion pollen grains** to be dispersed by the wind.

79

How grass flowers work

The flower head of a grass plant is made of many small flowers called florets. They are usually at the top of the plant to catch the wind, which is stronger farther away from the ground. In spring and summer, the florets open to scatter pollen and to capture pollen from other grass plants.

Bracts
Grass plants don't have sepals. Instead, flowers are protected by two boat-shaped structures called bracts. The smaller, inner one is called a palea. The larger, outer one is called a lemma.

Filament
The filaments holding the anthers are long and loose so the anthers can move easily in the wind.

Anther
Pollen is released from anthers, which hang outside the flower. When they move in the breeze, clouds of pollen blow away.

Stamen
The male part of a flower is called a stamen and consists of an anther attached to a thin stalk called a filament.

Stigma
Pollen from other flowers is captured by the stigma. In grass flowers, stigmas are divided into long, feathery arms to improve the chance of catching pollen.

Style
The style is a long, slender stalk that connects the stigma and the ovary. In wind-pollinated flowers, it holds the stigma in the air stream so it can more easily "catch" pollen.

Carpel
The female part of a flower is called a carpel. It is made up of the stigma, style, and ovary.

Pedicel
A stalk called a pedicel supports each floret.

Ovary
Hidden in the base of the female organ is the ovary, which contains an ovule. If the flower is fertilized, the ovule will develop into a seed. The ovary and seed together form a grain (such as a grain of wheat).

Conifer cones

Conifers don't have flowers, but they produce pollen in cones. Pollen blows from male cones to female cones, where it fertilizes ovules and seeds form. To prevent a tree from pollinating itself, the male cones are often at the bottom of the tree, while female cones are at the top.

Hay fever

The pollen from wind-pollinated plants is so abundant that we inhale it with every breath in spring and early summer. In some people, the body's immune system overreacts to the pollen particles. This causes the symptoms of hay fever: streaming eyes, a blocked or runny nose, and a scratchy throat.

ALDER TREE CATKINS SHED POLLEN IN SPRING

Pollen science

Pollen grains are very tough and can survive for centuries in mud. Some experts study the pollen grains in ancient mud or sedimentary rock to work out what kind of plants lived in an area in the distant past. This can reveal how the climate has changed over time. Forensic scientists also use evidence from pollen on shoes and clothes to help solve crimes.

55-MILLION-YEAR-OLD FOSSIL POLLEN FOUND IN CLAY

Pollen
Stamens produce pollen, a powdery substance that contains male sex cells.

1 Pollination
A fruit begins to form when a flower is pollinated. If a bee visits apple blossom, it accidentally transfers pollen from flower to flower. Some of the pollen rubs off on the tip of a flower's female parts—the stigma. A pollen tube grows down from the stigma to the ovary. Here, male sex cells from the pollen fuse with female sex cells inside an ovule. This is called fertilization.

Stigma

Stamen

Pollen tube

Ovary

Ovule

Petals fall off flowers after pollination.

2 Ovary swells
After fertilization, the ovules begin to develop into seeds, each containing a tiny embryo that may become a new apple tree. At the same time, the ovary wall around the ovules begins to swell to form the fruit's flesh. In apple flowers, the flower's base (receptacle) also swells, forming a thick layer of flesh around the ovary.

Colorful petals attract pollinators such as bees and wasps.

Withered stamen

Receptacle

Ovule

Ovary

From flower to fruit

Once a flower has been pollinated, its colorful petals wither and die and a fruit begins to grow, with seeds hidden inside it.

Fruits are part of a plant's strategy to make new plants. They are made by all flowering plants and help spread seeds to new homes, giving the plant's offspring a better chance of surviving. Edible fruits like apples and berries disperse seeds by packaging them in sweet, juicy flesh that animals find irresistible. The tastiest part usually develops from a small part of the flower called the ovary. It is a remarkable transformation and can take months to complete.

6,000 –the number of years people have been **cultivating peaches**.

Some farmers **hire honeybees** to pollinate the flowers on their farms.

81

3 Growing fruit
The apple continues growing for weeks, turning upside down as its weight makes it hang. Food transported from the tree's leaves is stored in the flesh as a substance called starch. This doesn't taste sweet, so the flesh is hard and bitter at this stage. The outer skin is still green.

True or false?
Not all fruits develop the same way. True fruits, such as peaches, peas, and grapes, grow from just the ovary of a flower and contain one or more fertilized seeds. False fruits, sometimes called accessory fruits, include other parts of the flower as well, such as the receptacle. Strawberries, pineapples, and apples are false fruits.

Ovary

Receptacle

FALSE FRUIT (APPLE)

Ovary

TRUE FRUIT (CHERRY)

Receptacle

Ovary

Ovary

Seed

The skin of an unripe fruit is usually green.

Apple seeds are white before ripening.

Ripening fruits often become colored.

4 Ripening
As an apple matures, its flesh softens and the store of starch is converted to sugar, making it taste sweet. The skin may change from green to red, helping attract animals. The seeds darken as they develop the protective outer coat that will help them survive the journey to a new home.

Remains of sepals

Types of fruits

We think of fruits as sweet, juicy, and tasty to eat, but not all fruits are like this. Some fruits are hard and stony, dry and papery, or as fluffy as cotton.

Scientifically speaking, a fruit is a mature, ripened flower ovary that contains seeds. For this reason, some things we consider vegetables, nuts, and seeds are actually fruits. All kinds of fruits, whatever form they take, have the same purpose: to help spread a plant's offspring.

⊙ INSIDE A FRUIT

After a flower is pollinated, the ovary develops into a fruit with seeds inside. The ovary wall has three different layers, and the way in which these develop varies from plant to plant. In fleshy fruits, the ovary wall typically grows into sweet flesh. In dry fruits, however, it might form a pod, a shell, or a structure to help a seed become airborne.

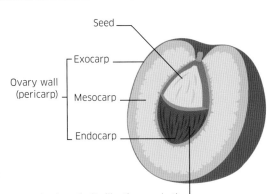

Seed
Exocarp
Ovary wall (pericarp)
Mesocarp
Endocarp

In stone fruits like the peach, the ovary's inner layer (the endocarp) forms a brittle shell around the seed.

⊙ DRY FRUITS

Many dry fruits have papery wings or feathery structures to catch the wind and help the seed travel far from the parent plant. Others are hard or heavy, so they roll away, and some split as they dry out, flinging seeds through the air.

STAR ANISE

Seed

Ovary wall (pericarp)

Schizocarp
A schizocarp is a dry fruit that splits into several parts as the fruit ripens. Each part contains one or more seeds. The fruits of carrots, parsnips, star anise, and geraniums are schizocarps.

Star anise is used as a spice in many Asian dishes.

Pericarp

Seed

PEA

Pod
Peas, beans, and most other members of the legume family have long fruits called pods. These dry out as they ripen and tear open along a seam, sometimes flinging out the seeds.

COTTON

Capsule
A capsule is a simple dry fruit that splits as it ripens to release many seeds. Cotton capsules have hairy seeds that catch the wind. These natural fibers have been spun into fabrics for more than 6,000 years.

Seed

Wing

MAPLE

Samara
A samara has a flat, papery wing formed from the ovary wall and a single seed. Trees such as maples produce samaras in pairs.

CORN

Grain
The fruits of grass plants are called grains. Each grain consists of a single seed fused with the flower's ovary wall. Wheat, rice, and corn all produce grains.

The parachute of hairs on milk thistle achenes forms from the flower's sepals.

The pericarp forms an inedible kernel.

Achene

MILK THISTLE

Achene
An achene contains a single seed that nearly fills the dry ovary wall but doesn't stick to it. The striped "seeds" of sunflowers and the pips of strawberries are achenes.

HAZELNUT

Nut
Scientifically speaking, nuts are fruits in which the ovary wall forms a hard shell (a kernel) that doesn't split when ripe. True nuts have a single seed inside.

55 lb (25 kg)–the weight of the **world's heaviest seed**, the coco de mer.

2,700 lb (1,225 kg)–the weight of the **world's largest fruit**, the giant Atlantic pumpkin.

83

FLESHY FRUITS

Fleshy fruits evolved to be sweet and nutritious because these features attract animals. Animals eat the sugary flesh, then discard the seeds or deposit them in droppings far from the parent plant–often with a supply of fertilizer.

Endocarp with seed inside

Mesocarp

Exocarp

CHERRY

Thick rind (exocarp)

Seeds

BUTTERNUT SQUASH

Ovary wall (pericarp)

KIWI FRUIT

Drupe
A drupe is a single fleshy fruit with a hard stone that contains one seed. Peaches, cherries, almonds, coconuts, and olives are all drupes.

Pepo
A pepo is a kind of berry with a thick rind, watery flesh, and many seeds. Pumpkins, melons, and cucumbers are all pepos.

Berry
A berry is a simple fleshy fruit formed from a flower with one ovary. Unlike a drupe, a berry has no stone as the whole pericarp becomes edible. Kiwi fruits, grapes, bell peppers, bananas, tomatoes, and even cucumbers are all berries.

Leathery exocarp

Mesocarp divided into segments

RED GRAPEFRUIT

Only the core develops from the ovary.

APPLE

Each pineapple segment develops from one ovary.

PINEAPPLE

One drupe

RASPBERRY

Hesperidium
A hesperidium is a kind of berry with a tough, leathery rind and a very juicy mesocarp divided into segments. This group includes all the citrus fruits.

Pome
The flesh of a pome develops not from an ovary but from another part of the flower. As a result, pomes are sometimes called false fruits. They include apples, pears, and quinces.

Composite fruit
A composite fruit, such as a pineapple or fig, forms from a cluster of tightly packed flowers. After pollination, the flowers' ovaries merge to form one fruit.

Accessory drupe
This fruit develops from a flower with multiple ovaries. It consists of many small drupes packed together, each with a single seed. Raspberries and blackberries are examples.

Berry or not?

Botanically speaking, some of the fruits we call berries are not really berries, as they aren't simple fruits formed from a single ovary. True berries include some surprising foods, from bananas and chilies to pumpkins and coffee.

Strawberries are false fruits. The pips (achenes) are the real fruits.

STRAWBERRY

RASPBERRY

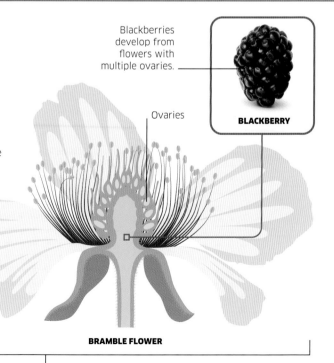

Blackberries develop from flowers with multiple ovaries.

BLACKBERRY

Ovaries

BRAMBLE FLOWER

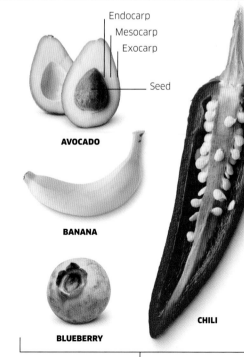

Endocarp

Mesocarp

Exocarp

Seed

AVOCADO

BANANA

BLUEBERRY

CHILI

Not berries

Berries

Natural glue

Not all sticky seeds use hooks to cling to animals. Instead, some plants coat their seeds with gluelike substances that stick to the feathers and beaks of birds. These seeds can be a nuisance to their carriers.

Mistletoe
Mistletoes are parasitic plants that grow on the branches of trees. Their sticky seeds cling to birds' beaks and are wiped off later on other trees—the perfect place for new mistletoe plants to take root.

Pisonia tree
The *Pisonia* tree grows on tropical islands and relies on seabirds to spread its incredibly sticky seeds to distant islands. Although the seeds eventually drop off, some birds become so heavily covered that they can't fly or they get stuck in the tree.

Spreading seeds

After flowering and producing seeds, plants have the challenge of making sure their offspring grow up in the best conditions.

Ideally, a plant's seeds will land and germinate far from the plant so that the seedling doesn't compete for light, nutrients, and water. Plants can't physically carry their offspring to new habitats like animals can, so they rely on other methods to ensure their seeds are dispersed. Many flowering plants use animals to do the job for them. Some plants reward animals with sweet-tasting fruit, while others stick their fruits to animals, hitching a free ride for the seeds inside.

Hooked hairs

Some plants have evolved fruits with hooks (burrs) that latch onto passing animals to be carried in their fur or feathers until they fall off far from the parent plant. Goosegrass is a common weed renowned for its clingy fruits. Although it feels sticky, every part of the plant, including its fruits, is actually covered in tiny hairs.

Burdock burrs
When the burdock flowers die away, just the prickly bracts remain. The burrs catch on passing animals to be dispersed.

Burrs
The hooked fruits are called burrs.

Goosegrass fruit

Squirrels **forget the location** of about 75 percent of the nuts they bury.

1 in (3 cm)—the diameter of a single spiky burdock burr.

300–400 seeds are produced by a **single** burdock plant every year.

85

In a tangle
Tiny hooked hairs tangle themselves in fur.

Clinging hairs
The tiny, hooked hairs that cover goosegrass plants and their small fruit easily cling onto passing animals to be spread far and wide. The hooks also help the plant clamber over other plants.

Goosegrass plant
Every part of the goosegrass plant is covered in tiny hairs.

Beasts' banquet

Animals are particularly attracted to fleshy fruits because they're a nutritious source of carbohydrates, minerals, and vitamins. As a result, animals make excellent seed dispersers, spitting and pooping out the seeds across a wide area.

Seeds are swallowed when animals eat fruits.

Some seeds benefit from passing through the digestive system, as it starts to break down the tough seed coat.

Animals will spit out or drop larger seeds that they cannot swallow.

When a seed takes root, the animal's dung can act as a fertilizer for the growing plant.

Poisonous fruit

Some fruits are poisonous to all but certain animals. This ensures they are eaten by only the best dispersers. Deadly nightshade is laced with toxic chemicals that are lethal to most mammals but harmless to some seed-spreading birds.

Buried treasure

Some animals, including squirrels, woodpeckers, and mice, stockpile seeds. Squirrels collect and bury surplus nuts in fall to provide food for winter. However, many of the planted seeds get forgotten, so they will germinate instead.

Flying and floating

Plants may grow rooted to one spot, but their offspring can travel great distances. Flying and floating seeds use wind and water to spread to new homes.

Seeds that fall straight to the ground from a tree are unlikely to thrive well in the shade of their parent. As well as being deprived of light, they end up competing with each other and with their parent for water and nutrients. Anything that helps a seed drift farther away—such as a wing that spins or a parachute of hair—improves the odds of survival. As a result, plants have evolved many different tricks and techniques to hitch a ride on the wind or water.

Blown away

Sycamore and maple trees produce winged fruits called samaras. The papery wings act like propeller blades, causing the fruits to spin as they fall and therefore slowing their descent. This allows the wind to blow them sideways, away from the parent tree.

Water dispersal

Seeds and fruits that fall into water have the potential to travel to the other side of the world. Floating seeds are usually buoyant, with a tough outer coat that resists saltwater.

Coconuts

Coconut palm trees grow on beaches. After falling, the heavy fruits often roll into the sea. Air spaces in the fibrous outer husk help the coconut float. By the time it washes up on a new beach, it is ready to sprout.

Mangroves

Mangrove trees grow in swamps on tropical coasts. Their seeds grow a long taproot that helps them float upright. When the water level drops at low tide, they anchor themselves in the mud.

Sacred lotus

This aquatic plant grows in rivers and has floating seed pods that detach and drift away. Later, the seeds fall out and sink to the riverbed, where they germinate.

Seed inside lotus pod

Strong backbone
A rigid edge keeps the samara stable as it rotates.

Tailspin

Samara wings are slightly pitched (tilted) like a propeller blade. This causes them to spiral as they descend. The tilt also gives the samara some lift, so it falls more slowly to the ground.

Hidden seed
A seed is hidden in the head of the samara.

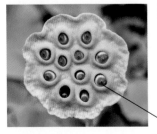

Wind dispersal

The maple seed's wing is just one of the ways plants take advantage of the wind to give their seeds the best chance of survival.

Hairy seeds
Hairy filaments extend from the seed coats of clematis seeds, allowing them to float off in the breeze when they detach from the plant.

Censers
Red campions produce seeds in pods called censers, which develop openings as they dry out. When the wind shakes the stalk, the seeds are flung from the opening.

Drifters
In strong winds, tumbleweeds break away from their roots and roll across the ground, scattering their seeds as they go. Each bush can produce as many as 50,000 seeds that need only the briefest of rain showers to begin growing.

Sideways drift
The slow descent of a spinning maple seed helps it drift away sideways and away from the parent tree, instead of falling directly under it.

Double-winged
The maple samara begins as a double samara, with two wings. As it matures and dries out, a seam develops down the center. The samara eventually splits along the seam, allowing each half to fall separately.

Tatar maple
The Tatar maple tree is found across parts of Europe and Asia. Its leaves and fruit turn a vibrant red in fall.

Under pressure
The pod uses fluid pressure to explode. As it matures, it fills with liquid, so the pressure within gradually increases.

Exploding plants

Throughout high summer, plants from beans to balsams crackle and pop as they take a more explosive approach to dispersing their seeds.

The fruits of some plants have evolved to violently break apart to make sure their seeds are flung far from the parent plant. An explosion is the only active way a plant can disperse its seeds widely. The seedheads of some explosive plants split along lines of weakness as they dry out, sending their seeds flying through the air. In other explosive plants, fluid builds up within a seed pod, creating pressure as the pod increases in size. When the tension becomes too great, the pod suddenly bursts and ejects the seeds.

Seeds are ejected at up to 60 mph (95 kph) and can fly 20 ft (6 m) away.

800 —the number of seeds a **Himalayan balsam plant** can fling out in one year.

The pods of popping cress eject their seeds at **22 mph (36 kph).** **89**

The seeds, juices, and fruit are toxic, reducing their chance of being eaten by animals.

When the pressure reaches a critical level, the pod detaches from the stem, leaving a hole for the seeds and slime to squirt out through.

Pea pods

Peas, beans, and other legumes produce seeds in pods. As the pods dry out and twist, their walls store energy. Eventually, the pods split along their seams, releasing the energy suddenly and flinging the seeds out with great force.

The pod splits along weak seams in its walls.

Seeds are flung away.

The pod curls as it splits.

Touch-me-not

Balsams are a family of plants found across the northern hemisphere and tropics. Their seed pods rely on fluid tension to fling seeds at speeds of up to 27 mph (43 kph). Just a drop of water can trigger the explosion, giving them their common name "touch-me-not."

The seeds and valves are flung away.

Plant stem

Seed

Valves splitting apart

Valve

Columella

1. Seed pods
Balsam seed pods are made up of five valves arranged around a central stalk called a columella.

2. Building tension
As the pod ripens, the valves fill with water, creating tension that forces them to start separating.

3. Pulling away
The valves curl and pull away from the columella at the center, shortening the pod.

4. Exploding
The valves reach a critical tension and break away from the columella. They coil as they break off, sending seeds flying.

Squirting cucumbers

One fruit that really goes off with a bang is the squirting cucumber. When ripe, the seed-filled pods of this poisonous plant break off their stalks and shoot away, propelled by an explosive jet of slime and seeds. Ripe pods are so sensitive that the slightest tap can trigger the reaction.

Sandbox tree

Sporting a trunk and branches covered in sharp, conical spikes, as well as poisonous sap and leaves, the sandbox tree is not the friendliest of plants. To disperse its seeds, its seedheads explode violently with a loud bang, earning this plant the nickname "dynamite tree."

The pumpkin-shaped seedheads explode when they dry out.

The seed casings and seeds fly like shrapnel in all directions and can injure nearby animals.

Hyacinth bulbs are poisonous.

Reproduction without sex

Many plants are able to clone themselves—a process known as asexual reproduction. Offspring produced in this way are genetically identical to their parents.

Asexual reproduction needs only one parent, which makes it quicker and easier than sexual reproduction. If the surrounding environment doesn't change much, the offspring have a high chance of survival because they have the same genes as their successful parent. However, offspring produced asexually are vulnerable to changes in the environment or new diseases, because they have no genetic variation. Across the plant kingdom, there are lots of different techniques for reproducing asexually.

BULBS
Examples: Hyacinth, tulip, and lily

Some plants survive winter underground as bulbs. These food storage organs consist of layers of special leaves wrapped tightly around each other. Many bulbs can reproduce asexually from "bulblets"—small buds that form at their base. The bulblets become whole new plants when a bulb starts growing in spring.

Bulblet

HYACINTH BULB WITH BULBLETS

HYACINTH FLOWER

GLADIOLUS PLANT

Cormels
New corms grow at the base of the original corm. These little offshoots are known as cormels.

Removing cormels
Gardeners sometimes remove the cormels from gladiolus bulbs and use them to grow new plants.

CORMS
Examples: Gladiolus, garlic, and crocus

A corm is a modified stem that stores food underground over winter. Corms look like bulbs but are more solid and don't contain layers of leaves. Like bulbs, they can reproduce asexually by making miniature corms at their base. These grow at the tips of short stems and are often discarded by bulb-eating animals, ensuring the plant survives.

UNFERTILIZED SEEDS
Examples: Dandelion

Dandelions have flowers with all the parts needed to reproduce sexually. However, their seeds form asexually without a need for pollination. Producing clones from seeds is known as agamospermy and helps dandelions spread rapidly to new habitats, which is partly why they are such common weeds.

DANDELION SEEDS

The titan arum's corm is the largest in the world and **weighs up to 200 lb (90 kg).**

In 2022, scientists in Australia reported that a seagrass plant had **covered 70 sq miles (180 sq km) of seafloor with clones of itself.**

91

RHIZOMES

Examples: Bamboo, turmeric, and iris

Rhizomes are rootlike stems that grow horizontally underground before producing new plants. Bamboo plants spread from rhizomes and can quickly invade the ground around them to form thickets.

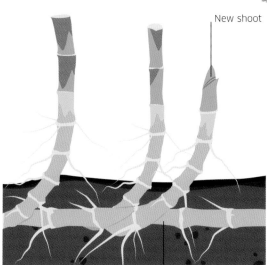

New shoot

Bamboo rhizome

SUCKERS

Examples: Quaking aspen, elm, and forsythia

Some trees, such as aspen, reproduce asexually from suckers—shoots that sprout from roots. In 1992, scientists reported the discovery of a 106-acre (42-hectare) stand of aspen tree clones in Utah. The trees had grown from suckers over thousands of years and their root systems are still linked, forming the world's largest organism.

CLONAL ASPEN COLONY IN UTAH

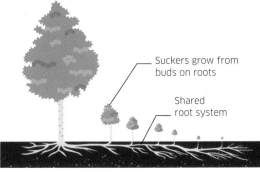

Suckers grow from buds on roots

Shared root system

ROOT SYSTEM OF AN ASPEN TREE

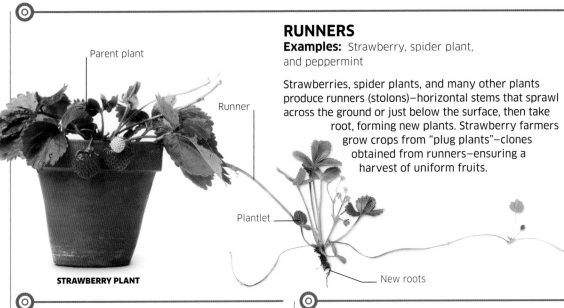

Parent plant

Runner

STRAWBERRY PLANT

TUBERS

Examples: Potato, peony, and cassava

Buried underground, tubers are swellings that store nutrients to help plants survive winter. Some tubers have buds on the surface from which new plants start to grow.

The "eyes" on potatoes are buds that can grow into new plants.

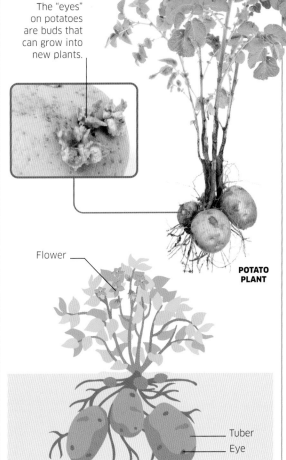

Flower

POTATO PLANT

Tuber

Eye

RUNNERS

Examples: Strawberry, spider plant, and peppermint

Strawberries, spider plants, and many other plants produce runners (stolons)—horizontal stems that sprawl across the ground or just below the surface, then take root, forming new plants. Strawberry farmers grow crops from "plug plants"—clones obtained from runners—ensuring a harvest of uniform fruits.

Plantlet

New roots

PLANTLETS

Examples: Mexican hat plant

The Mexican hat plant, also known as the "mother of thousands," produces hundreds of baby plants along the edges of its leaves. Each of these plantlets develops leaves and roots while still attached. When ready, they fall off the mother plant and take root in the soil below.

PLANTLETS

MEXICAN HAT PLANT

ECOSYSTEMS

In nature, all living things depend on relationships with other organisms and the physical environment. Together, the environment and its inhabitants make up an ecosystem. Plants are the most important members of every ecosystem on land, providing food and habitats to other organisms.

How ecosystems work

No living organism can survive on its own. Every animal and plant depends on a community of other living things to obtain nutrients, shelter, and other essential resources.

Communities of organisms and the environment around them make up what scientists call ecosystems. Plants are the most important parts of the world's terrestrial (land-based) ecosystems. They create shelter and habitats for wildlife and form the base of the food chain by capturing solar energy and converting it into food.

WHAT IS AN ECOSYSTEM?

An ecosystem consists of all the organisms in an area and their physical environment. Ecosystems can be as small as a pond or as large as a rainforest. Studying ecosystems helps scientists understand how different species interact and depend on each other.

Energy
The Sun is the energy source for nearly all ecosystems.

Rainfall
Environmental factors, such as rainfall, affect what kinds of organisms live in an ecosystem.

Community
The living organisms in an ecosystem make up a community. They depend on each other for resources such as food.

BIOMES

Large areas of Earth that are dominated by a particular kind of vegetation are known as biomes. Deserts and tropical rainforests are examples of biomes. Regions of the world that have similar climates also have the same biome types. The tropical rainforest biome is found in South and Central America, Africa, and Southeast Asia.

Tundra
Low-growing shrubs, mosses, and grasses are found in this area of long, icy winters and cool summers.

Boreal forest
These forests are dominated by evergreen conifer trees that thrive in cool summers and snowy winters.

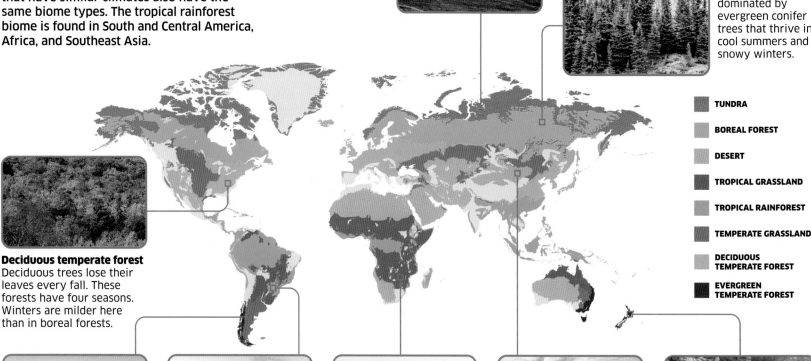

- TUNDRA
- BOREAL FOREST
- DESERT
- TROPICAL GRASSLAND
- TROPICAL RAINFOREST
- TEMPERATE GRASSLAND
- DECIDUOUS TEMPERATE FOREST
- EVERGREEN TEMPERATE FOREST

Deciduous temperate forest
Deciduous trees lose their leaves every fall. These forests have four seasons. Winters are milder here than in boreal forests.

Temperate grassland
Grasses dominate regions that are too hot and dry for forest but rainier than deserts.

Tropical rainforest
Warm and wet weather all year round allows many kinds of plants to grow in tropical rainforests.

Tropical grassland
These grasslands typically have a long dry season that makes it difficult for trees to thrive. Long grasses dominate the land.

Desert
Deserts are the driest regions on Earth. The few plants and animals living here have to survive with little water.

Evergreen temperate forest
In the southern hemisphere, areas of temperate forest usually have no winter frost. Trees keep their leaves and continue growing year round.

Rainforests are Earth's
oldest terrestrial ecosystems.

Only around **10 percent of the energy**
in a trophic level passes to the next level.

95

FOOD CHAINS

All organisms need energy to survive. A food chain shows how energy transfers from one living organism to another in an ecosystem. The different stages in a food chain are called trophic levels.

PLANTS

Producer
Plants and algae are producers. They use the Sun's energy to produce food through photosynthesis.

RABBIT

Primary consumer
Animals that eat plants (herbivores) are primary consumers. When they eat, the energy captured by plants transfers to their bodies.

OWL

Secondary consumer
Animals that eat other animals (carnivores) are secondary consumers. There are fewer carnivores than herbivores in an ecosystem.

WOLF

Tertiary consumer
Tertiary consumers are animals that eat primary and secondary consumers. Most food chains have a very small population of tertiary consumers.

PYRAMID OF ENERGY

This pyramid shows the energy stored in organisms at each trophic level. Energy is lost as it passes along a food chain, mostly as heat. Energy lost in dead matter or waste is used by decomposers, and the nutrients they take in are recycled into the soil and atmosphere.

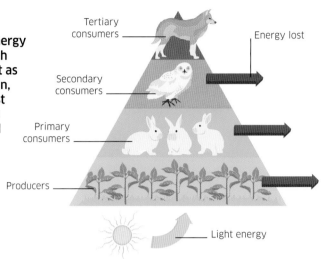

Tertiary consumers

Energy lost

Secondary consumers

Primary consumers

Producers

Light energy

CLIMATE AND SEASONS

The types of plants that grow in an ecosystem depend largely on its climate. Near Earth's equator, the climate is warm all year round. Closer to the poles, plants have to bear long and cold winters, when there is less sunlight and the ground may freeze. Plants that can survive freezing winters are described as hardy. Those that can't are described as tender.

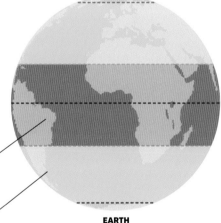

Regions near the poles have cool summers and freezing winters.

The region near the equator is the warmest, as it receives strong sunlight all year round.

Areas between the poles and the equator have a moderate climate without extreme seasons.

EARTH

-- Arctic Circle   -- Tropic of Cancer   -- Equator
-- Tropic of Capricorn   -- Antarctic Circle

RELATIONSHIPS IN ECOSYSTEMS

Every ecosystem involves a web of relationships between different species. Some relationships benefit both partners, such as when insects obtain nectar for pollinating flowers. Other relationships are harmful to one side but helpful to the other.

FLOWER

APHID

BLUE TIT

BIRCH TREE

Mutualism
A flower is pollinated by a bee, helping it make seeds, and the bee gains nectar in return.

Parasitism
A sap-sucking aphid gets food from its plant host, but the host is harmed as a result.

Predation
Predators are animals that hunt and kill other animals for food. Their victims are called prey.

Competition
Two trees growing close together compete for light and nutrients, resulting in weaker growth for both species.

BEE

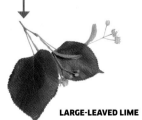

LARGE-LEAVED LIME

CATERPILLAR

OAK TREE

Nutrient cycles

The raw materials needed to build the bodies of all living things are continually recycled through ecosystems. Plants play an essential role in nutrient cycles by taking in vital elements such as carbon and nitrogen and converting them into organic matter.

All living organisms consist mostly of just four chemical elements—oxygen, carbon, hydrogen, and nitrogen—along with smaller amounts of other elements. Plants take in all these elements as simple molecules from the soil and air. Using the Sun's energy, the elements are recombined to make larger molecules such as carbohydrates, proteins, and fats—all of which are essential building blocks in animals' bodies as well as those of plants. When organisms die or when food molecules are used to release energy, these molecules break down and the elements return to the environment to be used again.

OTHER ELEMENTS

For healthy growth, plants need small amounts of the elements phosphorus, potassium, calcium, sulfur, magnesium, iron, copper, manganese, molybdenum, zinc, and boron. Most of these are absorbed in soluble form in soil water. Phosphorus (P) and potassium (K), as well as nitrogen (N), are added to fertilizers used by gardeners and farmers.

FERTILIZER

N   P   K
10   4   18

Fertilizers often show the quantities of nitrogen, phosphorus, and potassium as NPK numbers.

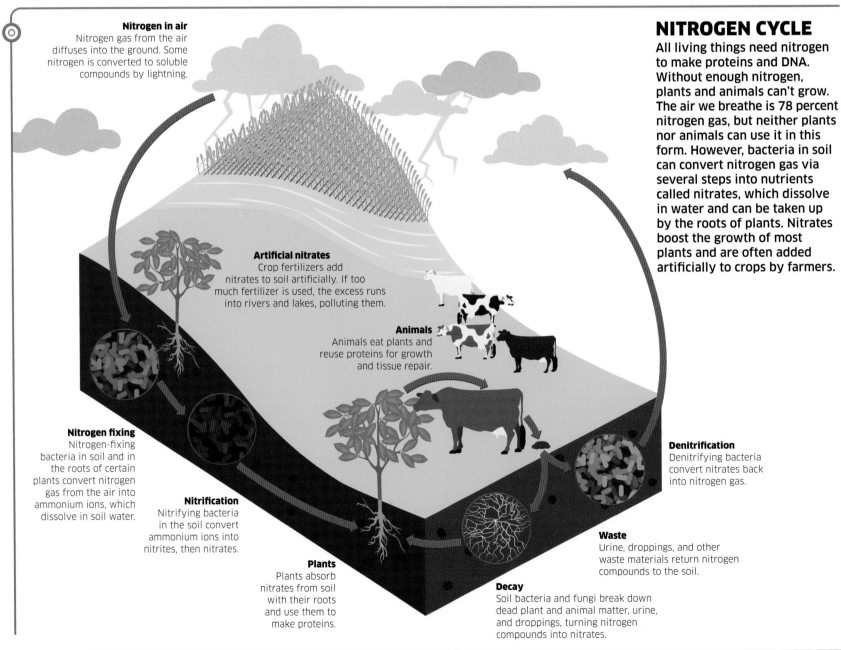

Nitrogen in air
Nitrogen gas from the air diffuses into the ground. Some nitrogen is converted to soluble compounds by lightning.

Artificial nitrates
Crop fertilizers add nitrates to soil artificially. If too much fertilizer is used, the excess runs into rivers and lakes, polluting them.

Animals
Animals eat plants and reuse proteins for growth and tissue repair.

Nitrogen fixing
Nitrogen-fixing bacteria in soil and in the roots of certain plants convert nitrogen gas from the air into ammonium ions, which dissolve in soil water.

Nitrification
Nitrifying bacteria in the soil convert ammonium ions into nitrites, then nitrates.

Plants
Plants absorb nitrates from soil with their roots and use them to make proteins.

Decay
Soil bacteria and fungi break down dead plant and animal matter, urine, and droppings, turning nitrogen compounds into nitrates.

Waste
Urine, droppings, and other waste materials return nitrogen compounds to the soil.

Denitrification
Denitrifying bacteria convert nitrates back into nitrogen gas.

NITROGEN CYCLE

All living things need nitrogen to make proteins and DNA. Without enough nitrogen, plants and animals can't grow. The air we breathe is 78 percent nitrogen gas, but neither plants nor animals can use it in this form. However, bacteria in soil can convert nitrogen gas via several steps into nutrients called nitrates, which dissolve in water and can be taken up by the roots of plants. Nitrates boost the growth of most plants and are often added artificially to crops by farmers.

82 million tons—the amount of nitrogen fertilizer **washed from farmland** into rivers and oceans worldwide each year.

45 percent of the dry weight of plants (their weight without water) is **carbon**.

97

CARBON CYCLE

Carbon forms the backbone of all organic molecules in living things. Plants and algae take in carbon dioxide from the atmosphere and, through the process of photosynthesis, turn it into energy-rich sugar molecules, which are used as building blocks for larger molecules. Animals get carbon and energy by eating plants. When they use energy, they breathe out carbon dioxide as a waste product, returning carbon to the atmosphere. Humans have upset the carbon cycle by extracting and burning the fossilized remains of ancient organisms as fuels (such as coal and oil), causing a sudden rise in carbon dioxide levels in the atmosphere.

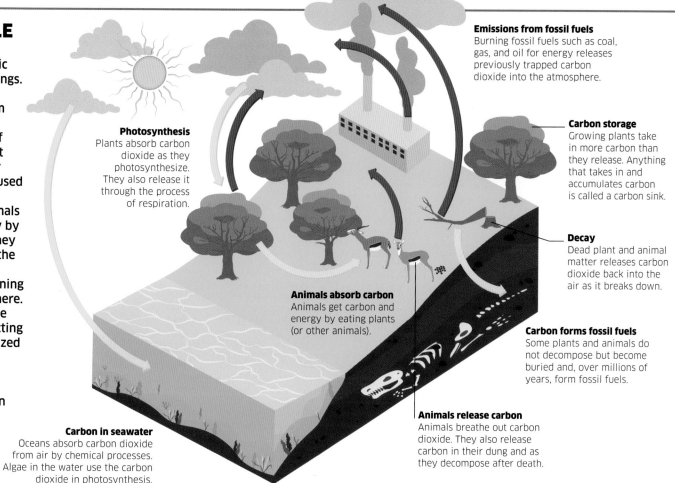

Emissions from fossil fuels
Burning fossil fuels such as coal, gas, and oil for energy releases previously trapped carbon dioxide into the atmosphere.

Photosynthesis
Plants absorb carbon dioxide as they photosynthesize. They also release it through the process of respiration.

Carbon storage
Growing plants take in more carbon than they release. Anything that takes in and accumulates carbon is called a carbon sink.

Decay
Dead plant and animal matter releases carbon dioxide back into the air as it breaks down.

Animals absorb carbon
Animals get carbon and energy by eating plants (or other animals).

Carbon forms fossil fuels
Some plants and animals do not decompose but become buried and, over millions of years, form fossil fuels.

Animals release carbon
Animals breathe out carbon dioxide. They also release carbon in their dung and as they decompose after death.

Carbon in seawater
Oceans absorb carbon dioxide from air by chemical processes. Algae in the water use the carbon dioxide in photosynthesis.

WATER CYCLE

Water is the main ingredient of all living things, making up about 70 percent of the weight of most organisms. Water molecules contain the elements hydrogen and oxygen, which, like carbon, are essential parts of all organic molecules. The water cycle is powered by the Sun's warmth, which causes water from the sea and land to evaporate, form clouds in the atmosphere, and fall back down as rain or snow. Plants take up water through their roots and combine it chemically with carbon dioxide in photosynthesis to make food molecules.

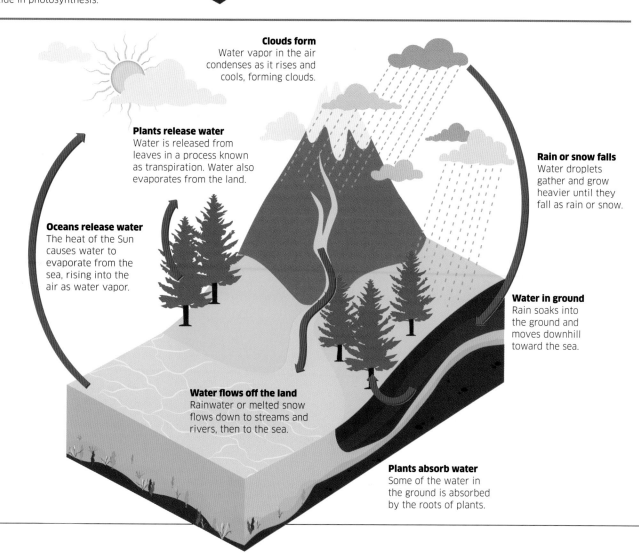

Clouds form
Water vapor in the air condenses as it rises and cools, forming clouds.

Plants release water
Water is released from leaves in a process known as transpiration. Water also evaporates from the land.

Rain or snow falls
Water droplets gather and grow heavier until they fall as rain or snow.

Oceans release water
The heat of the Sun causes water to evaporate from the sea, rising into the air as water vapor.

Water in ground
Rain soaks into the ground and moves downhill toward the sea.

Water flows off the land
Rainwater or melted snow flows down to streams and rivers, then to the sea.

Plants absorb water
Some of the water in the ground is absorbed by the roots of plants.

98 ecosystems ∘ **RAINFORESTS**

2.3 million sq miles (6 million sq km)—the area of the Amazon Rainforest.

Rainforests

Warm and wet all year round, tropical rainforests provide ideal growing conditions for plants. They have a greater diversity of plant and animal life than any other ecosystem.

Rainforests cover only 6 percent of Earth's surface but are home to more than half the world's plant and animal species. Unaffected by the ice ages, they have existed for more than 70 million years, making them the oldest ecosystem on land. The mass of vegetation acts as a vast carbon store, but their destruction releases the carbon into the air, accelerating global warming.

Location

Tropical rainforests lie near the equator between the Tropic of Cancer and the Tropic of Capricorn. The largest areas of rainforest are in South America, central Africa, and Southeast Asia.

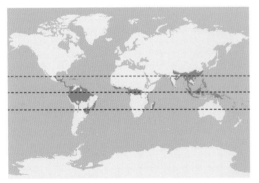

- -- Tropic of Cancer
- -- Tropic of Capricorn
- -- Equator
- ■ Tropical rainforests

Climate

Sunlight is intense between the Tropics, so tropical rainforests are warm all year round. The air is humid and the rainfall is frequent and often heavy.

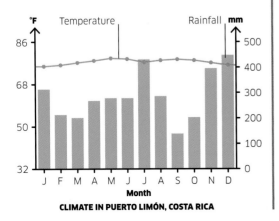

CLIMATE IN PUERTO LIMÓN, COSTA RICA

Tree frogs
In most parts of the world, frogs are confined to wet places like ponds, but rainforests are so damp that frogs live in the treetops.

Costa Rica rainforest
Costa Rica is a small country in Central America. More than half the land area is tropical rainforest.

Smooth trunks
Rainforest trees typically have smooth trunks with few branches below the canopy. This helps keep them from being smothered by climbing plants.

Sloth
Many rainforest plants produce toxic chemicals to protect them from animals. However, the sloth can withstand these poisons by eating small amounts of leaves from many different trees.

Lianas
These climbing plants have long, woody stems that hang from trees and form bridges in the canopy, helping climbing animals move from tree to tree.

Buttress roots
These large roots are found on the biggest trees in the rainforest. They stabilize the tree in the shallow soil, preventing it from falling in storms.

Tapir
This ground-dwelling animal forages on the forest floor and in rivers for soft vegetation, fruit, and small animals.

Fallen tree
Sunlit clearings form when trees fall down, fueling rapid growth of small plants that race to fill the gap.

A raindrop can take **10 minutes** to fall from the canopy to the forest floor.

4 sq miles (10 sq km) of rainforest contains around **1,500** plant species.

99

Kapok tree
One of the tallest trees in the rainforest, the kapok rises high above the canopy of other trees, supported by buttress roots.

Canopy
The treetops form a dense layer of vegetation called the canopy, which gets most of the sunlight. The canopy is home to fruit-eating animals such as monkeys and parrots.

Epiphytes
The boughs of rainforest trees are festooned with epiphytes—plants that grow on other plants. Epiphytes get all the water they need from frequent downpours and don't need roots in the ground.

Attracting pollinators
The flowers of *Heliconia* plants use bright colors to attract pollinators such as hummingbirds in the dense shade of the understory.

Climbing plants
Many rainforest plants try to reach the sunlit canopy by climbing up other plants.

Macaw
This colorful parrot uses a strong beak to crack open nuts and seeds. Macaws also swallow clay to neutralize poisons from rainforest plants.

Leafcutter ants
Insects are the main herbivores in rainforests. Leafcutter ants carry inedible leaves back to their nest and feed them to a fungus. The ants then eat the fungus.

Forest floor
Only 2 percent of the sunlight reaches the forest floor, so plants grow slowly here. Young trees remain small until a larger tree falls, creating a light-filled clearing.

Soil
Dead matter is recycled so quickly by fungi and other decomposers that rainforest soil is low in nutrients. Most of the nutrients are locked up in the living vegetation.

Recyclers
Dead leaves falling to the forest floor are quickly recycled by fungi in the warm and humid conditions. The stinkhorn fungus releases a foul smell to attract flies, which spread its spores.

Buttress roots

In rainforests, the battle for light is won by the tallest trees. These towering giants risk being blown over in storms, so their roots grow into stabilizing buttresses.

Rainforests have shallow soil, so the roots of trees don't grow deep. Instead, they snake sideways across the forest floor and grow upward along their tops. Roots that align with the prevailing wind grow tallest for support. In Africa, chimpanzees use these buttress roots as drums to communicate over long distances, each chimp identifying itself with a signature rhythm.

134°F (56.7°C)—the **highest temperature** recorded on Earth was in Death Valley in the Mojave Desert in the US.

Water storage
Cacti such as the saguaro have ribbed stems that can expand to store water.

DRY SEASON

WET SEASON

Saguaro cactus
A large saguaro cactus can hold up to 6.6 tons of water in its enormous, branching stems.

Nesting owls
Holes in saguaro cacti make ideal nesting sites for birds such as pygmy owls. High up and protected by prickly spines, the chicks are safe from most predators.

Root system
The roots of saguaro cacti stay close to the surface and spread sideways to cover a wide area. This helps them absorb a large amount of water quickly after heavy rain.

Night flowers
Most desert cacti flower at night, when pollinators such as bats and moths are active in the cooler air.

Desert ironwood
The leaves of many desert plants have a soft covering of silvery hairs that reflect sunlight, protecting them from damaging ultraviolet rays. The hairs also trap air, reducing water loss.

Jojoba
The leaves of the jojoba plant are held vertically, with edges pointing upward. This protects them from the fierce midday heat, when the Sun is directly overhead.

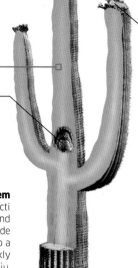

Desert in bloom
After winter rains, the Sonoran Desert can turn into a blaze of color as wildflowers appear. These plants are "ephemerals"— species that complete their life cycle in a matter of days. Their seeds may lie dormant for years, waiting for rain. Then they sprout, burst into flower, and set seed before dying as the ground dries out.

Sonoran Desert
The Sonoran Desert stretches from California and Arizona into northwest Mexico, covering an area of 124,000 sq miles (320,000 sq km). Although hot and dry most of the year, it receives heavy downpours in winter that support more than 3,000 different plant species, as well as hundreds of animal species.

Prickly pear
Prickly pear cacti protect their stems with long spines and tiny, hairlike ones that detach and lodge in the skin of animals. Their fruits are eaten by birds, jackrabbits, and ground squirrels.

Barrel cactus
Cacti have spines instead of leaves. This protects them from animals and helps conserve water. Photosynthesis takes place in their swollen stems, which double as water-storage organs.

Ground squirrel
Desert mammals such as ground squirrels avoid the daytime heat by hiding underground in burrows.

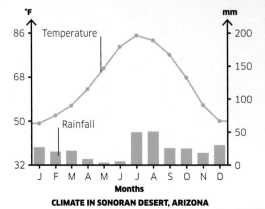

Location
Deserts are found on every continent and cover more than a fifth of the world's land area. Most of the world's major deserts lie near the Tropics of Cancer and Capricorn.

-- Tropic of Cancer
-- Tropic of Capricorn
-- Equator
■ Deserts

°F — Temperature
86 —
68 —
50 —
Rainfall
32 —
J F M A M J J A S O N D
Months
CLIMATE IN SONORAN DESERT, ARIZONA
mm
— 200
— 150
— 100
— 50
— 0

Climate
Deserts get less than 10 in (250 mm) of rain a year, and some deserts get almost none. Brief downpours can soak the parched ground, but the water quickly evaporates or drains away through sandy soil. Cloudless skies make deserts very sunny but not necessarily hot—some are bitterly cold, especially at night.

20 percent of the land in the world's deserts is **covered by sand.**

The Atacama Desert in Chile is the **world's driest desert.** Parts of it get less than 0.01 in (2 mm) of rain a year.

103

Organ pipe cactus
Like most cacti, the organ pipe cactus stores water in fleshy stems and conserves it by growing very slowly. It can live for more than 150 years.

Ocotillo
This spiny shrub saves water by shedding its small leaves in dry spells and regrowing them after rain.

Joshua tree
A mature Joshua tree can survive for a year without rain by storing water in its trunk and branches.

Mesquite tree
The mesquite tree provides much-needed shade to desert animals. Its branches have sharp thorns that deter grazing animals from eating it.

Dormant seeds
Mesquite trees produce seeds in pods. They can stay dormant for decades after falling to the ground and germinate only when there's enough water.

Jackrabbit
Jackrabbits survive on a diet of mesquite and creosote leaves as well as grasses and cacti. Their long ears help them keep cool.

Creosote bush
Small, waxy leaves mean that water is less able to evaporate through the surface. The creosote bush also has a deep root system. It can live for 100 years.

Desert agave
Succulent plants such as the agave store water in their fleshy leaves, which are covered in a layer of waterproof wax. The agave's leaves also have jagged edges and sharp tips for protection.

Deep taproot
To reach underground water, the mesquite tree has a central taproot that can grow to 100 ft (30 m) long—the height of a 10-story building.

Roadrunner
These ground-dwelling birds use speed to catch insects, reptiles, and other small animals. They nest in bushes or cacti.

Kangaroo rat
These nocturnal rodents feed on the seeds of desert plants. They don't need to drink, as their bodies make water chemically from food.

Yucca
The spiky leaves of yucca plants are arranged in a rosette shape, which funnels dew and rain toward the stem, then the roots. A long taproot reaches moisture deep underground.

Deserts

Deserts are the driest places on Earth. They can be scorching by day and freezing at night, with little shelter from wind or Sun. Yet deserts are full of life.

Plants must be tough to survive in deserts. It rains very little, and when it does rain, the ground soon dries out again. Desert plants need to take in water quickly, then hold onto it for weeks or even months. They also need to protect their precious water stores from thirsty animals.

Boreal forests

A vast swathe of conifer forest forms a ring around Earth's North Pole, crossing Canada, northern Europe, and northern Asia. This ecosystem is known as boreal forest.

Boreal forest occupies a tenth of Earth's land surface, which is nearly twice the area covered by tropical rainforest. For most of the year, it is bitterly cold and covered in snow, so only the hardiest plants and animals can survive. In summer, the snow melts and the trees bask in sunlight for up to 20 hours a day, bringing the forest to life. The harsh climate is not good for agriculture, so this biome has only a small human population. Much of it is unspoiled wilderness.

Summer visitors
Migratory birds fly north to boreal forests in summer to feed on caterpillars and other insects and raise their young. The magnolia warbler spends summer in Canada but winter in the Caribbean and Central America.

Conifer cones
Conifers make seeds in cones instead of flowers. Cones open to release seeds in hot weather, when seeds have the best chance of germinating in the warm ground.

Storm protection
The narrow, tapering shape of conifers helps them resist wind. This is important, as their roots are shallow and provide poor anchorage.

Layered branches
Layered branches with an open area in between help wind pass through. The tapering shape also means that the upper branches don't shade the lower ones.

Understory plants
Only small plants thrive under the dense evergreen canopy. In early summer, shrubs such as wild roses flower to attract pollinating bees. Later, the roses produce red fruits called hips that provide food for birds.

Ground cover
Much of the ground is boggy in summer after snow melts. The damp conditions are ideal for mosses and lichens, which carpet the ground and grow on dead trees.

Summer

The summer growing season in Canada's boreal forests is short, but the long days and short nights trigger a spurt of plant growth. Food for animals is abundant, but they must race to raise their young, then fatten up for winter before the time of plenty ends again.

Beaver
Beavers fell trees in the forest, then use the wood to build dams. This floods parts of the forest, creating wetlands for fish, water birds, and amphibians.

Berry banquet
Many understory plants produce berries in summer, including juniper bushes, blueberries, bilberries, and lingonberries. Brown bears feast on the berries, helping them gain weight in preparation for winter.

Up to **3 billion birds** migrate to Canada's boreal forest every spring.

Temperatures in the boreal forest of northeastern Russia can plunge to −94°F (−70°C) in winter.

105

Location

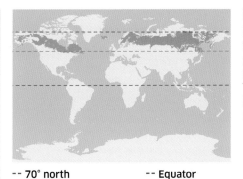

Boreal forests are found in the northern parts of Asia, Europe, and North America. They mainly lie between 50° and 70° north of the equator.

-- 70° north
-- 50° north
-- Equator
■ Boreal forest

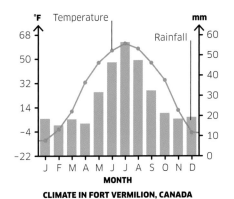

°F Temperature
mm Rainfall

MONTH
CLIMATE IN FORT VERMILION, CANADA

Climate

Boreal forests have harsh winters, with freezing temperatures and only 5–6 hours of sunlight a day. Summers are the opposite, with warm weather and long days. Most of the rain falls in spring or summer, adding to melting snow to make the ground wet.

Winter

In winter, the nights are much longer and the ground freezes, making it hard for plants to absorb water. Growth stops and food is in short supply. Animals that don't fly away or hibernate must work hard to find food in the frozen wilderness.

Larches are among the few conifers that shed their needles in winter.

Evergreen foliage
Unlike deciduous trees, most conifer trees stay green all year round. Their narrow needles lose little moisture, helping them endure the lack of water while the soil surface is frozen.

Drilling in
Woodpeckers drill into bark to find insect larvae. They can also crack open pine cones with their powerful bills.

Digging for food
Caribou (reindeer) use their hooves to dig through snow to reach edible lichens.

Snow cover
A layer of insulating snow helps burrowing animals such as mice survive in winter.

Hibernation
Grizzly bears hibernate in dens for 5–7 months, surviving on fat reserves built up in summer. Females give birth in winter, but the cubs stay inside the den until April or May.

Gray wolf
Wolves hunt and eat caribou and hares.

Winter coat
The snowshoe hare turns white in winter for camouflage. It stays active in winter, surviving on a diet of twigs, buds, and conifer needles.

Coping with snow
Many conifers have a triangular shape and sloping branches. This allows heavy snow to slide off without breaking branches.

Beavers spend winter in lodges built under piles of logs and vegetation. They pile up sticks at the bottom of a pond to provide food for winter.

Deciduous forests

**Dominated by trees that lose and regrow their leaves
every year, deciduous forests have a cycle of four distinct
seasons each year.**

Trees such as oak, beech, chestnut, maple, and elm are found in
deciduous forests. Their dead leaves pile up on the ground year
after year, building up to form a very rich soil that supports
many other plants. The rich soil makes this ecosystem ideal
for agriculture, which is why some of the world's most densely
populated areas are in zones of deciduous forest.

Four seasons

Deciduous forests change color with the seasons. In a European oak
woodland, the fresh, bright green of new spring foliage darkens in
summer before turning gold and red in fall as leaves die. In winter,
the trees are bare but occasional snowfalls may carpet the ground.

Leaves open
The warmth of spring
triggers the opening of leaf
buds that have been closed
since fall.

Fruits of the forest
In summer, fruits such
as acorns develop from
blossoms pollinated in
spring. Green at first, they
turn brown later as they
ripen. Squirrels and jays
hoard the ripe acorns for
winter, when food is scarce.

Insects emerge
As soon as leaves open,
caterpillars and other
insects hatch from their
eggs and begin feeding.

Waking up
Badgers become
active in spring. They
leave their burrows
at night and forage
for plants or small
animals such as
insects, worms, slugs,
and mice. Cubs don't
leave their nests
until late spring.

Bird life
The abundance of insect
life in spring attracts
migrating birds, such as
blackcaps. Songbirds fill
the air with their calls
as they search for mates.
Nesting birds collect
hundreds of caterpillars
from the trees as they
raise their chicks.

Spring flowers
On the woodland floor,
spring flowers such as
bluebells, primroses, and
wild garlic burst into life.
They grow and flower
quickly to make the most
of the light before the
trees develop their full
canopy, casting the forest
floor into shade.

Life in the shade
The forest floor
becomes darker in
summer, but ferns
flourish in the shade.
In sunny clearings
where trees have
fallen, brambles,
foxgloves, and
nettles flourish.

Varied diet
The diet of
these woodland
deer includes
brambles, ivy, and
the leaves of any
shrubs and trees
they can reach.

Location

Most of the world's deciduous forests are in the northern hemisphere. The largest areas are in eastern North America, western Europe, and east Asia.

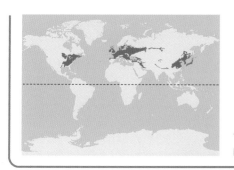

-- Equator
■ Deciduous forests

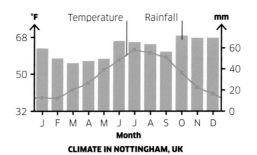

°F   Temperature   Rainfall   mm

Month

CLIMATE IN NOTTINGHAM, UK

Climate

Deciduous forests flourish in places with a mild (temperate) climate. Summers are warm but not very hot, winters are cool, and there is plenty of rain all year round.

Fall colors

As days shorten and temperatures drop in fall, trees prepare for winter and stop growing leaves. The green chlorophyll in leaves breaks down, changing their color. The leaves die and fall.

Waiting for spring

Although deciduous trees look totally bare in winter, they already have tiny versions of next year's leaves packed in buds all over their twigs.

Surviving winter

Squirrels don't hibernate. They survive winter on a diet of stashed acorns and beechnuts. They avoid the coldest weather by hiding in a nest of twigs and leaves built in a tree hollow or in a fork between branches.

Mushroom season

Fungi live unseen in the soil or in decaying organic matter for most of the year. When the cool, damp weather of fall arrives, their fruit bodies appear as mushrooms on the ground or bracket fungi on rotting logs and tree trunks.

Leaf litter

Dead leaves don't go to waste. They are food for armies of tiny animals, from earthworms to mites and even greater numbers of microscopic organisms. All their actions recycle the leaves into rich soil.

Winter berries

A few evergreen plants, such as holly, keep their foliage in winter. The red fruits of holly ripen in winter, providing food for blackbirds, thrushes, and other birds.

Winter sleep

Badgers spend all or most of the winter asleep in their burrows, where females give birth. In mild winters, they might leave the burrow to feed from time to time.

The earliest, two-legged **ancestors of humans** evolved in tropical grasslands.

Location

There are two main types of grasslands: temperate and tropical. The largest areas of temperate grassland are the Eurasian steppes and the North American prairies. Tropical grasslands occur in Africa, Australia, and parts of South America.

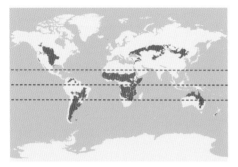

-- Tropic of Cancer   ▓ Temperate grassland
-- Tropic of Capricorn   ▓ Tropical grassland
-- Equator

Temperate grassland climate

The largest areas of temperate grassland occur in places with long, hot summers and very cold winters. Wildflower meadows occur in a wide range of climates. The most species-rich meadows grow where the soil is dry or low in nutrients, preventing grasses from growing very densely.

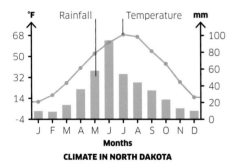

°F — Rainfall — Temperature — mm

CLIMATE IN NORTH DAKOTA
Months

Tropical grasslands

Tropical grasslands are also called savannas and typically have a short rainy season and a long dry season that limits the growth of trees. African savannas have scattered trees, but wild elephants push them over to eat the branches and prevent forests from becoming established. These grasslands are also home to huge herds of grazing animals such as zebras and wildebeest.

Grasshopper
Grasshoppers use biting mouthparts to chew the edges of grass blades. Their green or brown camouflage makes them hard to spot, but they are easy to hear—males rub their legs against their wings to create a song to attract females.

Caterpillars
Caterpillars of many butterfly species feed in wildflower meadows. Marbled white caterpillars eat grass. Adult butterflies scatter eggs from the air and the caterpillars hatch out the next spring.

Rabbit
Rabbits are grazing animals, with grass forming most of their diet. They make a tasty snack for stoats and buzzards, so they never stray far from their underground warren.

Dandelion
Plants such as dandelions are quick to colonize open or disturbed ground due to their ability to produce hundreds of windborne seeds, each carried by a parachute of tiny hairs.

Clover
As well as providing nectar for pollinators such as bees, clover plants capture nitrogen from the air and turn it into nitrates—nutrients that are essential for the growth of all plants.

Rhizomes
Some meadow grasses can spread rapidly by producing rhizomes—stems that grow sideways underground. These produce new grass plants that are genetically identical to the parent plant.

European wildflower meadow

Wildflower meadows are areas of permanent grass where many species of wildflowers grow. The diverse plant life provides food and habitats for small mammals, birds, and many kinds of insects. In temperate parts of the world, such as Europe, wildflower meadows occur in places trampled or grazed by large mammals or regularly flooded by rivers.

Bumblebee nest
Abandoned burrows make ideal bumblebee nests, which contain up to 400 bees each. Bumblebees feed on the nectar of wildflowers, which they help pollinate.

2 million wildebeest migrate **across the Serengeti grasslands of** East Africa each year in search of fresh grazing grounds.

109

Swallow
Swallows skim over grasslands on summer days, snatching insects in midair.

Secure nest
The harvest mouse builds a nest by weaving grass into a large ball and securing it between plant stems.

Flower crab spider
Instead of spinning a web, the flower crab spider hides in a flower and waits to pounce on visiting insects. It can change its color to match the flower for camouflage.

Knapweed
Knapweed flowers and the related cornflowers are a magnet to meadow butterflies such as blues, marbled whites, and meadow browns.

Harvest mice
These small rodents use their tails to grip grass plants as they search for seeds and small insects to eat.

Plantain
Like daisies and dandelions, plantains have a rosette of leaves that lie flat against the ground, helping them survive in areas that are trampled or grazed by animals.

Grasses
Grass leaves (blades) are long and narrow, with growing points (meristems) near the base, where the leaf joins the stem.

Mole
Moles use their spadelike paws to dig tunnels and hunt for earthworms. By digging up the earth, they aerate the soil, allowing more types of plants to grow.

Creeping buttercup
The stems of buttercups grow low against the ground before growing roots to produce new plants.

Taproot
Many grassland wildflowers, such as dandelions and wild carrots, have a deep central root (a taproot) to find water in dry spells.

Butterflies
Adult butterflies only feed on nectar, which they suck from flowers through a long tongue called a proboscis. They are most active in spring and summer, when meadow flowers are in bloom.

Grasslands

Take a close look at a grassland and you'll discover a multitude of different plants and animals, from colorful wildflowers to tiny camouflaged herbivores and carnivores.

There are grasslands on every continent except Antarctica. The largest areas tend to occur where rainfall is higher than in deserts but too low to support the growth of forest. Grasslands also develop in places with lots of grazing animals or regular wildfires. This is because grasses, unlike most plants, have their main growing points (meristems) at the base of their leaves, so they can regrow quickly after damage.

110 ecosystems ○ **MOUNTAIN ECOSYSTEMS**

45,000 species of **alpine plants** grow in the Andes Mountains.

Mountain ecosystems

A mountain can capture a whole world of different ecosystems in a single place. As you climb higher, the climate and vegetation change, mirroring the changes that occur as you travel toward Earth's poles.

Mountains are challenging places for plants. As height increases, temperatures fall, winds strengthen, and sunlight becomes more harsh because there is less air and dust to filter out harmful ultraviolet rays. The lush forest that might cloak the foot of a mountain gives way to conifer forest higher up, then grassy meadows like arctic tundra, and finally icy peaks that never thaw. Higher up, changeable weather and steep slopes speed up the process of erosion, preventing soil from building up and thus making water harder to obtain from the loose, rocky ground.

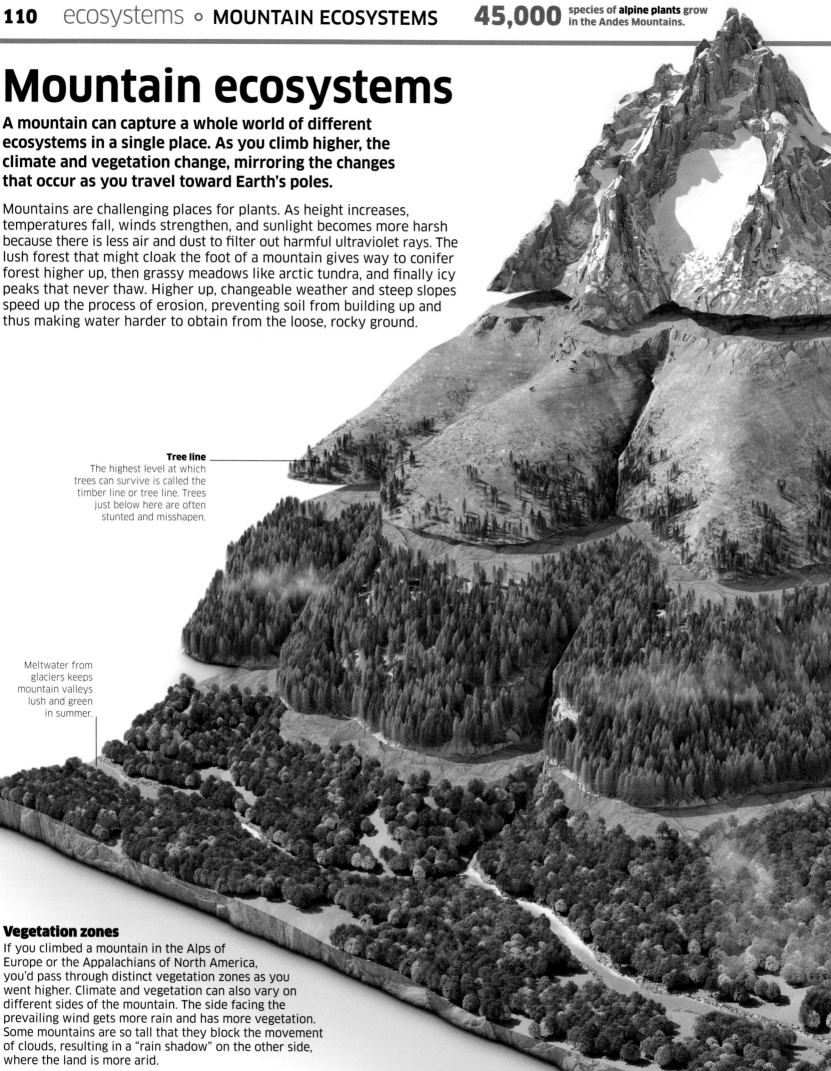

Tree line
The highest level at which trees can survive is called the timber line or tree line. Trees just below here are often stunted and misshapen.

Meltwater from glaciers keeps mountain valleys lush and green in summer.

Vegetation zones

If you climbed a mountain in the Alps of Europe or the Appalachians of North America, you'd pass through distinct vegetation zones as you went higher. Climate and vegetation can also vary on different sides of the mountain. The side facing the prevailing wind gets more rain and has more vegetation. Some mountains are so tall that they block the movement of clouds, resulting in a "rain shadow" on the other side, where the land is more arid.

The plants of alpine grasslands often grow in **low, compact mounds** to help them endure powerful winds.

Many high-altitude plants are covered in **silvery hair** to reflect powerful ultraviolet rays in mountain sunlight.

111

Frozen zone
Few plants can endure the Arctic-type conditions at the summit of a mountain, where there may be permanent snow and ice. Lichens cling to bare rock, and mosses flourish in sheltered crevices.

Snow line
This is the lowest point of permanent snow, though glaciers may extend farther down mountain valleys.

Alpine grassland
Above the tree line, it is too cold for large plants. Grasses and cushion-shaped alpine plants survive here in an ecosystem similar to the tundra grasslands of the far north. Buried under snow in winter, plants burst to life in spring and produce brightly colored flowers to attract butterflies and other pollinators.

Montane forest
Higher up, deciduous trees peter out and evergreen conifers such as pine, spruce, and fir take over. These trees can better withstand the heavy snow and freezing nights of winter in the mountains. This ecosystem resembles the boreal conifer forests of Canada, Scandinavia, and Russia.

Lowland forest
The base of a mountain has similar vegetation to the surrounding area. In temperate climates, this is typically deciduous forest, dominated by trees such as oak, maple, beech, and birch.

Location
Mountains are found on all the world's continents. Some of the longest mountain ranges are the Andes in South America, the Himalayas in Asia, and the Rocky Mountains in North America.

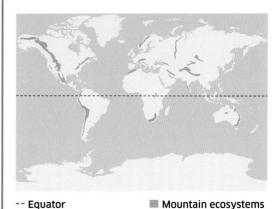

-- Equator   ■ Mountain ecosystems

Agricultural zones
In the Andes Mountains of South America, farmers use the different vegetation zones to grow crops from different climates. Tropical fruits like bananas are grown in the lowland rainforest zone, whereas wheat, potatoes, apples, and other crops of temperate countries are grown higher up. The alpine grassland is used for rearing llamas.

- ■ Coffee
- ■ Banana
- ■ Corn
- ■ Apple, grapes
- ■ Wheat
- ■ Barley
- ■ Potatoes
- ■ Llama pasture

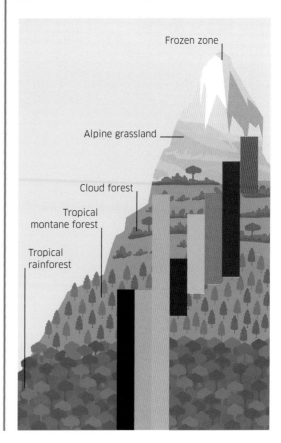

Frozen zone

Alpine grassland

Cloud forest

Tropical montane forest

Tropical rainforest

112 ecosystems ○ **MANGROVE FORESTS**

Mangroves cover **less than 1 percent of Earth's surface** but are found along the coast of more than 100 tropical and subtropical countries.

Mangrove forests

Specially adapted to saltwater habitats, mangrove trees thrive along tropical and subtropical coasts.

Mangrove trees grow in dense forests, also known as mangrove swamps, in shallow coastal waters, tidal estuaries, and salt marshes. They have a thick tangle of roots that keeps them propped up above the water and mud. The mass of roots slows down the movement of seawater, allowing sediment to settle and build up into nutrient-rich mud. This unique habitat provides valuable shelter and safe breeding sites for fish and other marine wildlife. It also stabilizes coastlines by reducing erosion by waves.

Australian mangrove forest

Australia has around 4,400 sq miles (11,500 sq km) of mangroves. Found primarily on the northern and eastern coasts of the continent, these regions represent around 6 percent of the world's total mangrove forest area and contain half the world's mangrove tree species.

Coastal trees
Mangrove trees include many unrelated species that have adapted to coastal habitats in the same way, evolving a tolerance of saltwater and stiltlike roots to support them above the water or mud.

Nesting sites
Shorebirds use mangrove trees as nesting sites. The lesser noddy builds a sturdy platform from mangrove leaves, seaweed, and droppings.

Salt glands
Some mangrove trees have glands on their leaves to get rid of salt. Other species let salt build up in the bark or in old leaves, then shed them.

Mud crabs
Mud crabs eat dead mangrove leaves. Their droppings add nutrients to the mud, helping mangrove trees grow.

Breathing roots
Some mangrove trees have special roots that grow upward from the mud. These act like snorkels, absorbing air to keep submerged roots supplied with oxygen.

The striated heron creeps around in the soft mud among mangrove roots to look for fish, crabs, and other marine invertebrates.

Floating fruit
The fruits of mangrove plants can float. They drift away and lodge in muddy crevices, where they start growing.

Up to 2 percent of the world's
mangrove forest area is **lost each year.**

At the current rate of destruction, **mangrove
forests could disappear entirely** by 2100.

113

Location

Most mangrove forests occur on tropical coasts in the intertidal zone (the area between high and low tide). However, there are also areas of mangrove forest outside the tropics.

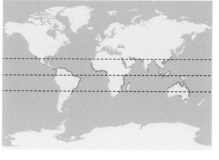

-- Tropic of Cancer -- Equator
-- Tropic of Capricorn ■ Mangrove forests

Under threat

As well as providing a refuge for wildlife, mangrove forests protect coasts from erosion by absorbing the force of storms. In recent decades, much of the world's mangrove forest has been destroyed by urbanization, agriculture, tourism, and land reclamation. Major efforts are now underway to protect and restore this threatened ecosystem, for instance by replanting trees (right).

Thick leaves
Most mangrove leaves have a thick, waxy cuticle or dense hairs to reduce water loss, because fresh water is in short supply.

Seed

Seedling

Flying fox
Flying foxes are the largest members of the bat family. They feed on the flowers and fruits of tropical trees and are important pollinators and seed dispersers.

Knee roots spread sideways in a series of loops, providing anchorage. Their exposed tops absorb air.

Propagules
The seeds of some mangroves germinate into spear-shaped seedlings called propagules while still attached to the tree. When big enough, they break off and float away.

Mudskipper
Mudskippers are fish that can live in and out of the water. They move on land with great agility, basking in the mud or on mangrove roots.

Fish nursery
Many ocean fish lay their eggs under mangrove trees. The roots keep out large predators, allowing the young fish to develop in safety.

Predators
Crocodiles and alligators wait for fish and other animals to leave the shelter of the tangled mangrove roots.

Pelicans dive from perches in mangrove trees to scoop fish and shrimp from the water with their huge bills.

Leaves, twigs, bark, flowers, and seeds from mangroves fall into the water, fertilizing the mud.

Kelp forests

Around the world's cooler shorelines, giant kelp—the world's biggest seaweed—forms underwater forests that provide shelter to thousands of fish, invertebrates, and marine mammals.

Kelps are not plants but multicellular algae that live in cool, nutrient-rich waters on rocky coasts. They need sunlight to photosynthesize, so they flourish best in shallow coastal waters where there is plenty of light. Like the trees in a forest, kelps create a three-dimensional ecosystem that provides habitats and food for many marine organisms, as well as shelter from storms and hiding places to evade predators.

California kelp forest

Along the coast of the northeast Pacific Ocean, currents of cold water bring nutrients from the deep ocean to the surface, sustaining an abundance of sea life. Some of the world's most diverse kelp forests are found here.

Sea otter
Sea otters feed on sea urchins and shellfish found on the seafloor. They sleep in the sea, wrapped in long strands of kelp.

Giant kelp
The largest species in kelp forests, giant kelp can grow as tall as a rainforest tree.

Elk kelp
Elk kelp is the second-largest kelp in California's kelp forests. Its name comes from its branching blades, which resemble an elk's antlers.

Blades
Leaflike structures called blades form the top part of kelp. They are flexible to reduce damage by waves and slimy to reduce water loss at low tide.

Floats
Kelps have air chambers called bladders to help them float near the surface. Here, the sunlight is stronger, meaning photosynthesis occurs faster.

Stipe
A long stalk called a stipe holds kelp to the seafloor. It is thick and flexible to withstand tides and waves.

Holdfasts
Kelps stay anchored to rocks on the seafloor with rootlike structures called holdfasts.

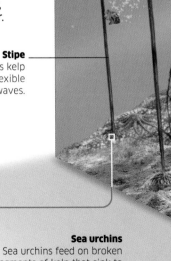

Sea urchins
Sea urchins feed on broken fragments of kelp that sink to the seafloor. However, they sometimes eat living kelp, too.

Sunflower sea star
These starfish feed on sea urchins and help keep their populations under control.

Bullwhip kelp

Storm protection
Dense kelp forests dissipate the energy of incoming waves, providing shelter to coastal wildlife and slowing the erosion of beaches.

Feather boa kelp
Small blades line this kelp's stipe, making it look like a feather boa.

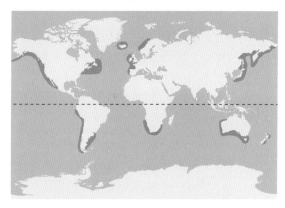

Microscopic algae
The sunlit sea surface teems with single-celled algae called phytoplankton. They form the base of most marine food chains, providing food for many sea creatures, including shrimp, snails, and jellyfish.

Snowy egret
Seabirds such as the snowy egret use the kelp canopy as a perch when hunting.

Sea lions
These marine mammals hunt fish that live in kelp forests.

***Laminaria* kelp**
The leathery blades of these kelps generally last for about a year.

Location
Kelp forests are found along temperate coastlines where the waters are shallow enough to allow sunlight to penetrate.

-- Equator   ■ Kelp forests

Under threat
More than 95 percent of the kelp in California's kelp forests has been devoured by purple sea urchins, whose numbers have exploded in recent years. Scientists think there are two causes. One is a fall in the population of sunflower sea stars—the urchin's main predator—due to disease. Another is climate change. In 2014, a heatwave reduced nutrient levels in the water, preventing the kelp from growing tall enough to reach the surface. The sea urchins devoured the weakened kelp, creating dead zones that stretched for miles.

Spiny lobster
Kelp forests provide ideal habitats for lobsters and their larvae. Adult spiny lobsters prey on the kelp-eating sea urchins.

Seagrass
Patches of seagrass grow where sunlight reaches the shallow sea floor. Seagrass is the only flowering plant that lives in seawater.

California moray eel
The moray eel is nocturnal. It hides in a crevice by day, with only its head protruding. At night, it patrols the kelp forest looking for smaller fish to eat.

Garibaldi fish
Fish such as Garibaldis use kelp forests to hide from predators.

***Pterygophora* kelp**
This kelp can live for 25 years and has woody stems with annual growth rings.

PURPLE SEA URCHINS FEEDING ON KELP

The fight for light

Plants must have sunlight for photosynthesis, but finding a sunny spot in a crowded habitat such as a forest is difficult. As a result, plants compete with each other for light, sometimes with deadly consequences.

Plants compete for light in lots of different ways. Some plants grow as tall as they possibly can, becoming towering trees that cast neighbors into gloomy shade. Other plants cheat their way up by climbing on top of larger plants, borrowing their support while stealing their light. The strangler fig tree uses both tactics to win territory in its tropical rainforest habitats.

1 Germination
Strangler fig seeds are deposited on trees in the sticky droppings of animals that feed on figs. The seeds germinate, fed by nutrients in the droppings, and roots emerge.

Finding light

Plants have many tactics to reach sunlight while staying rooted to the same spot.

Waiting game
Many rainforest trees spend their early years living in deep shade and growing slowly. When a mature tree topples in a storm, light floods through the canopy and the waiting saplings race to fill the gap.

Climbers
Using clinging roots or wiry tendrils to hold on to other plants, climbing plants can reach the light without wasting valuable resources producing their own woody trunks or stems.

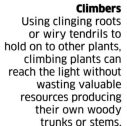

Epiphytes
Epiphytes take root on top of other plants, allowing them to start life in a sunny spot without growing tall. They flourish best in very rainy forests, because they can't reach the ground with their roots.

Springing to action
In places where trees shed their leaves in winter, sunlight reaches the forest floor in winter and early spring. Spring flowers such as snowdrops grow quickly from bulbs and bloom before the trees sprout new leaves.

2 Roots reach down
The fig's roots grow downward, clinging to the bark of the host tree. They grow slowly at first.

3 Cage forms
More roots develop. Once they reach the forest floor, they begin to thicken and wrap around the tree's trunk, forming a cage. Meanwhile, shoots grow upward and invade the canopy.

The strangler fig

Strangler figs grow in lush tropical forests, where the fight for light is intense. Their grisly name is well deserved. After sprouting high on the branch of another tree, a strangler fig grows around it in a tight cage and gradually smothers it, starving it of light, water, and nutrients.

Foods that come from climbing plants include grapes, cucumbers, figs, runner beans, and pumpkins.

An ancient strangler fig in Anantapur, India, covers an area as large as **three soccer fields**.

117

Keystone species

Fig trees are considered to be "keystone species," which means they play an important role in the health of an ecosystem. Many mammals and birds depend on figs when other food is scarce. The branches and hollow trunks provide habitats for insects, birds, reptiles, and amphibians. Figs also have an essential bond with their pollinating wasps—neither can survive without the other.

BLACK-CAPPED SQUIRREL MONKEY

EPAULETTED FRUIT BAT

TRUMPETER HORNBILL

The strangler fig's branches grow higher, shading the host tree and depriving it of light.

A dense network of roots now covers the tree trunk.

4 Growth accelerates
As more roots reach the forest floor, the plant absorbs more water and nutrients from the soil. The strangler fig can now grow faster and larger.

The strangler fig's roots take water and nutrients from the soil, slowly starving the host tree.

5 Host dies
Starved of light, water, and nutrients, the host tree dies and begins to rot. The death of the host tree can take anywhere from 10 to 200 years.

6 Hollow cage
Eventually, the host tree rots away completely. The cylindrical cage of fig roots remains, supporting the strangler long after the host tree has disappeared.

Hitchhikers

In a forest, it can take years for a plant to grow tall enough to reach sunlight. So instead of getting there the hard way, some plants take a sneaky shortcut.

Epiphytes are plants that start life high on the branches of trees, saving themselves the trouble of growing their own trunk. Most live in tropical forests, where they make up a quarter of all plant species. They are especially common in rainforests, where water is so plentiful that plants can survive without roots in the ground. Even so, epiphytes need special adaptations to cope with life high in the treetops, where they are exposed to wind and strong sunlight. They don't usually steal resources from the host tree—instead, they harvest nutrients and water from the air or debris around their roots. They provide food, habitats, and breeding grounds for many animals.

Spanish moss is an epiphyte that dangles from trees in strands up to **100 ft (30 m)** long.

Blue morpho
Butterflies such as the blue morpho feed on the nectar of flowering epiphytes and occasionally drink from bromeliad ponds.

Storing water
High in the canopy, epiphytes have to endure the full force of the Sun and dry spells with no water. Cacti are ideally suited to such conditions, as their thick stems can store water. The dragon fruit cactus is an epiphyte in Central and South America's rainforests, where its long, vinelike stems drape over the boughs of trees.

Absorbing rain
Air plants take in water through their leaves and use their roots only for clinging. The leaves are covered in tiny, absorbent scales—seen here with a microscope— that capture rain as it trickles past.

Around **70 percent** of orchids are epiphytes.

One seed capsule of the epiphytic orchid *Cycnoches chlorochilon* can contain **4 million seeds**.

119

Watertight reservoir

Tank bromeliad plants have thick, overlapping leaf bases that funnel rain into the plant's watertight center. It collects in a pool, forming a reservoir for dry spells and providing a habitat for aquatic animals.

Treetop pond
Poison dart frogs use bromeliad plants as treetop ponds to raise their young, safe from the predators of the forest floor. The female frog carries each tadpole on her back to its own private pond and returns every few days to lay sterile eggs, which the tadpole eats.

Water
Rain collects in the plant's base, providing a store of water for hot, dry spells.

Crab nursery
The bromeliad crab lays her eggs in a bromeliad and looks after the babies, cutting up insects to feed to them, adding snail shells for calcium to build their shells, and killing the damselfly larvae that would otherwise eat the baby crabs.

Holding tight
The roots of epiphytic orchids wrap around branches, providing anchorage. The stout roots also store water and are green so they can photosynthesize.

Aerial roots
Some epiphytes collect rain as it trickles through a mass of dangling roots.

The ant plant

Many plants form close partnerships with other species, often to the advantage of both. The ant plant creates a custom home for an ant colony, while the ants that live inside it defend the plant and help feed it.

A close relationship between different species is called symbiosis. Plants rely on symbiotic relationships with animals to pollinate their flowers and to spread their seeds, while symbiotic relationships with fungi help roots absorb nutrients from the soil. When a symbiotic relationship benefits both partners, it is also described as mutualistic.

Perfect partners

Plants form symbiotic relationships with many different species, but some of the most spectacular examples involve ants. Usually, both partners gain from the arrangement, but in some cases, the relationship is one-sided.

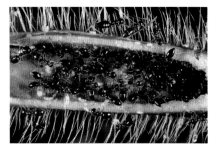

Devil's gardens
The *Duroia* tree of the Amazon Rainforest has hollow stems that are home to leafcutter ants. The ants attack all other kinds of plants in the area by injecting them with acid from their stingers. This creates clearings—"devil's gardens"—giving the *Duroia* more space to grow. But the *Duroia* is also harmed as the ants eat its leaves.

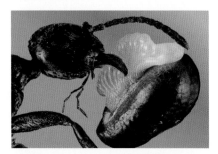

Seed sowers
Some seeds have a fleshy growth called an elaiosome, which is packed with nutrition. Ants carry these seeds home and feed the elaiosomes to their larvae before dumping the seeds in waste heaps—the ideal place for a new plant to germinate.

Whistling thorn trees
In Africa, the whistling thorn tree provides homes for ants inside hollow thorns. In return, the ants defend the tree from large herbivores, including elephants and giraffes. The tree's name comes from the whistling sound made when wind blows through the thorns.

Extrafloral nectaries
Nectaries are usually found in flowers, where the sugary drink they make helps attract pollinators. However, some plants have "extrafloral nectaries"—nectaries outside flowers. These attract predatory insects such as ants or ladybugs, helping ward off plant-eating insects.

Defensive army
If an animal tries to eat the ant plant's foliage, the ants swarm out to attack it with their biting mouthparts.

Fruit
Ant plants produce small, juicy fruits containing seeds. The ants chew through the fruits, collect the seeds, and plant them to grow new nests.

Ant plants
Ant plants (*Myrmecodia*) grow high in the canopy of Southeast Asia's rainforests. They are epiphytes, which means they grow on other plants and can't reach the soil with their own roots. This makes nutrients hard to obtain, so they get ants to help them. Inside an ant plant are hollow chambers that ants use as nurseries for eggs and larvae or as chambers for storing waste. The waste rots and breaks down, providing nutrients the plant can absorb.

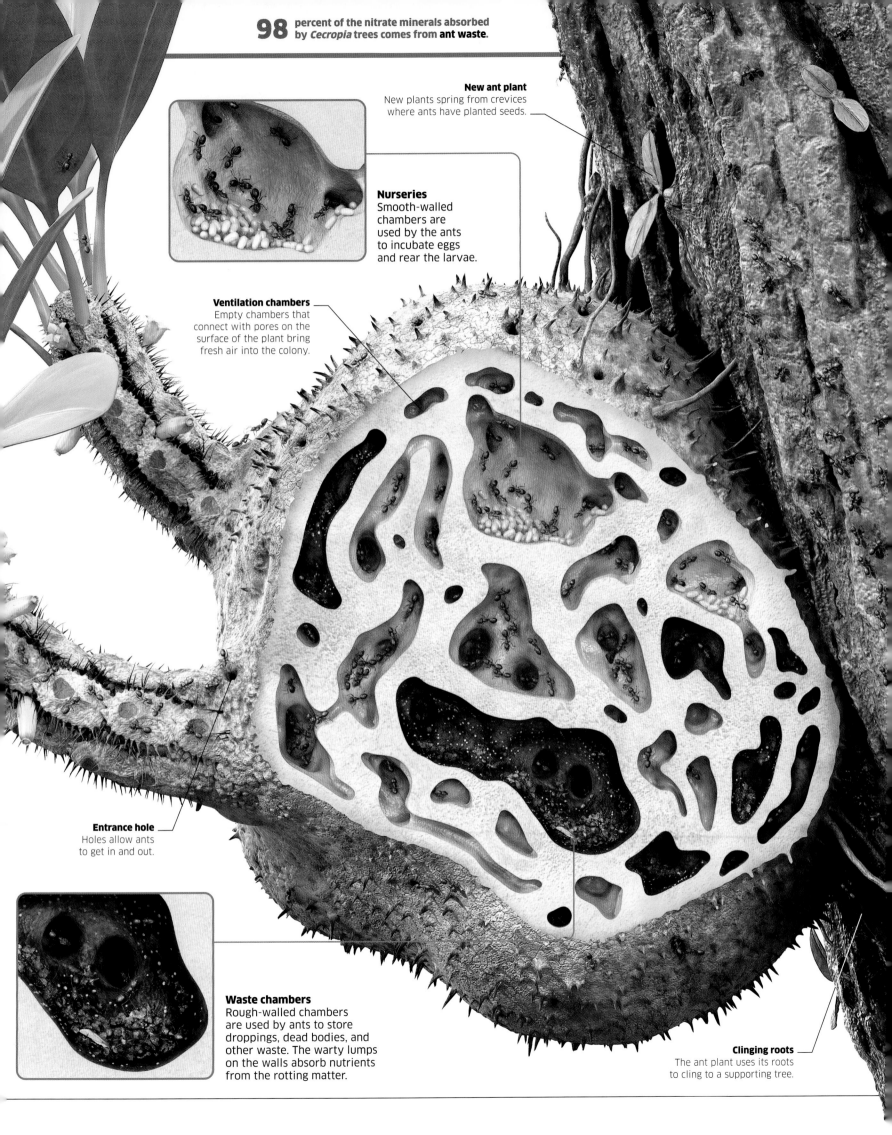

New ant plant
New plants spring from crevices where ants have planted seeds.

Nurseries
Smooth-walled chambers are used by the ants to incubate eggs and rear the larvae.

Ventilation chambers
Empty chambers that connect with pores on the surface of the plant bring fresh air into the colony.

Entrance hole
Holes allow ants to get in and out.

Waste chambers
Rough-walled chambers are used by ants to store droppings, dead bodies, and other waste. The warty lumps on the walls absorb nutrients from the rotting matter.

Clinging roots
The ant plant uses its roots to cling to a supporting tree.

Carnivorous plants

Carnivorous plants turn the tables on animals, catching and killing them for food.

Plants can't survive with only air and water. They also need certain nutrients from soil, such as nitrates, which are essential for making the proteins needed for growth. In boggy or waterlogged soil, where organic matter breaks down very slowly, these nutrients are in short supply. Carnivorous plants solve the problem by killing and digesting animals.

Trigger hairs
Each trap typically has six trigger hairs, three on either side.

2 Snapping shut As the fly searches for nectar, it touches sensitive trigger hairs. The trap will only close if the fly touches hairs twice within 20 seconds. This helps prevent accidental closure.

Venus flytrap
The Venus flytrap plant has mouthlike traps at the ends of its leaves. When the trap is sprung, the mouth closes and the teeth interlock before the prisoner has time to escape.

1 Attracting prey Bright colors and a sweet scent make the open traps irresistible to flies and other insects.

The two halves of the flytrap are convex. When triggered by a moving fly, they pop into a concave shape, which closes the trap in an instant.

Each trap can only digest three to five meals before dying.

A Venus flytrap can imprison a fly in **one-tenth of a second.**

English naturalist Charles Darwin called the Venus flytrap **one of the most wonderful plants** in the world.

123

Digestive glands

The inner surface of a Venus flytrap is dotted with tiny glands that secrete acid and digestive enzymes.

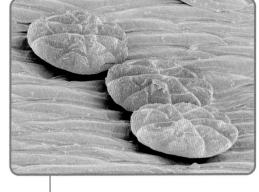

3 Imprisoned

Tiny insects can escape between the teeth, but large insects are imprisoned. As they struggle, they touch the trigger hairs again. If the plant counts five more touches, it starts producing digestive juices.

4 Decomposing body

The jaws close tightly to form a watertight seal, allowing a pool of digestive juice to build up. The victim drowns, and digestive enzymes break down its body into simple nutrients that can dissolve in the fluid and be absorbed by the plant.

After about a week, only an undigested husk remains. The trap reopens to let it fall out.

Trap types

Carnivorous plants produce five different types of traps: sticky flytraps, suction traps, pitfall traps, lobster-pot traps, and snapping cages (like the Venus flytrap). All are hard to escape, and all turn their victims into nutrients for the plant to use.

Sticky flytraps

The leaves of the Cape sundew are lined with tentacles, each of which has a droplet of glue on its tip. If an unfortunate fly gets stuck and tries to fly free, its struggles make ever more tentacles stick to it. To seal its fate, the entire leaf curls around it.

A sticky droplet at the end of each tentacle attracts prey.

Suction traps

Bladderworts capture tiny aquatic organisms in underwater suction traps. When passing prey brush against the trap's trigger hairs, the trap sucks in the victim in less than a thousandth of a second. This may be the fastest movement in the plant kingdom.

Pitfall traps

Pitcher plants grow jug-shaped traps called pitchers from the tips of their leaves. Insects lose their footing on the slippery surface and fall into a pool of slimy digestive fluid.

Lobster-pot traps

The traps of corkscrew plants work like the lobster pots that people use to catch lobsters. Each trap consists of a special, Y-shaped leaf with openings that microscopic organisms can enter. The inside of the trap is lined with bristles that all point in one direction, preventing the victim from backing out.

Victims are funneled into digestive chambers.

Buried in boggy soil, the Y-shaped traps consist of special leaves wound into spiral shapes with hollows inside.

Slitlike openings allow tiny soil organisms to swim inside.

Monkey cup pitchers are so named because
monkeys sometimes drink from them.

16 in (41 cm)—the height of
the **largest known** pitcher.

Lid
The lid (operculum)
keeps out the rain so
that the digestive juice
in the trap isn't diluted.

Nectar glands
Nectar glands on the
underside of the lid
attract insects and
other animals.

Slippery lip
The lip (peristome) is
extremely slippery when
wet, making it almost
impossible for insect prey
to keep their footing.

Wings
On the outside of most
pitchers are hairy wings,
which act as ladders to
help insect victims crawl
up to the trap.

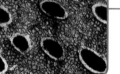

Digestive glands
Glands on the inner lining of the
pitcher, seen here through a
microscope, secrete digestive
fluids into the water.

Wax crystals
Lining the inner wall are
loose wax crystals that make
the surface too slippery for
victims to climb up.

Slimy fluid
The fluid in the trap contains substances
that make it slightly slimy. This ruins the
wings of flies and makes it difficult for
small animals to wriggle out. As the victim
struggles in the goop, acid and digestive
enzymes begin to digest its body.

Shrew bathrooms
As well as getting
nutrients from rotting
corpses, pitcher plants
sometimes feed on poop.
Tree shrews and rats love
to lick nectar from the lids
of monkey cup pitchers.
While feeding, they sit
over the cup and use the
opening as a toilet.

Pitcher dwellers
A few mosquito species
lay eggs in pitchers. Their
larvae can withstand the
plant's digestive enzymes.

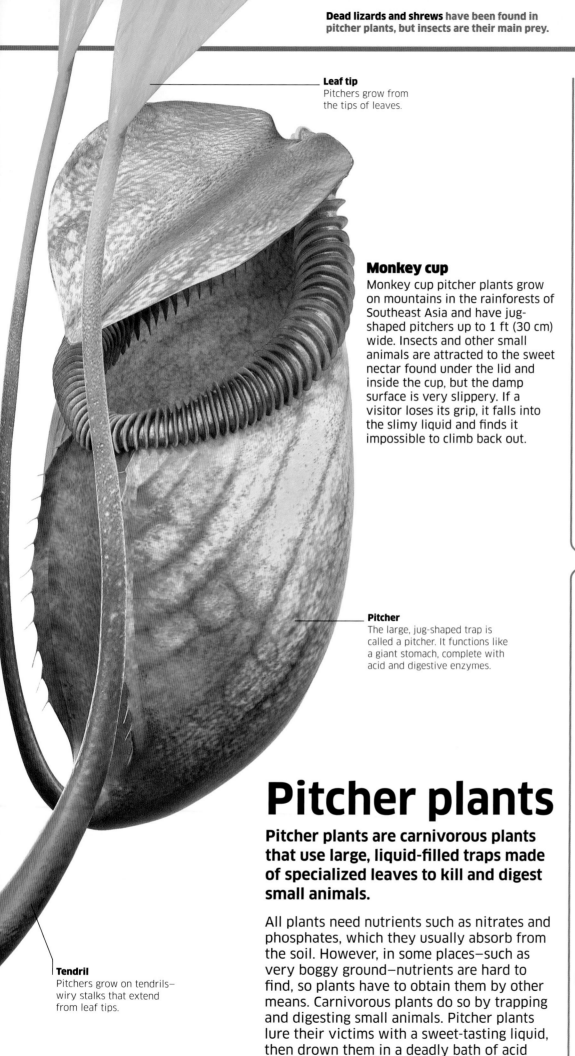

Leaf tip
Pitchers grow from
the tips of leaves.

Monkey cup

Monkey cup pitcher plants grow
on mountains in the rainforests of
Southeast Asia and have jug-
shaped pitchers up to 1 ft (30 cm)
wide. Insects and other small
animals are attracted to the sweet
nectar found under the lid and
inside the cup, but the damp
surface is very slippery. If a
visitor loses its grip, it falls into
the slimy liquid and finds it
impossible to climb back out.

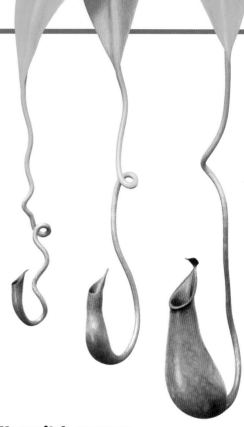

How pitchers grow

To make a pitcher, the plant first grows a new
leaf. A tendril (a wiry stalk) extends from the
tip of the leaf and then curves upward, while
a bud forms at its end. The bud balloons in size,
forming a hollow container. Finally, the lid opens
and the rim rolls back to form the slippery lip.

Cobra lily

The cobra lily is a kind of pitcher plant that
grows in boggy places in parts of North America.
Flies enter the trap through a small entrance
hole, but when they search for the exit, they get
confused by light shining through windowlike
spots at the top. They bump into these false exits
repeatedly, become exhausted, and eventually
fall into the deadly liquid below. Trapped at the
bottom, they will drown and be digested.

Pitcher
The large, jug-shaped trap is
called a pitcher. It functions like
a giant stomach, complete with
acid and digestive enzymes.

Entrance

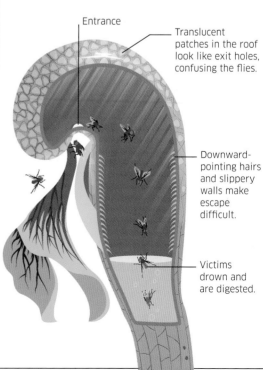

Translucent
patches in the roof
look like exit holes,
confusing the flies.

Downward-
pointing hairs
and slippery
walls make
escape
difficult.

Pitcher plants

**Pitcher plants are carnivorous plants
that use large, liquid-filled traps made
of specialized leaves to kill and digest
small animals.**

All plants need nutrients such as nitrates and
phosphates, which they usually absorb from
the soil. However, in some places—such as
very boggy ground—nutrients are hard to
find, so plants have to obtain them by other
means. Carnivorous plants do so by trapping
and digesting small animals. Pitcher plants
lure their victims with a sweet-tasting liquid,
then drown them in a deadly bath of acid
and digestive juices.

Victims
drown and
are digested.

Tendril
Pitchers grow on tendrils—
wiry stalks that extend
from leaf tips.

Parasitic plants

Most plants collect water and nutrients from the soil and energy from the Sun, but some are parasites that steal their food from other plants instead.

Parasites are organisms that live on or inside other organisms and steal from them. Some parasitic plants (called holoparasites) have no leaves and spend their entire life as a network of threads within another plant, like a fungus, and emerge only to flower. Others (hemiparasites) have leaves but steal from a host plant, too. Parasites may not cause noticeable damage, but some are devastating to crops such as rice and maize.

Mistletoe

This evergreen parasite can photosynthesize, but it also sucks water and nutrients from host trees such as apples, poplars, and hawthorns. It doesn't kill its victims but can weaken them over time.

Hydnora

This unusual plant, known in its native southern Africa as "jackal food," lives underground, stealing nutrients from the roots of other plants. Its fleshy flower gives off the smell of poop to attract pollinating beetles.

Flesh mimic
The blotchy red color of *Rafflesia* mimics decaying flesh. The flower also generates heat, helping its foul smell travel farther and making it more attractive to flies.

Victim
Rafflesia's victim is a plant called *Tetrastigma*, which grows as a vine (a climbing plant) in the rainforests of Indonesia.

Inside the vine
Rafflesia seeds germinate if they land in a wound on a suitable vine. The parasite then invades the vine and grows as microscopic strands in its veins. After about two years, flower buds form.

Rafflesia

The Indonesian plant *Rafflesia* is a holoparasite that spends nearly all its life as thin threads inside rainforest vines, where it steals water and nutrients. Flower buds break out of the vines and open to form flowers about 3 ft (1 m) wide. These record-breakers are the largest individual flowers in the world and attract pollinators by releasing a smell like rotting flesh.

Flower bud
The only visible parts of *Rafflesia* are its flowers and fruits. The flower buds take up to a year to mature, but the flowers last only a week after opening.

Tree shrew
Tree shrews eat *Rafflesia*'s berrylike fruits, which contain thousands of tiny seeds.

Spiky disk
Inside the flower is a disk covered with spikes. Their purpose is a mystery. Male or female sex organs are located under the disk.

Pollination
Rafflesia is pollinated by the oriental latrine fly, which lays its eggs on dead animals. It can carry pollen a great distance away to other *Rafflesia* flowers.

Self-defense

Plants have evolved an arsenal of defenses to help them stand their ground against all sorts of plant eaters, from microscopic bacteria to herbivores as large as elephants.

Plants are under constant attack from other organisms and must protect themselves if they are to survive. All plants pack their cells and tissues with substances that animals find difficult to digest, but many plants go further, using armored surfaces, poisons, insect repellents, foul-tasting chemicals, or even animal helpers. Some plants try to evade herbivores altogether, whether by growing in inaccessible places or by hiding from view.

◎ PHYSICAL DEFENSES

Many plants have thorns (modified stems), spines (modified leaves), or prickly leaf or stem surfaces to stop animals from eating them. Some plants even have glasslike crystals inside their leaves that irritate the mouth and gut when eaten.

Thorns are modified stems, which is why they can branch.

Thorns
The honey locust tree of North America produces clusters of long, vicious thorns. These may have been essential during the last ice age, when mammoths fed on the region's trees and shrubs.

◎ CHEMICAL WEAPONS

Many plants use poisons to defend themselves against hungry animals. If an animal takes a bite from a poisonous plant and gets a nasty stomachache, it won't try eating the plant again. If the poison is lethal, the herbivore species will die out if it does not evolve to instinctively avoid the plant.

Stinging nettle
The leaves of stinging nettles are covered in tiny, needlelike hairs. When touched, they pierce the skin and break off, injecting a cocktail of chemicals that cause pain and irritation.

Stings cover the leaves and stems of stinging nettles. At the base of each sting is a chamber containing a toxic liquid.

Ricin, a deadly poison from castor beans, has been used by people as a **chemical weapon**.

Less than one-tenth of a gram of ricin can **kill an adult** human.

129

OAK LEAF

The waxy cuticle of leaves repels water, causing rain to form beads that roll off easily.

Waterproof coat
Most leaves are covered with a waxy layer called a cuticle. As well as preventing water loss, this waterproof coat stops microbes such as fungi and bacteria from getting in. When a plant detects an invading microorganism, it responds by thickening its cuticle. It can also add antifungal chemicals to the cuticle to kill off infections before they take hold.

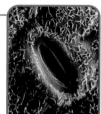

Stomata
Small openings called stomata on the surfaces of leaves close when a plant senses an invasion.

DUMB CANE PLANT

Needle-shaped crystals

Raphides
Raphides are needle-shaped crystals hidden inside leaves. They make an animal's mouth sore if it chews the leaves, but they are even more effective in poisonous plants—the needles poke holes in the mouth, throat, and gut to speed up the action of toxins.

Chili
The fruits of chili plants are protected by the chemical capsaicin, which produces a burning sensation in an animal's mouth. Eating whole raw chilies can be painful for humans, but small amounts add a hot flavor to food, making chili a very popular spice.

Lily of the valley
All parts of this pretty woodland plant, including its bell-shaped flowers and shiny red berries, contain poisons that can stop an animal's heart.

Manchineel
One of the most toxic trees in the world, manchineel contains a white sap that can cause blistering and burning if touched. Just standing beneath this tree in the rain is enough to burn the skin.

Wolfsbane
The poisonous roots of this plant contain a nerve toxin that can stop a person's heartbeat. Wolfsbane was once used to poison arrow tips for hunting wolves and bears. The ancient Romans also used it as a method of execution.

Ragwort
Some animals steal the chemical weapons made by plants. Cinnabar moth caterpillars are immune to the poison in ragwort and store it in their bodies to ward off predators such as birds. Their bright colors serve as a warning.

INSECT DEFENDERS
Some plants send out a call for help when herbivores attack. When chewed by caterpillars, cabbage plants release a scent that attracts parasitic wasps. The wasps lay eggs inside the caterpillars, and the wasp larvae devour the caterpillars from within. The relationship between cabbage and these wasps is described as mutualistic, which means that both partners benefit. The plant gets protection from herbivores, and the wasp gets food for its offspring.

Parasitic wasp larvae
A female white butterfly parasite wasp can lay as many as 50 eggs in a host caterpillar. These wasps are very effective in controlling caterpillar infestations.

Wasp larvae emerge from the dead body of a host caterpillar.

MOVEMENT
It's rare for plants to flee from herbivores by moving, but a few species do it. When touched, the leaves of the sensitive plant fold and collapse, hiding the plant from herbivores and scaring away flying insects.

The sudden movement relies on fast-acting electrical signals that trigger the movement of water in hinge cells at the base of each leaflet.

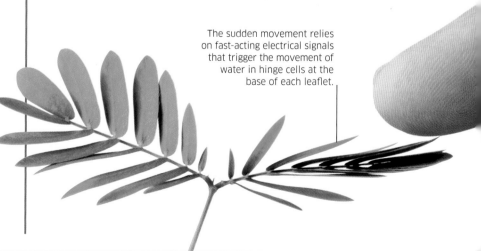

PEOPLE AND PLANTS

When people first figured out how to grow edible plants, it triggered the birth of civilization. Since then, we've learned how to cultivate thousands of plant species and converted nearly half the world's wilderness into farmland. Now our ever-expanding population is putting wild plants at risk.

Food from plants

Plants are vital to our survival. As well as giving us oxygen to breathe and materials to build with, plants create our food.

All the food we eat comes from plants in one way or another. Most of our diet comes directly from plants in the form of fruit, vegetables, and grain products such as wheat and rice. However, even animal foods like meat and dairy products come from animals that obtained their nutrients from plants. Humans consume an enormous variety of different plants, but only a small number make up the majority of our diet. Compared to animal foods, plant foods are less rich but are healthier. Producing plant foods also uses less energy per meal and does less harm to the environment than producing animal foods.

Plant parts

Not all parts of plants are edible. Depending on the species, we eat different parts, such as leaves, roots, stems, fruits, or seeds. Even the flowers of some plants are edible. Plant foods fall into three main groups according to the part we eat: grains (grass seeds), fruits (sweet fruits), and vegetables (everything else, including fruits that aren't sweet).

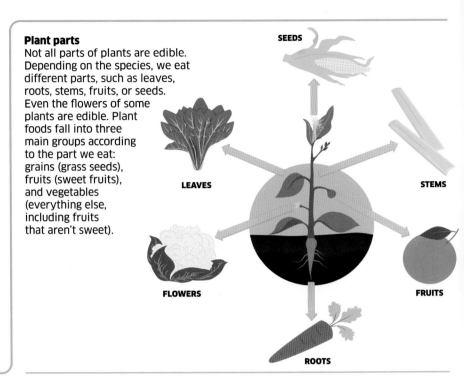

SEEDS

LEAVES

STEMS

FLOWERS

FRUITS

ROOTS

ESSENTIAL NUTRIENTS

The World Health Organization (WHO) recommends that people eat at least five portions of fruit and vegetables a day—about 14 oz (400g) in total. Plant foods are rich in all the main nutrients we need to stay healthy: carbohydrates, proteins, fats, and fiber. They also contain essential vitamins and minerals.

Carbohydrates

Carbohydrates, such as starch and sugar, provide our bodies with energy, but excessive amounts can cause weight gain, tooth decay, and diseases such as diabetes. Carbohydrates are found in all plant foods. Root vegetables and grains are richest in starch, while fruits are high in sugars.

RICE

SUGAR CANE

SWEET POTATO

Protein

We need proteins to build, repair, and maintain our bodies. We can't store proteins, so we need a constant supply. Animal foods such as meat and cheese are rich in proteins, but so are the seeds of plants—especially seeds of plants from the pea family (Fabaceae). These include lentils, beans, and peanuts.

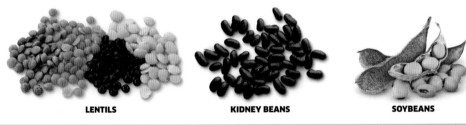

LENTILS

KIDNEY BEANS

SOYBEANS

Lipids

Our bodies need lipids (fats and oils) to make cell membranes and hormones and to store energy. In general, fats from plant foods are healthier than fats from animal foods. Nuts and seeds are a good source of healthy fats. They also contain omega fatty acids, which protect against heart disease.

CASHEWS

AVOCADO

LINSEED

ALMONDS

OLIVE OIL

Fiber

This is a type of carbohydrate found only in plant foods. We can't digest fiber, but it is still important to our health. It helps in digestion and protects us from heart disease, certain cancers, and some kinds of diabetes.

BLACK-EYED
PEAS

PIGEON
PEAS

BROCCOLI

CHICKPEAS

WHOLE-WHEAT BREAD

The **first cultivated potatoes** were grown 7,000 years ago in Peru, South America.

About half of the world's food energy comes from **only three crops**: wheat, maize, and rice.

133

DRINKABLE PLANTS

We don't just eat plants, we use them to make drinks as well. Two of the world's favorite beverages—tea and coffee—come from plants. Juices are made by pressing fruits or other parts of plants, and alcoholic drinks are made by using the fungus yeast to ferment sugars from plants.

TEA LEAVES   **TEA**

COFFEE BERRIES

COFFEE

Tea
Dried leaves of the tea plant are steeped in hot water to make this refreshing hot drink. Tea contains caffeine, a compound that stimulates the nervous system.

Coffee
Rivaling tea in popularity, coffee is made from the roasted and ground beans (berries) of the coffee plant. It has a higher concentration of caffeine than tea.

CACAO PODS WITH BEANS

HOT CHOCOLATE

Cacao
The beans of the cacao tree are used to make chocolate and cocoa powder, which can be mixed with milk or hot water to make a hot chocolate drink.

KOLA NUTS   **COLA DRINK**

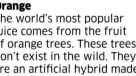

ORANGE FRUIT   **ORANGE JUICE**

Kola
Though no longer used as an ingredient, the kola plant of Africa gives cola its name. Other plants used in cola include orange, lime, lavender, cinnamon, coriander, nutmeg, and vanilla.

Orange
The world's most popular juice comes from the fruit of orange trees. These trees don't exist in the wild. They are an artificial hybrid made by breeding mandarins with pomelos.

BEER

BARLEY PLANT

GRAPES   **WINE**

Barley
This grain is used to make beer. It is brewed with yeast, which feeds on sugars in the grains to produce alcohol.

Grapes
Wine is made by mixing crushed grapes with yeast, which produces alcohol from the fruit's sugars.

CROP PRODUCTION

Billions of tons of crops are grown across the world every year to meet the demand for food for people and livestock (farm animals). Grains such as wheat and rice make up one-third of the total weight of cultivated plant food. However, the world's largest single crop by weight is sugar cane.

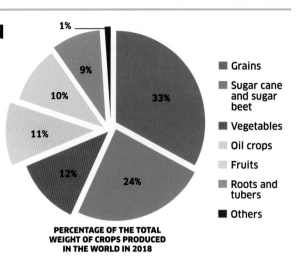

- Grains
- Sugar cane and sugar beet
- Vegetables
- Oil crops
- Fruits
- Roots and tubers
- Others

1%
9%
10%
33%
11%
12%
24%

PERCENTAGE OF THE TOTAL WEIGHT OF CROPS PRODUCED IN THE WORLD IN 2018

AGRICULTURE AND THE ENVIRONMENT

As the world's population has grown, the area of land used for agriculture has increased, causing natural habitats to disappear. About 46 percent of Earth's habitable land is now used for agriculture. If the population keeps rising, we will need to find more sustainable ways of producing food.

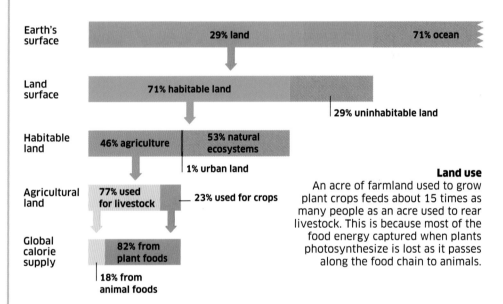

Earth's surface — 29% land — 71% ocean

Land surface — 71% habitable land — 29% uninhabitable land

Habitable land — 46% agriculture — 53% natural ecosystems — 1% urban land

Agricultural land — 77% used for livestock — 23% used for crops

Global calorie supply — 82% from plant foods — 18% from animal foods

Land use
An acre of farmland used to grow plant crops feeds about 15 times as many people as an acre used to rear livestock. This is because most of the food energy captured when plants photosynthesize is lost as it passes along the food chain to animals.

Climate change
Modern agriculture contributes to global warming by releasing the greenhouse gases methane (from livestock), nitrous oxide (from fertilizer use), and carbon dioxide (from machinery). As weather patterns change, some parts of the world may become too hot to grow staple foods such as maize (left).

Indoor farming
In the future, more crops may be grown indoors or in greenhouses, where farmers can carefully control the temperature; light level; and the amount of water, nutrients, and carbon dioxide that plants receive. In vertical farming, crops are grown in racks stacked one above the other, giving greater yields than traditional farming.

Grain crops

**Grains are cultivated grasses. They have been sown
by farmers for at least 9,000 years and are the source
of most of the world's food.**

Wheat, rice, maize, millet, rye, and oats are the most important
grain crops. All belong to the grass family (Poaceae) and
are grown for their edible seeds. Modern varieties of these
plants are very different from their wild ancestors and
produce bumper seedheads with huge grains.

WHEAT GRAINS

Each kernel
develops from
a separate flower.

A single ear of
maize has up
to 600 kernels.

WHEAT
Triticum aestivum
Cultivated in: Temperate parts of the world with
good rainfall
Height: Up to 3 ft (1 m)

The first plant to be cultivated, wheat triggered
the birth of farming and the growth of the first
civilizations. Today, it is one of the most widely
grown crops in the world. Wheat grains are ground
into flour and used to make bread, pasta, noodles,
cakes, and cookies. The stalks are used as
animal food.

A brown husk
surrounds each
grain of rice.

RICE
Oryza sativa
Cultivated in: Hot
countries, especially
in Asia
Height: Up to 4 ft (1.2 m)

Rice is a staple food for more
than half the world's population.
It grows in flooded fields called
paddies that are drained before
the crop is harvested. The
seedheads are then milled
to remove the husk and bran,
leaving the white rice grains.

MAIZE
Zea mays
Cultivated in: Worldwide
Height: Up to 10 ft (3 m)

First cultivated in Central America,
maize has been grown as a crop for
almost as long as wheat. Its seeds, called
kernels, form on large ears. Maize is grown
for human consumption (sweetcorn), as
animal feed, to make cornstarch and corn
syrup, and is fermented to make alcohol and
biofuel. The flour is used to make flatbreads.

MILLET
Panicum miliaceum
Cultivated in: Asia, Africa,
Europe, and North America
Height: Up to 4.3 ft
(1.3 m)

Millet grows well in hot,
dry places where wheat
and rice are difficult to
grow. It is a staple food
in much of Africa and
parts of Asia and
is used to make
flatbreads and
oatmeal. In other
parts of the world,
millet is mainly
used to feed animals.

OATS
Avena sativa
Cultivated in: Cool temperate
regions, mainly Europe and USA
Height: Up to 5 ft (1.5 m)

Oat flour is no good for making
bread, so oats are mainly grown
for animal food, breakfast grains,
and high-fiber snacks. Rolled oats,
which are used to make oatmeal,
are whole grains that have been
steamed and flattened.

OAT GRAINS

Vegetable crops

Vegetables include any fresh, edible parts of a plant, from flowers and fruits to leaves, buds, stems, and roots. They are a vital part of a healthy diet.

Some of the foods we call vegetables—including tomatoes, peppers, cucumbers, and pumpkins—are considered fruits by scientists because they develop from flowers. However, most people use the word vegetable for any plant part used in savory foods. Farmers have been breeding and changing vegetable crops for thousands of years. Many of today's varieties, from cabbages to cauliflowers, are artificial creations that don't exist in the wild.

GOURD FAMILY
Cucurbitaceae

Types: Cucumber, gourd, melon, pumpkin, squash, and zucchini

Origin: Central and South America

The plants of the gourd family are vines (climbing plants) that produce fleshy fruits. Harder types like pumpkins are usually cooked to soften them. Softer, sweeter types like melons are sold as fruits.

PUMPKIN

LEGUME FAMILY
Fabaceae

Types: Beans, lentils, peas, and soybeans
Origin: Central and South America, Europe, and Middle East

Legumes are grown for their edible seeds, but the fresh pods are eaten as vegetables, too. All legumes are high in protein, which makes them an important part of vegetarian diets.

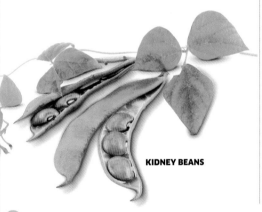

KIDNEY BEANS

BRASSICA FAMILY
Brassicaceae

Types: Broccoli, cabbage, cauliflower, and radish

Origin: Asia and Europe

There are thousands of species in the brassica family, but just one of them—the wild cabbage—is the original source of many common vegetables. Over centuries, farmers bred the plant to enlarge different parts of it. The top leaf buds became cabbages, side buds became sprouts, flower buds became broccoli and cauliflower, and leaves became kale.

Radishes are edible roots with a powerful, spicy flavor.

ONION FAMILY
Amaryllidaceae

Types: Garlic, leek, onion, and spring onion
Origin: Asia

Members of this family are grown for their strongly flavored, edible bulbs. Young onions grown from seed can be eaten raw, but most are cooked to make them sweeter and less overpowering. Chopped onions are often used as the base in savory dishes, as their flavor complements many other foods.

ONION

SOLANUM FAMILY
Solanaceae

Types: Bell pepper, chili, eggplant, potato, and tomato
Origin: Americas

This family includes some of the most widely grown vegetables in the world, such as tomatoes and potatoes. Grown for thousands of years in the Americas, they weren't introduced to Europe and Asia until the 16th century, after which they transformed the way people cook.

Bell peppers come from a cultivated variety of *Capsicum annuum*, the species that also gives us chili peppers.

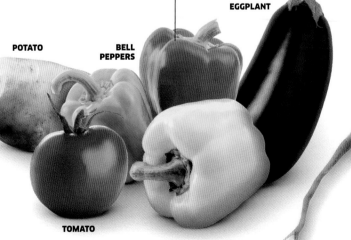

POTATO

BELL PEPPERS

EGGPLANT

TOMATO

APPLE
Malus domestica
Origin: Central Asia
Cultivated in: Worldwide

Scientists think the modern apple originated in Central Asia around 4,000 years ago, when the crab apple tree and another wild species bred and formed a hybrid. Today, there are more than 7,500 different apple varieties. Most are not grown from seeds but from cuttings grafted onto other apple trees. This ensures each variety always looks and tastes the same.

ORANGE
Citrus sinensis
Origin: China and Southeast Asia
Cultivated in: South America, USA, India, China, and Mediterranean countries

Oranges originated in tropical Asia and are now the most cultivated fruit trees in the world. The most common type is also called the sweet orange to distinguish it from the bitter variety used to make marmalade. Oranges are grown for eating fresh, juicing, and making flavorings.

Depending on the variety, it takes 6–14 months for oranges to ripen before picking.

Fruit crops

Sweet, juicy, and deliciously fragrant, fruits are the tastiest parts of plants. Growing them is big business, with hundreds of millions of tons sold worldwide every year.

The scientific meaning of "fruit" is different from its everyday meaning. To a botanist, a fruit is simply the ripened ovary of a flower, whether it's edible or not. To most people, however, a fruit is something not just edible but sweet-tasting and often colorful, too. Fresh fruits are an important part of a healthy diet. Fruits can also be used to manufacture jellies, juices, ice creams, and other products. In addition, the scents and colors of fruits can also be extracted to make natural dyes, flavorings, and perfumes.

BANANA
Musa acuminata
Origin: Malaysian archipelago and Papua New Guinea
Cultivated in: All tropical regions

There are many different kinds of bananas, including green, yellow, and brown ones; sweet ones; and a starchy cooking banana called a plantain. However, the vast majority are Cavendish bananas, a sweet yellow variety. All Cavendish banana plants are genetically identical and are now under threat from a fungal disease.

Banana hand
Bananas grow in bunches called hands, each fruit forming from a single flower in a cluster.

MELON
Cucumis and *Citrullus*
Origin: Africa and Southwest Asia
Cultivated in: China, Turkey, Iran, and India

Melons are related to pumpkins and squashes but are softer and sweeter. They grow on vines that scramble over the soil. With the ground to provide support, the fruits can grow huge. The largest on record reached 351 lb (159 kg), which is twice the weight of an adult human.

CANTALOUPE MELON

PEACH
Prunus persica
Origin: China
Cultivated in: China, Italy, Spain, Greece, and Turkey

Peaches and nectarines (which belong to the same species) originated in China, where these trees have been cultivated for possibly as long as 8,000 years. Also known as stone fruits, these fruits each contain a single large seed. In China, the peach is a symbol of immortality and is often given to wish a person a long life.

Edible skin
The velvety, yellowish-red skin of the peach is edible and hides a stony core.

A pomegranate contains around **600 seeds**.

50 different chemicals are used to make **artificial strawberry flavor**.

137

PINEAPPLE
Ananas comosus

Origin: South America

Cultivated in: Brazil, Philippines, Costa Rica, and Indonesia

Pineapple plants are members of the bromeliad family of tropical America, which is where most pineapples are still grown. Each fruit forms from a cluster of dozens of individual flowers that fuse to form a multiple fruit. Pineapples were introduced to Europe in the 16th century but proved very difficult to grow. As a result, they were rare and incredibly expensive, costing the equivalent of $7,800 each in today's money.

Maturing fruit
The fruit takes 10–12 weeks to mature.

PASSION FRUIT
Passiflora edulis

Origin: South America

Cultivated in: Australia, Brazil, Columbia, Ecuador, Kenya, and West Indies

Passion fruits come from a tropical climbing plant native to South America that is now cultivated in many tropical and semitropical places. Inside the fruit are dozens of seeds embedded in a juicy, jellylike flesh that has an intense fragrance. Passion fruits are used to make ice cream, soft drinks, and desserts.

STRAWBERRY
Fragaria

Origin: Throughout northern hemisphere

Cultivated in: Worldwide

Scientifically speaking, strawberries are false fruits and the pips on the outside are the real fruits, but this hasn't stopped them from being one of the world's most popular fresh fruits. Strawberry plants are grown in rows and multiply by producing horizontal stems called runners.

Pips on surface
Each strawberry has about 200 pips.

GRAPE
Vitis

Origin: Middle East

Cultivated in: Europe, China, USA, South America, and Australia

Grapes have been cultivated for at least 8,000 years. They grow on vines (climbing plants) and can be eaten fresh, dried to make raisins and sultanas, or used to make wine. Seedless grapes are mutant varieties that are grown from cuttings.

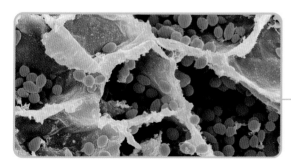

Yeast
Yeast (seen here as orange disks), a type of single-celled fungus, grows on grape skin and helps turn grape juice into wine.

Cranberry harvest

The easiest way to harvest cranberries is to flood the boggy fields in which they grow, then corral the floating fruits into containers.

Cranberries don't grow in water. Like blueberries and bilberries, they grow on small shrubs in damp heathland. Harvest takes place when the berries turn bright red. After flooding the field up to about knee height, farmers wade through it pushing wheeled "eggbeaters"–spinning contraptions that loosen the berries from the shrubs. The cranberries contain just enough air to float.

VANILLA
Vanilla planifolia
and *Vanilla tahitensis*
Origin: Caribbean and
Central America
Part used: Seed pod

The vanilla plant is the only
orchid that produces edible
seed pods. The dried pods
or the seeds inside them are
used to flavor sweet foods
like ice cream and cakes, and
extracts are also used to
make perfume. Vanilla is
the second most expensive
spice after saffron.

The green pods turn
black when dried.

DRIED VANILLA PODS

SAFFRON
Crocus sativus
Origin: Iran and the Middle East
Part used: Flower style and stigma

This spice is made from the red styles and stigmas of crocus
flowers. These tiny parts have to be picked by hand, making
saffron the most expensive spice in the world. Luckily, only
a few styles are needed to add a complex flavor and intense
red-yellow color to food.

Precious harvest
Around 80,000
flowers are needed
to make just
1.1 lb (0.5 kg)
of saffron.

Herbs and spices

**Some plants have very powerful tastes or smells, often to
ward off herbivores. Used in tiny amounts, these potent
ingredients can transform the flavor of what we eat.**

Herbs are mostly leaves, whereas spices come from seeds, flowers,
stems, bark, and roots. While herbs taste best when fresh, spices are
often dried and may be ground into a powder. In many parts of the
world, regional foods get their flavor from the herbs and spices that
grow in the area. However, some herbs and spices are so tasty that they
are used everywhere. In the past, sailors made great fortunes shipping
precious spices like pepper and cinnamon across the world, and only
the richest people could afford to use them.

GINGER
Zingiber officinale
Origin: Southeast Asia
Part used: Underground stem

Ginger comes from the rhizomes (underground
stems) of a small tropical plant that only exists
now as a cultivated plant and not in the wild.
Whether used fresh or dried, it adds gentle
heat to food. In Europe, it's traditionally used
in sweet foods like cakes and cookies, but in
Asia, it's a popular spice in hot, savory dishes.

Underground stem
Although sometimes described as a root, ginger
is a swollen stem that grows underground.

PEPPER
Piper nigrum
Origin: India
Part used: Fruits

Peppercorns–the dried fruits
of a tropical Indian plant–were
once so valuable, they were used
as money. They make white
pepper if picked ripe and
black pepper if picked unripe
and boiled before drying.
The spice has a sharp, hot
flavor and is added as
a seasoning both during
and after cooking.

Unripe
peppercorns
are green.

**DRIED
BLACK
PEPPER**

Beekeepers sometimes use lemon grass extract to make **bees swarm**.

Black peppercorns were found **stuffed in the nose** of the mummy of the Egyptian pharaoh Ramesses II.

The Carolina reaper pepper is so hot that **people wear gloves** to handle it.

141

CINNAMON
Cinnamomum verum
Origin: Southeast Asia
Part used: Bark

Cinnamon has a warming and scented flavor that is used in sweet foods in Europe and savory dishes in Asia. It is supplied as a powder or curled sticks of bark. The outer bark of the cinnamon tree is stripped off so that the inner bark can be harvested. It curls into brown "quills" as it dries.

The cinnamon tree's inner bark is used to make the spice.

CINNAMON QUILLS

BASIL
Ocimum basilicum
Origin: India
Part used: Leaves

Like other members of the mint and rosemary family (Lamiaceae), basil produces aromatic oils that act as natural insect repellents. These oils give the herb its flavor. Basil is a tropical plant but is cultivated worldwide. It is especially popular in Italy, where it's used to flavor pizzas and make a pasta sauce called pesto.

Aromatic leaves
Basil's softly fragrant leaves give out a strong aroma when crushed.

LEMON GRASS
Cymbopogon citratus
Origin: Southeast Asia
Part used: Stem and leaf

Lemon grass is one of many plants that defend themselves from insects with aromatic oils that smell like lemon. Fresh stems and leaves are used to add zesty flavor to Southeast Asian dishes, particularly in Thailand and Vietnam. Extracts are also used to perfume soaps, candles, and household cleaning products.

Lemon grass grows in dense tussocks.

CUMIN
Cuminum cyminum
Origin: West Asia
Part used: Seed

Cumin is a member of the parsley family and is sold as ground or whole seeds. It has a warm, earthy flavor and is used in curries, stews, pickles, and as a part of spice mixes such as garam masala and curry powder.

Seedheads
Cumin seeds are hand-picked from dried seedheads.

Feel the heat

Chili plants were cultivated in South America for more than 5,000 years before Portuguese traders introduced them to the rest of the world in the 16th century. The spice became hugely popular, especially in Asia. The fiery heat comes from the chemical capsaicin, which triggers pain receptors. It is so powerful that it is used in weapons such as pepper sprays and even grenades. The strength of chili varieties depends on how much capsaicin they contain and is measured in Scoville Heat Units (SHU). The SHU number tells you how many times an extract from the chili has to be diluted before the heat can't be tasted.

0 SHU
Bell pepper

500 SHU
Pimento

8,000 SHU
Jalapeño

50,000 SHU
Cayenne pepper

350,000 SHU
Scotch bonnet

1,040,000 SHU
Ghost pepper
(Bhut jolokia)

1,380,000 SHU
Naga viper

2,200,000 SHU
Carolina reaper

Making chocolate

Solid chocolate is so complicated to make that the recipe wasn't discovered until 1847, when British chocolatier (chocolate maker) Joseph Fry made the world's first chocolate bar. Even today, chocolatiers keep their methods secret, as tiny changes to the process can have a big impact on the finished product. Skilled chocolate makers repeatedly heat and cool chocolate until it has the perfect crystal structure to make it taste smooth and creamy as it melts in the mouth.

1 Harvest
Cacao pods are harvested when ripe, cut open, and the beans and pulp are removed.

2 Fermenting
The beans are left for about a week while the pulp softens, making it easier to remove.

3 Drying
The beans are dried in sunlight to prevent mold. They can now be shipped to factories.

4 Roasting
At a chocolate factory, the beans are roasted to develop their flavor.

5 Shelling
The brittle, roasted beans are cracked to remove the shells, which are then discarded.

6 Grinding
The cracked insides of beans are called nibs. They are ground into thick liquid: chocolate liquor.

7 Blending
Chocolate liquor is blended with sugar, cocoa butter (fat from the liquor), and sometimes milk.

8 Molding
After heating and grinding to make the chocolate smoother, it is poured into molds.

Cacao flower
The tree's small flowers are pollinated by midges. After pollination, the petals drop off and the flower's ovary grows into a cacao pod.

Unripe pod
Cacao pods grow directly on the tree's trunks and branches. They change color as they ripen, turning from green to orange, red, or even purple.

Moth caterpillar
Cacao harvests can be damaged by pests called cocoa pod borers. These moth caterpillars burrow into pods and devour the soft pulp that surrounds the cacao beans.

The word chocolate comes from the Aztec word xocolatl, which means "bitter water."

6.385 tons (5.793 tonnes)—weight of the **world's largest** chocolate bar.

143

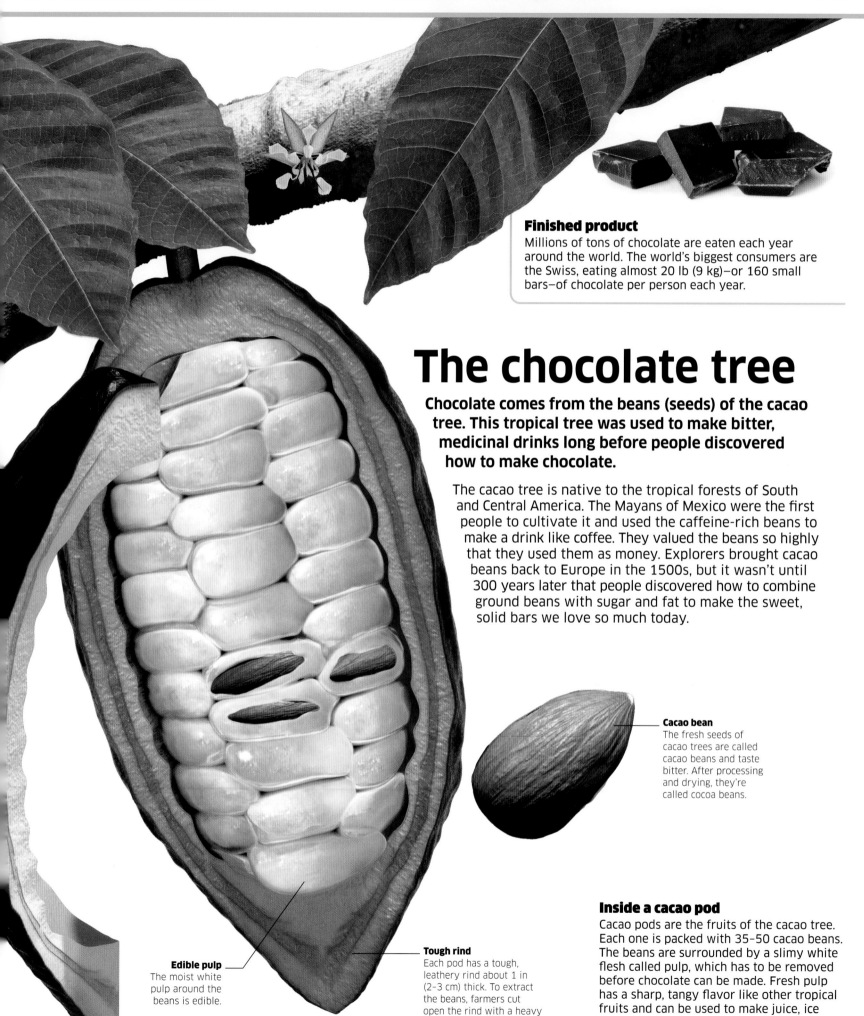

Finished product
Millions of tons of chocolate are eaten each year around the world. The world's biggest consumers are the Swiss, eating almost 20 lb (9 kg)—or 160 small bars—of chocolate per person each year.

The chocolate tree

Chocolate comes from the beans (seeds) of the cacao tree. This tropical tree was used to make bitter, medicinal drinks long before people discovered how to make chocolate.

The cacao tree is native to the tropical forests of South and Central America. The Mayans of Mexico were the first people to cultivate it and used the caffeine-rich beans to make a drink like coffee. They valued the beans so highly that they used them as money. Explorers brought cacao beans back to Europe in the 1500s, but it wasn't until 300 years later that people discovered how to combine ground beans with sugar and fat to make the sweet, solid bars we love so much today.

Cacao bean
The fresh seeds of cacao trees are called cacao beans and taste bitter. After processing and drying, they're called cocoa beans.

Edible pulp
The moist white pulp around the beans is edible.

Tough rind
Each pod has a tough, leathery rind about 1 in (2–3 cm) thick. To extract the beans, farmers cut open the rind with a heavy knife called a machete.

Inside a cacao pod
Cacao pods are the fruits of the cacao tree. Each one is packed with 35–50 cacao beans. The beans are surrounded by a slimy white flesh called pulp, which has to be removed before chocolate can be made. Fresh pulp has a sharp, tangy flavor like other tropical fruits and can be used to make juice, ice cream, or jam.

144 people and plants ○ **HEALING PLANTS**

44,000 tons of aspirin (40,000 tonnes) are made every year worldwide.

Healing plants

For thousands of years, people have used the healing properties of plants to treat illness. Some of today's most effective and widely used medicines are based on plants.

Before modern medicine, people relied on plants to treat everything from minor wounds and headaches to serious illness. Ancient healers thought their herbal remedies had magical properties and often mixed plants with other ingredients believed to have special powers, including salt, honey, worms, dung, and dead animals. Discovering what worked and how much to take was a matter of trial and error. Today, scientists carry out careful trials of drugs from plants to see if they genuinely work. Their research has proved that plants make many potentially life-saving compounds.

ALOE VERA
Aloe vera
Location: Arabian peninsula
Part used: Leaves

Aloe vera is a desert plant that stores water in a kind of jelly that fills its thick, spiky leaves. Long ago, people discovered that swallowing the jelly triggers bowel movements, helping a person go to the bathroom. The active ingredient is aloin, a substance now used as a laxative (a drug to cure constipation). Some people also use the jelly from *Aloe vera* to soothe sunburn and sore skin.

WILLOW
Salix
Location: Central and Southern Europe
Part used: Bark

The ancient Egyptians were among the first to discover the pain-relieving properties of willow bark. In the 19th century, scientists discovered the active ingredient and used it to make aspirin. This cure for headaches and fever is now one of the world's most used drugs.

WILLOW BARK

Water store
The natural jelly in *Aloe vera* is used to make soap, skin moisturizers, and cosmetics.

YEW
Taxus baccata
Location: Europe, North Africa
Part used: Leaves and bark

The bark, leaves, and seeds of the yew tree are extremely toxic to animals. Though dangerous to eat, the bark contains a chemical called paclitaxel, which is used in chemotherapy to treat cancer. It isn't a cure, but it can extend a person's life.

ROSY PERIWINKLE
Catharanthus roseus
Location: Madagascar
Part used: Roots and leaves

The rosy periwinkle plant is used to make two anticancer drugs: vincristine and vinblastine. Vincristine increases the chance of surviving childhood leukemia from 10 percent to 95 percent.

PEPPERMINT
Mentha x piperita
Location: Europe, Middle East
Part uses: Leaves and stem

Peppermint is a hybrid species—a cross between watermint and spearmint. Some people use an oil extracted from the leaves to soothe an upset stomach or treat digestive problems, though the medical benefits are not yet scientifically proven.

Half a ton of rosy periwinkle is needed to make just 0.04 oz (1 g) of the cancer drug vinblastine.

Tonic water containing quinine **glows in the dark** if you shine ultraviolet light on it.

145

OPIUM POPPY
Papaver somniferum
Location: Europe, Asia
Part used: Seed pods

People have used the seed pods of the opium poppy for thousands of years to treat toothache and coughs, and as a sedative to help them sleep. Powerful and highly addictive painkillers, such as morphine and codeine, are made from the milky juice produced when the unripe seed pods are slit open.

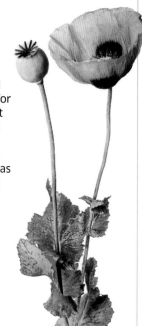

CHINESE MAGNOLIA VINE
Schisandra chinensis
Location: China, Korea, Japan
Part used: Fruit

The bright red berries of the Chinese magnolia vine contain several compounds that have been used to treat liver disease, cancer, and problems with the immune system. The berries are known as the "five-flavor fruit" because they taste sweet, salty, bitter, spicy, and sour at the same time.

ARTEMISIA
Artemisia annua
Location: Asia, Europe
Part used: Leaves

Also known as sweet wormwood, the *Artemisia* plant has long been used as a folk remedy for malaria and to reduce fever and swelling. A drug called artemisinin has since been produced and is used for treating malaria, though some resistance to its effects is already developing.

CITRUS
Citrus
Location: China, Southeast Asia
Part used: Fruit

Scurvy is a potentially fatal disease that develops if a person doesn't get enough vitamin C. For hundreds of years, scurvy was common among sailors on long sea voyages until it was discovered that eating citrus fruits could prevent it.

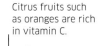

Citrus fruits such as oranges are rich in vitamin C.

FOXGLOVE
Digitalis
Location: Europe, West Asia, Northwestern Africa
Part used: Whole plant

Foxgloves are tall plants with bell-shaped flowers. All parts of the plant contain the deadly poison digoxin, which can stop a person's heart. However, tiny amounts can stabilize an irregular heartbeat, making digoxin a life-saving drug.

Energy from plants

Plants don't just provide us with raw materials for making things—they also give us energy. The fossil fuels we use to generate electricity, heat our homes, and power our cars come from the ancient remains of plants or algae that lived millions of years ago. In many parts of the world, people rely on firewood for heating and cooking.

Environmental cost

When fossil fuels are burned, they generate energy we can use to power and heat our homes. However, doing so releases large amounts of carbon dioxide into the atmosphere. This extra carbon dioxide is warming the planet and causing glaciers to melt, sea levels to rise, and weather to become more extreme.

Future materials

Most modern buildings are constructed with concrete and cement, but the manufacture of these materials is harmful to the environment. To improve matters, scientists, engineers, and architects are turning to the natural world. They hope that new materials made from plants and fungi will lower carbon emissions and make the construction industry more sustainable.

Hemplime

Also called hempcrete, hemplime is a building material made by mixing fibers of the hemp plant with sand or lime. The resulting blocks can be used like concrete but are lighter and provide better insulation.

Mycelium

The fast-growing, rootlike fibers of fungi, known as mycelium, can be dried and molded to create building materials and insulation, as well as fabrics and packaging (shown here).

Made from plants

For thousands of years, people have used the plants growing around them to build houses and create essential items for day-to-day life.

Sturdy timber beams form the framework of buildings, while the soft fibers of plants such as cotton are spun into textiles. Unlike plastics and many other synthetic materials, materials from plants are renewable, which means we'll never run out of them. They are also biodegradable, which means they break down naturally when thrown away.

Cotton

The fluffy fruits of cotton can be spun into thin threads and woven to make all sorts of textiles, for anything from dish towels to comforters. Cotton is the world's largest nonedible crop, but it requires lots of water to grow, making it environmentally harmful.

Wood

Household furniture is often made from the wood of fast-growing conifer trees, such as pine.

Jute

Beneath a carpet, there is often a layer of a tough, coarse material known as jute, which is made from the fibers of the jute mallow plant.

Paper

Paper is made from wood pulp—a soggy mixture of plant fibers, generally from trees, and water. It is spread out thinly and left to dry, then cut into sheets. In the home, it is used widely and found in items such as wallpaper, toilet paper, and books.

The people of Peru have been using cotton to make fabric for at least **8,000 years**.

The world's **first electric light bulb** used a thin filament of cotton to emit light.

147

Plant-based home

Wherever you look in a house, you can find something that was once a plant. Some of these plant-based materials—for example, timber, cotton, and linen—are so common, it's easy to forget they have come from the plant kingdom.

Viscose
Also called rayon, viscose is an artificial textile made from plants. Wood pulp or bamboo is chemically treated, then spun into fibers to make thread. Viscose fabric has a soft and silky feel, making it ideal for clothing.

Denim
Denim, often used to create jackets or jeans, is made from the fluffy, white fibers of the cotton plant.

Linen
Made from the stem of the flax plant, linen has been used to make bedding and clothing for thousands of years. Today, this quick-drying, breathable fabric is used in homes for bedsheets, curtains, table cloths, and bath towels.

Timber
Timber can easily be cut into strong, load-bearing beams and floorboards, as well as doors.

Wicker
Rushes, reeds, and sedges are tall, stiff, grasslike plants that grow near water. They can be bent and woven into shape to make wicker laundry baskets.

Bamboo
The tough but flexible stems of bamboo plants can be used to make fencing and furniture. In some parts of the world, giant bamboo canes are used to make scaffolding.

Coir
Coir comes from the fibrous shells of coconuts. It's tough and hard-wearing—ideal for brushes and brooms, mattress stuffing, and doormats.

Rubber
This stretchy, waterproof material is made from the milky sap of the rubber tree. It can be molded into different shapes and is used to make kitchen gloves, dog toys, and rain boots.

148 people and plants ○ **PLANTS IN DANGER**

About 2,500 plant species are
classified as **critically endangered**.

Plants in danger

**More than a quarter of the plant species known to science
are endangered due to changes to the natural world.**

The world's plants are disappearing at an alarming rate. Loss of wild
habitats such as rainforests is the main cause, but plants are also
threatened by pollution, climate change, disease, plant-eating animals
such as goats, and invasive plants introduced from one part of the
world to another. The rarest plants are considered extinct in the wild
and survive only as specimens in plant collections. Scientists classify
endangered plants into five main groups depending on how likely they
are to disappear: least concern, near threatened, vulnerable,
endangered, and critically endangered.

SANDER'S ORCHID
Paphiopedilum sanderianum
Origin: Borneo
Status: Critically endangered

Scientists thought this unusual
orchid was extinct until it was
rediscovered in the wild in
1978. It is renowned for its
very long, curled tepals,
which can reach 3 ft (1 m)
in length. The remaining
plants grow protected in
Gunung Mulu National
Park, a world
heritage site.

Tepal

MANDRINETTE
Origin: Mauritius
Status: Critically endangered

Fewer than 50 mandrinette plants exist
in this species' native island of
Mauritius in the Indian Ocean. These
rare shrubs are unable to breed
naturally in the wild because a closely
related introduced species—the Chinese
hibiscus—hybridizes with them.
Scientists hope to one day reestablish
the species in the wild using plants bred
in botanical gardens.

WOOD'S CYCAD
Encephalartos woodii
Origin: South Africa
Status: Extinct in the wild

Cycads are palmlike plants that have existed since
before the age of the dinosaurs. Wood's cycad is
one of several species that are extinct in the wild.
Only a handful survive in botanical gardens and all
are male, which means the species can no longer
reproduce sexually.

DARWIN'S SICYOS
Sicyos villosa
Origin: Floreana Island, Galápagos, Ecuador
Status: Extinct

All that remains of this extinct species is a
pressed specimen in the herbarium at Cambridge
University in the UK. The plant was discovered
on a Pacific island by English naturalist Charles
Darwin in 1835 before the species was wiped out
by introduced goats. DNA from Darwin's specimen
reveals it was a relative of cucumbers.

GHOST ORCHID
Dendrophylax lindenii
Origin: Florida, USA
Status: Endangered

Named for its striking white flowers, which smell
like apples, the ghost orchid grows on trees in
tropical swamps. It has no leaves and relies instead
on its roots to photosynthesize. Ghost orchids need
long-tongued moths for pollination and do not
survive for long if taken from their usual habitat.

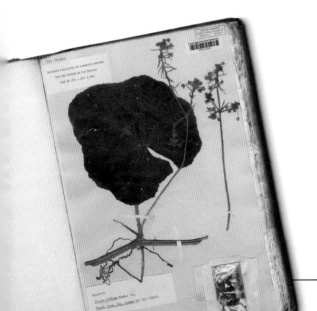

Male cones
Wood's cycad
produces pollen
in male cones. As
female cones no
longer exist, the
species cannot
produce seeds.

NEPENTHES ARISTOLOCHIOIDES

Origin: Sumatra, Indonesia
Status: Critically endangered

Prized by plant collectors for its unique shape, this carnivorous pitcher plant is on the verge of extinction because so many have been taken from the wild. It grows only on the peaks of a few mountains on the island of Sumatra in Southeast Asia. It preys on small insects, which crawl or fly through the opening, then drown in a pool of sticky slime.

Cycads are often mistaken for palms, as their huge leaves have the same featherlike shape. In fact, they are more closely related to conifers.

Slow grower
Cycads grow slowly, the trunk increasing only 1 in (2-3 cm) a year.

DRAGON BLOOD TREE
Dracaena cinnabari

Origin: Yemen
Status: Vulnerable

This umbrella-shaped tree grows only on a few desert islands in the Arabian Sea and is named for its red sap, which is traditionally used as a medicine and a dye. Overcollection, grazing by introduced goats, and global warming have all contributed to its decline.

CAFE MARRON
Ramosmania rodriguesii

Origin: Rodrigues Island, Mauritius
Status: Critically endangered

This wild coffee plant was considered extinct until 1979, when a teacher showed his class the only existing image of the plant—a drawing from 1877. A boy raised his hand and said he'd seen the plant near his house. Scientists confirmed the discovery and took cuttings back to Kew Botanic Gardens in the UK. Seeds were later produced, raising hopes that the plant can be reestablished in the wild.

FRANKLIN TREE
Franklinia alatamaha

Origin: Georgia, USA
Status: Extinct in the wild

This beautiful shrub has large, honey-scented flowers and leaves that turn fiery red in fall. It hasn't been seen in the wild since 1803, but thousands of specimens still exist in parks and gardens thanks to American botanist William Bartram, who collected seeds. He named the plant after the American statesman Benjamin Franklin.

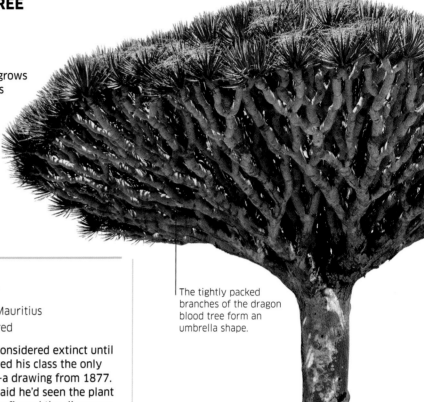

The tightly packed branches of the dragon blood tree form an umbrella shape.

HAWAIIAN SILVERSWORD
Argyroxiphium sandwicense

Origin: Maui, Hawai'i, USA
Status: Critically endangered

The Hawaiian silversword grows only on Haleakalā volcano on the island of Maui in Hawai'i. It nearly became extinct in the early 20th century because tourists would uproot the ball-shaped plants and roll them downhill for fun. Grazing by sheep and goats made the problem worse.

Tiny hairs give the leaves a silvery color.

COMMON IVY
Hedera helix
Origin: Europe, West Asia, North Africa
Invasive in: USA, Australia, New Zealand

This fast-growing climbing ivy scrambles up trees, using its clinging roots to grip bark. Outside its native range, it grows so densely that it starves trees of light and can pull them down with its weight. It can also damage buildings by piercing brickwork with its roots.

Aerial roots form along the stems of ivy to allow it to cling to vertical surfaces.

PARROT'S FEATHER
Myriophyllum aquaticum
Origin: South America
Invasive in: Every continent except Antarctica

This plant's feathery leaves and small pink flowers make it an attractive addition to ponds. However, it spreads quickly from fragments that break off and grow into new plants. Huge mats of parrot's feather clog waterways and shade out the native aquatic plants. The mats are also a breeding ground for mosquitoes.

Tiny white flowers grow where the leaves join the stem.

Invasive plants

When plants from one part of the world are introduced elsewhere, they sometimes grow out of control and become a menace. We call these problem plants "invasive."

Ever since people started traveling around the world, they've taken useful plants with them to sow as crops or plant in gardens. Most plants introduced to new places do little harm, but a few escape into the wild and change the way ecosystems work. Without their natural predators or diseases to keep them in check, invasive plants grow faster and more strongly than native species. They can spread like wildfire by cloning themselves or by producing huge numbers of seeds. Native plants may struggle to compete with the invaders. The imported plants may also bring new pests and diseases that can wipe out plants in the new habitat.

PURPLE PAMPAS GRASS
Cortaderia jubata
Origin: South America
Invasive in: USA, Australia, New Zealand, South Africa

Purple pampas grass makes a beautiful ornamental plant, but a single plant produces millions of seeds. It has escaped from gardens and spread quickly in many countries. Some countries now ban its sale.

JAPANESE KNOTWEED
Fallopia japonica
Origin: China, Japan, Korea
Invasive in: USA, Canada, Europe, New Zealand

One of the world's worst invasive plants, Japanese knotweed was a popular garden plant until people discovered how difficult it is to kill. It can regenerate from tiny fragments, and its thick roots can damage buildings and drains.

The USA spends **$100 million a year** destroying invasive aquatic plants.

A single multiflora rose can produce **500,000 seeds** a year.

151

TAMARISK
Tamarix ramosissima

Origin: Europe, Asia, Africa
Invasive in: Southwestern USA

In the 19th century, this shrub was deliberately planted along arid riverbanks in hot, dry parts of the USA to control erosion, but it spread quickly and replaced native willow and cottonwood plants. In the 1990s, scientists tried to kill tamarisk by introducing a leaf-eating beetle from Asia, but that escaped into the wild and became a pest, too.

Tamarisks have distinctive feathery pink flowers.

TREE OF HEAVEN
Ailanthus altissima

Origin: China
Invasive in: USA, Europe

This ornamental tree was planted in Europe and the USA in the 1700s but fell out of favor because of its foul smell and its ability to spread quickly from shoots that grow at the base. It also harbors the spotted lanternfly–a notorious insect pest that ruins fruit crops. Cutting back the tree of heaven makes it grow all the more vigorously.

Winged invaders
The tree of heaven produces thousands of windborne seeds that spread to new areas and germinate easily.

WATER LETTUCE
Pistia stratiotes

Origin: Unknown, but possibly South America
Invasive in: All tropical countries

Water lettuce grows in slow-moving water, floating on the surface with roots dangling below. It forms dense mats that block sunlight and deprive the water of oxygen, killing aquatic life. Like other invasive water plants, it probably spread around the world as tiny fragments carried in the ballast water of ships.

Water lettuce spreads to cover the surface of the water.

MULTIFLORA ROSE
Rosa multiflora

Origin: China, Japan, Korea
Invasive in: Eastern North America

This invasive rose is named for its clusters of large flowers, which produce more fruits and more seeds than wild roses. It was introduced to North America as a hedge plant but quickly spread after birds distributed the seeds. Its leaves open earlier in spring than those of other plants and are shed later, allowing it to outcompete native species. It is also difficult to eradicate without digging up every last fragment of its root system.

Thickets
As well as spreading by seed, the multiflora rose has long, arching stems that take root wherever they touch the ground, creating a thicket.

Flower clusters
The flowers grow in clusters of more than a dozen, while native roses produce only a few flowers on each branch.

THE FUNGUS KINGDOM

Neither plants nor animals, fungi make up one of the major kingdoms of life. Fungi are nature's great recyclers, turning leftover organic matter into useful nutrients that other organisms can use. However, just like animals and plants, some are dangerous or even deadly.

154 the fungus kingdom ○ **WHAT IS A FUNGUS?**

148,000 fungus species have been **described and named** by scientists.

What is a fungus?

Fungi are not plants, not animals, and not bacteria. Instead, they belong in a kingdom of their own.

For centuries, scientists classified fungi as members of the plant kingdom, because mushrooms appear to sprout from the ground like plants. However, we now know that fungi work in a very different way from plants or any other organisms. While plants make food from light and animals get food by eating, fungi grow inside their food and digest it externally. The main body of most fungi is the mycelium—a network of threads that lives inside whatever the fungus is feeding on. While most fungi live as a mycelium, some spend part or all of their lives as single cells called yeasts.

◎ FRUIT BODIES

A mushroom might look like a whole organism, but it is just one small part of a fungus that lives mostly hidden from view. Just as a tree produces fruits to help spread its seeds, fungi produce "fruit bodies" such as mushrooms to help spread their spores. There are many other kinds of fruit bodies, too, from cups and balls to fruit bodies that look like jelly or hair.

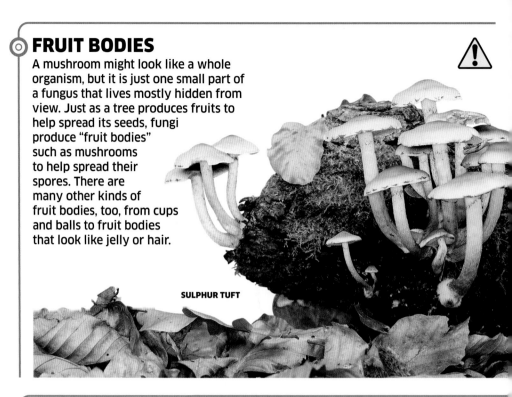

SULPHUR TUFT

◎ TYPES OF FUNGUS

The many thousands of different species in the fungus kingdom are divided into a family tree with five main groups. Each has a scientific name that is long and tricky to pronounce: Basidiomycota, Ascomycota, Zoopagomycota, Chytridiomycota, and Mucoromycota. We sometimes simplify these.

Basidiomycetes
The fungi in this group produce fruit bodies such as mushrooms, brackets (shelflike growths on tree trunks), or jellies when they have mated. More than 31,000 basidiomycete species have been named so far. The edible mushrooms we buy in stores belong to this group.

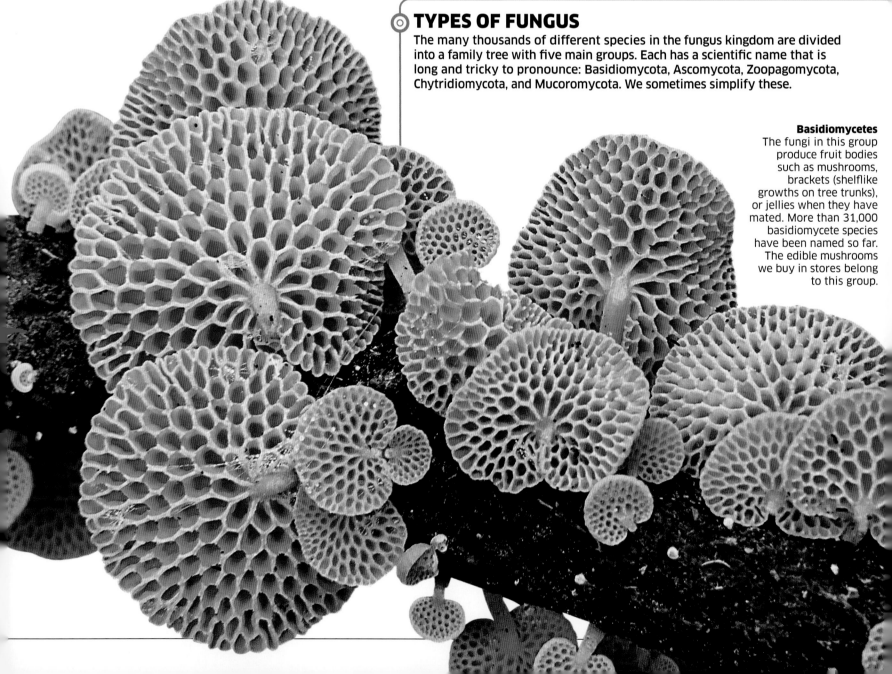

There are microscopic fungi in **every breath of air** you inhale.

The death cap is the **world's most poisonous** mushroom.

FUNGUS NAMES

Like all organisms, each type of fungus has a Latin scientific name with two parts: first a genus, then a species. For example, the edible mushroom most commonly sold in stores is *Agaricus bisporus*. Many fungi also have a common name that describes what the visible part looks like.

CAULIFLOWER FUNGUS
(*SPARASSIS CRISPA*)

COAL FUNGUS
(*DALDINIA CONCENTRICA*)

This species is also called King Alfred's cakes, after an English king who fell asleep watching cakes bake and let them burn.

WITCHES' BUTTER
(*EXIDIA GLANDULOSA*)

YELLOW BRAIN FUNGUS
(*TREMELLA MESENTERICA*)

JELLY EAR
(*AURICULARIA*)

Ascomycetes

This is the largest fungus group, with 83,000 named species, but there are thousands more still to be studied. Ascomycetes that grow in rotting wood produce fruit bodies shaped like tiny flasks, cups, or balls. Other species produce the blue-green mold on rotting fruit. Spores are typically made in sacs of eight, called asci, which is where the group's name comes from.

GREEN ELFCUP

Chytrids

Also called water molds, these fungi live in water and wet soil. Some feed on rotting matter, but others are parasites that cause disease in animals and plants. When chytrids find food, they grow as a ball on its surface or in its cells, with rootlike threads penetrating the food. Chytrid spores have tiny tails and can swim.

Zoopagomycota

Members of this group infect and often kill other small organisms, including insects. The insect-feeding species grow into the victim's living body and emerge as a mass of white threads to release spores after the victim dies.

This fly has been eaten alive by the fungus *Entomophthora*.

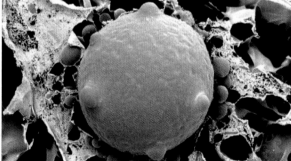

CHYTRID SEEN THROUGH A MICROSCOPE

This tropical species is widespread and is even considered an invasive species in some parts of the world.

ORANGE PING PONG BAT

Mucoromycota

These fungi are mostly microscopic but become visible as mold when they grow on decaying food. For example, *Rhizopus* forms a fluffy white or black growth on damp bread.

Slime mold

These fruit bodies look like tiny fungi, but they are not fungi. They are slime molds, which are some of the oddest organisms known.

Slime molds have strange lives that switch between very different forms. One form is a microscopic single cell called an amoeba. From time to time, a much larger, slithering, slimy mass—a plasmodium—forms. You might spot one in summer on a lawn, a path, or an old log. A plasmodium has no fixed shape and moves by flowing. It feeds by absorbing small molecules or engulfing larger bits of food. Slime molds can disperse to new homes by making spores in tiny fruit bodies. Once classed as fungi, they are now put in a different kingdom of life: kingdom Protista.

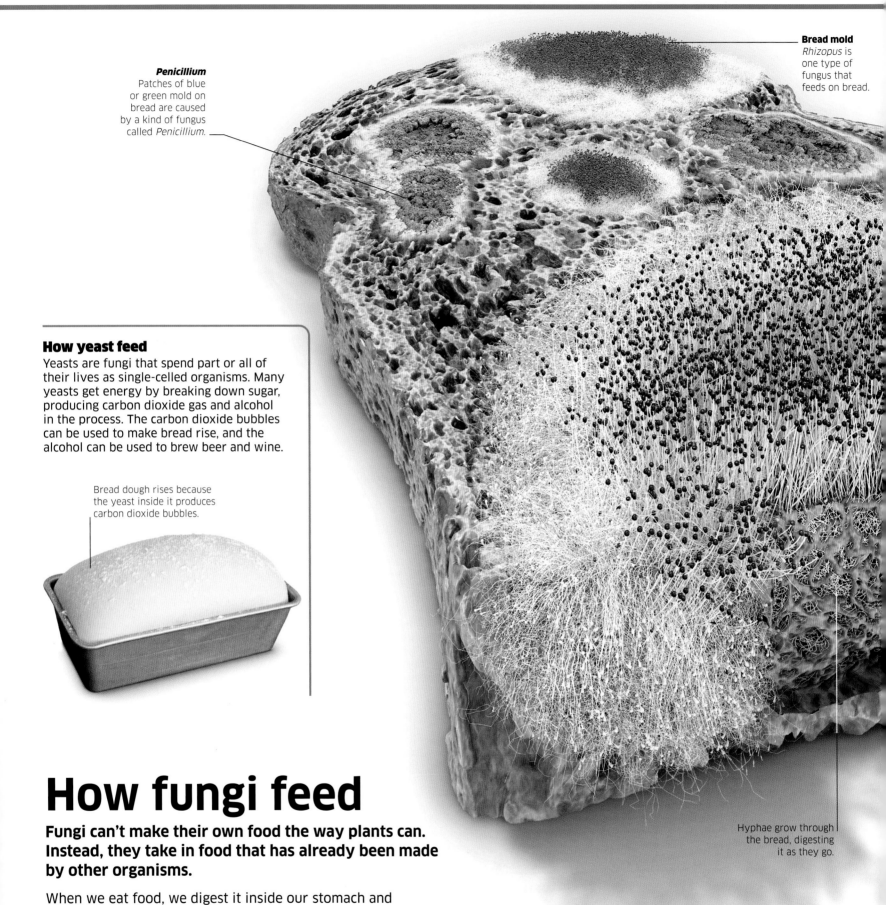

Penicillium
Patches of blue
or green mold on
bread are caused
by a kind of fungus
called *Penicillium*.

Bread mold
Rhizopus is
one type of
fungus that
feeds on bread.

How yeast feed

Yeasts are fungi that spend part or all of
their lives as single-celled organisms. Many
yeasts get energy by breaking down sugar,
producing carbon dioxide gas and alcohol
in the process. The carbon dioxide bubbles
can be used to make bread rise, and the
alcohol can be used to brew beer and wine.

Bread dough rises because
the yeast inside it produces
carbon dioxide bubbles.

Hyphae grow through
the bread, digesting
it as they go.

How fungi feed

**Fungi can't make their own food the way plants can.
Instead, they take in food that has already been made
by other organisms.**

When we eat food, we digest it inside our stomach and
intestines. The big molecules in food are broken down by
digestive enzymes into smaller ones that can be absorbed and
used for energy and growth. Fungi, however, digest food outside
their bodies. They grow through food as a network of tiny
threads called hyphae. The hyphae secrete digestive enzymes
into food, then absorb the small molecules released as food
breaks down. Every organic substance made by animals, plants,
and microorganisms can be broken down in this way by fungi.

Moldy bread

Bread is an ideal source of food for *Rhizopus*,
a fast-growing fungus that causes bread mold.
Rhizopus's hyphae grow into the bread, digesting
it with enzymes. After several days, the fungus
starts to make spores. Thousands of tiny spore-
making structures grow up from the surface,
covering the bread with fuzzy gray mold.

The oyster mushroom can **break down some plastics** while trying to eat them.

Some fungi can **infect ants and control their brains** while feeding on them.

159

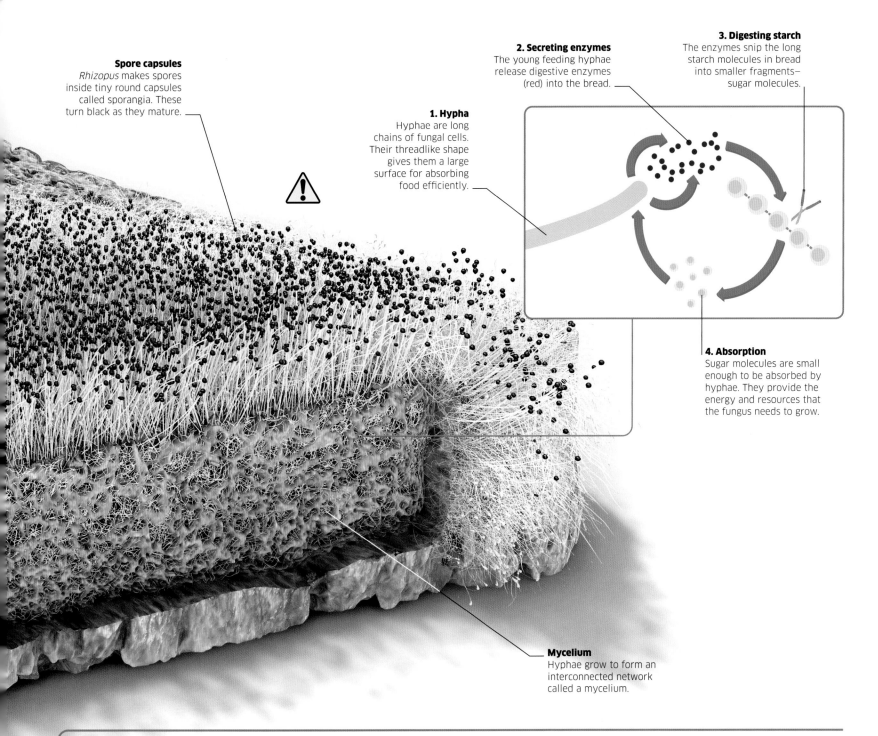

Spore capsules
Rhizopus makes spores inside tiny round capsules called sporangia. These turn black as they mature.

1. Hypha
Hyphae are long chains of fungal cells. Their threadlike shape gives them a large surface for absorbing food efficiently.

2. Secreting enzymes
The young feeding hyphae release digestive enzymes (red) into the bread.

3. Digesting starch
The enzymes snip the long starch molecules in bread into smaller fragments—sugar molecules.

4. Absorption
Sugar molecules are small enough to be absorbed by hyphae. They provide the energy and resources that the fungus needs to grow.

Mycelium
Hyphae grow to form an interconnected network called a mycelium.

Ecological roles

Fungi can occupy several different positions in food chains, either as consumers of living matter or as decomposers of dead matter. They play a very important role in all ecosystems, as they recycle nutrients in soil, allowing plants to use them again.

Decomposers
Organisms that break down dead organic matter and waste are called decomposers. Decomposer fungi may feed on whole dead organisms or parts such as leaves, skin, fur, feathers, and dung.

Parasites
Parasites are organisms that live on or inside other living organisms and feed on them, usually doing harm. The pear rust fungus is a parasite of pear trees. It causes red blisters in leaves when it produces spores.

Partners
Many fungi form helpful partnerships with other organisms. In lichens, for example, algae give the fungi food made by photosynthesis, and fungi in turn provide the algae with mineral nutrients, water, physical support, and protection.

160 the fungus kingdom ∘ **HOW FUNGI GROW**

The average fungal hypha is about a
fortieth of the width of a human hair.

Finding food

In some fungi, the mycelium actively
searches for new sources of food. When it
finds suitable food, it sends signals back to
the rest of the mycelium, changing the pattern
of growth. Hyphae can bunch together to
form thick cords. Water and nutrients move
rapidly through these cords.

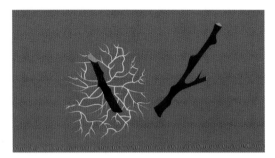

1 The mycelium grows out of a food source
such as a twig.

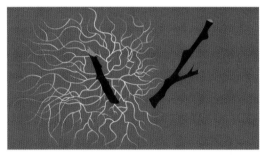

2 The mycelium finds a new source of food
and grows into it.

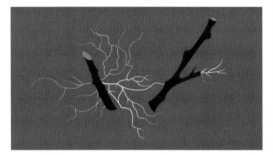

3 Messages sent back to the original mycelium
tell it to stop searching in other directions.

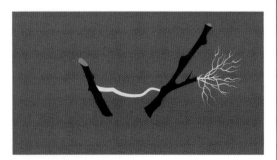

4 A cord carries resources from the old site
to the new one. The mycelium grows out
of the new site in search of yet more food.

How fungi grow

**A fungus starts life as a single cell called a spore.
If conditions are right, the spore germinates.**

Tiny threads called hyphae start to grow away from the spore,
extending into the food. They grow at their tips, branching
repeatedly to form an interconnected network called a mycelium.
The mycelium is the main body of most fungi and is usually hidden
from view inside the matter the fungus is growing through. The
hyphae may grow haphazardly at first, but they become evenly
spaced to absorb food more efficiently as the mycelium expands.

Decaying acorn
Fungal spores spread in the air around us and are quick to
colonize dead matter. After a spore germinates on a dead
acorn's surface, hyphae begin feeding and grow into it,
branching as they go to form a mycelium. Hyphae of some
fungi grow into the ground and explore their surroundings.
If a new source of food is discovered, a thick cord of hyphae
forms a kind of highway between the two locations.

New mycelium
After the fungus discovers
a new source of food in
the nearby acorn cup,
hyphae spread through it.

Cord
A thick cord of hyphae
connects the mycelium
in the two food sources.

The **world's largest fungus** is a honey mushroom mycelium that occupies 3.5 sq miles (9.5 sq km) of soil.

A mycelium can **split into two organisms and later rejoin to become one again.**

161

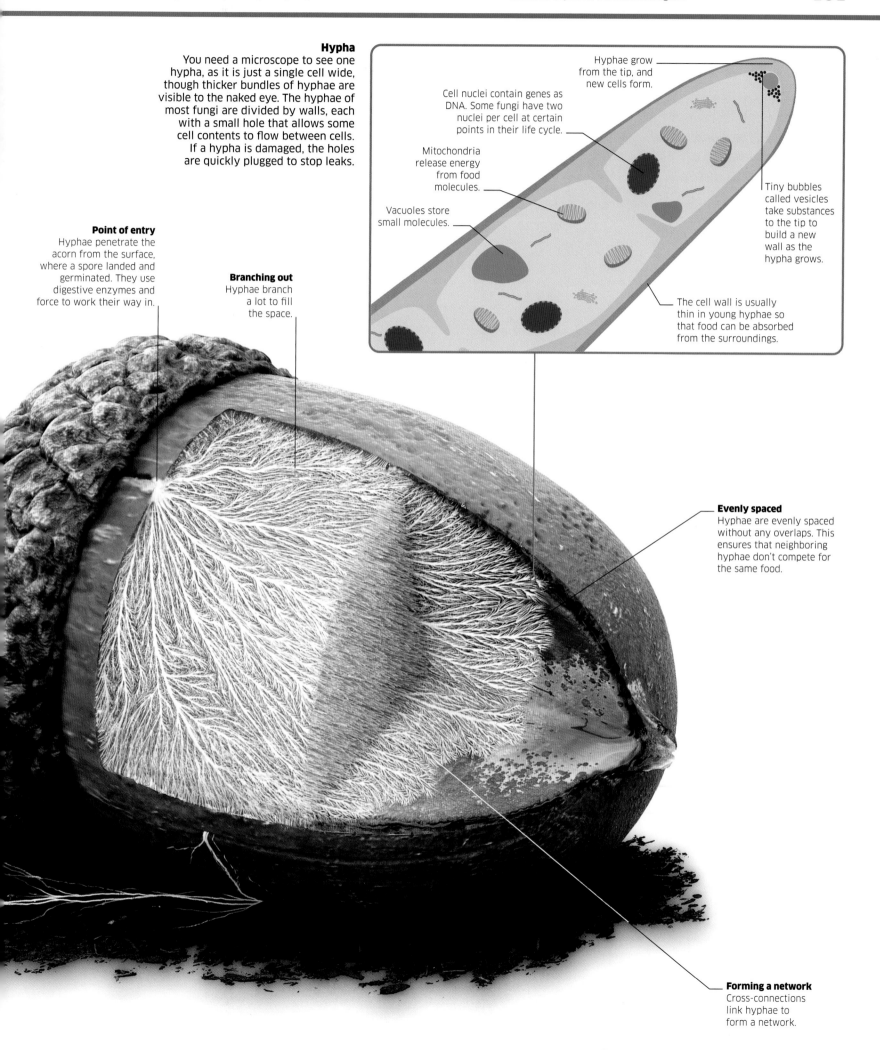

Hypha
You need a microscope to see one hypha, as it is just a single cell wide, though thicker bundles of hyphae are visible to the naked eye. The hyphae of most fungi are divided by walls, each with a small hole that allows some cell contents to flow between cells. If a hypha is damaged, the holes are quickly plugged to stop leaks.

Hyphae grow from the tip, and new cells form.

Cell nuclei contain genes as DNA. Some fungi have two nuclei per cell at certain points in their life cycle.

Mitochondria release energy from food molecules.

Vacuoles store small molecules.

Tiny bubbles called vesicles take substances to the tip to build a new wall as the hypha grows.

The cell wall is usually thin in young hyphae so that food can be absorbed from the surroundings.

Point of entry
Hyphae penetrate the acorn from the surface, where a spore landed and germinated. They use digestive enzymes and force to work their way in.

Branching out
Hyphae branch a lot to fill the space.

Evenly spaced
Hyphae are evenly spaced without any overlaps. This ensures that neighboring hyphae don't compete for the same food.

Forming a network
Cross-connections link hyphae to form a network.

Fungus life cycles

A life cycle is the sequence of stages that an organism passes through between its birth and the birth of its own offspring. Fungus life cycles vary a great deal and may involve sexual stages (with two parents) and asexual stages (with one parent).

The life of a fungus starts as a spore. Threadlike hyphae grow from the spore to form a mycelium. At some point, this mycelium may meet another mycelium of the same species. If their hyphae join to mate, they can produce spores with a mix of genes from both parents. Some fungi make fruit bodies immediately, while others make them much later after mating. This whole process is called sexual reproduction. Many fungi can also make spores without mating in what is called asexual reproduction. Offspring produced this way have exactly the same genes as the parent.

Mating molds

Mucor is a mold that grows on food. When two individuals of different sexes meet, they mate. Their cell nuclei join, mix genes, then divide to create new nuclei. These nuclei have a mix of genes from both parents.

Pin mold
Mucor is also called pin mold because its spore-making structures (sporangia) look like pins. Some of these form from a sexually produced survival spore, but most develop asexually from unmated mycelia.

Moldy strawberry
Mucor grows as mold on strawberries and other food. It becomes visible when it starts making spores.

1 A *Mucor* hypha of one sex detects a hypha of the opposite sex. Side branches grow toward each other.

2 Bulges called gametangia form on both side branches.

3 The bulges join to form a zygote. A thick wall then develops around them, forming a structure called a zygospore.

4 Inside the zygospore, cell nuclei from the two parents join. They divide to produce nuclei with a mix of both parents' genes. Zygospores survive conditions that kill hyphae.

There are **no visible differences between sexes** in most fungi, so in
Mucor, scientists call them plus and minus instead of male and female.

163

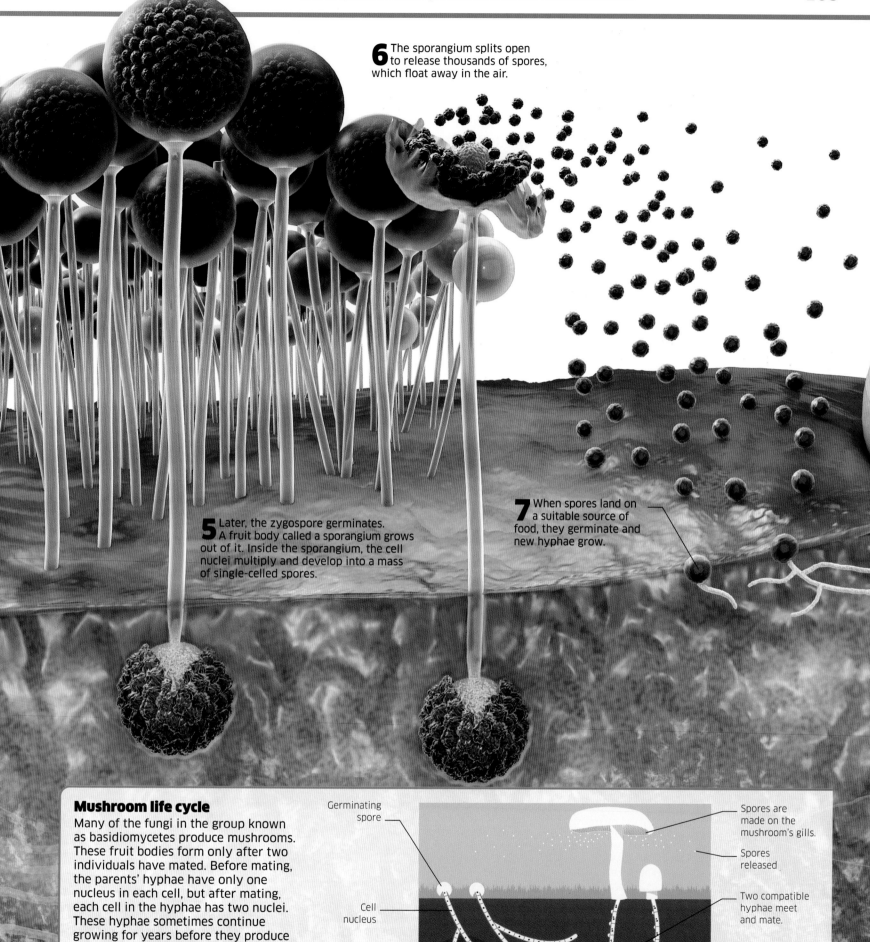

6 The sporangium splits open to release thousands of spores, which float away in the air.

5 Later, the zygospore germinates. A fruit body called a sporangium grows out of it. Inside the sporangium, the cell nuclei multiply and develop into a mass of single-celled spores.

7 When spores land on a suitable source of food, they germinate and new hyphae grow.

Mushroom life cycle

Many of the fungi in the group known as basidiomycetes produce mushrooms. These fruit bodies form only after two individuals have mated. Before mating, the parents' hyphae have only one nucleus in each cell, but after mating, each cell in the hyphae has two nuclei. These hyphae sometimes continue growing for years before they produce mushrooms. Spores are made on the mushroom's gills, where the parental cell nuclei combine, mix up their genes, then split to produce spores with one nucleus each.

Germinating spore

Cell nucleus

Hypha growing into soil

Spores are made on the mushroom's gills.

Spores released

Two compatible hyphae meet and mate.

After mating, the hyphae have two nuclei in each cell—one from each parent.

How mushrooms grow

Mushrooms are just the visible parts of fungi that live mostly hidden from view in the ground or inside decaying plant matter. The scientific name for mushrooms and related structures is fruit bodies because these structures help fungi reproduce sexually, just as flowers and fruit help plants reproduce.

Fruit bodies form only after a fungus has mated with another individual, but it may take months or even years before they appear. They grow only when conditions are ideal: the fungus must have enough food and water and just the right temperature. Once fruit bodies start growing, they develop quickly—some can reach full size overnight. Most mushrooms live for only a matter of days, but tough brackets on trees can last for months. Mushrooms die when it's frosty or very dry, but brackets survive, and jelly fungi can sometimes rehydrate after drying out.

Mushroom season
Different species produce fruit bodies at different times of year and at different stages in their lives. In temperate regions (between tropical and polar regions), most fruiting occurs in fall, with a smaller peak in spring. Because of climate change, the fall fruiting season is growing longer, and some fungi now fruit in both spring and fall.

SULFUR TUFT MUSHROOMS

Fly agaric mushroom
The fly agaric mushroom starts to develop underground. It pushes through the surface and expands into a full mushroom in just a few days. Its gills, with their precious spores, are protected by two "veils" of tissue: one that surrounds the whole mushroom and a second one that protects the delicate underside of the cap.

Second veil
A second veil protects the underside of the cap. It tears open as the cap expands, exposing the gills.

Scales
Fragments of the veil remain stuck on top, forming white scales.

Universal veil
A protective veil of tissue covers the young mushroom. As the mushroom expands, the veil tears open, exposing the cap.

Emerging mushroom
The mushroom pushes its way above ground.

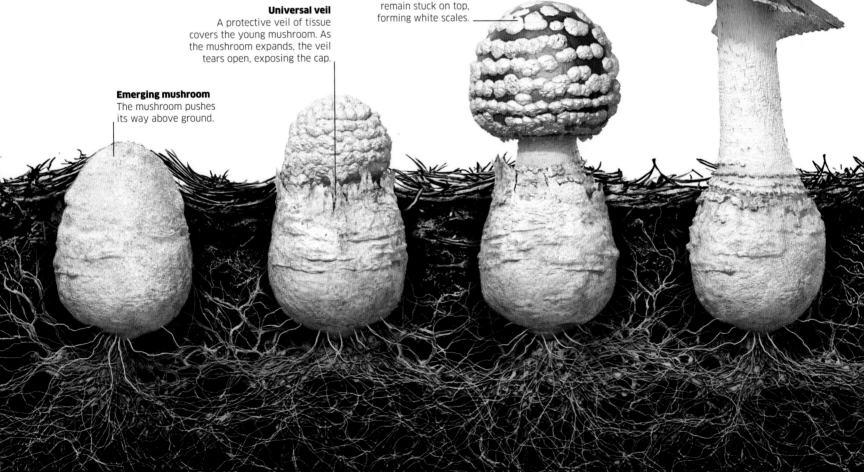

44 lb (20 kg)—the top weight of a giant **puffball**.

A few mushroom species **glow in the dark,** emitting a ghostly light called foxfire.

165

Mature cap
The cap flattens as it matures, exposing the gills.

Cap
The top part of a mushroom is called the cap and varies in color depending on the species. The cap of a fly agaric is red or a paler color with white scales.

Gills
On the underside of the cap are hundreds of vertical plates, called gills. These release millions of tiny white spores into the air, each a mere hundredth of a millimeter wide.

Ring
The remains of the second veil may form a ring around the mushroom's stem.

Stipe
A mushroom's cylindrical stem is called a stipe. The stipe holds the cap above the ground so that spores have a better chance of blowing away.

Volva
Some mushrooms have a swollen based called a volva, sometimes with the torn remains of the universal veil still attached.

Mycelium
The main body of the fungus is the mycelium, which is hidden in whatever the fungus is growing in. The mycelium of a fly agaric mushroom grows in the soil and forms a partnership with tree roots.

166 the fungus kingdom • **FRUIT BODIES**

5 ft (1.5 m)—the **diameter** of the biggest recorded giant puffball.

Fruit bodies

Mushrooms and other kinds of fruit bodies come in a huge range of colors, shapes, and sizes. Scientists have described about 100,000 different types so far.

The most common fruit body color is brown. Many are whitish-gray, pink, red, or black. A few are blue, green is rare, and some can change color. Fruit bodies can be many different shapes: bells, balls, brackets, cones, cups, crusts, saucers, and more. Their surface may feel smooth, scaly, slimy, sticky, greasy, hairy, leathery, or hard. Some fruit bodies have stems and others don't. And some smell horrible.

CATERPILLAR FUNGUS
Cordyceps militaris
Location: Asia, Europe, and the Americas
Size: Up to 3.5 in (9 cm) tall

The caterpillar fungus kills insects. Its spores stick to the insect before threadlike hyphae force their way into its body and digest it. Fruit bodies then grow out of the victim to release more spores and infect more insects.

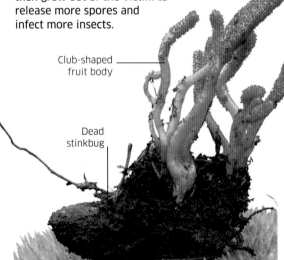

Club-shaped fruit body

Dead stinkbug

BOG BEACON
Mitrula paludosa
Location: Europe
Size: Up to 1.5 in (4 cm) tall

Bog beacons are seldom seen, but when you do find them, they usually occur in groups. They only appear in wet places, such as ditches or slow-moving streams, where they feed on dead leaves, mosses, and algae.

The cap slowly turns blue when cut.

Pores on cap's underside

SATAN'S BOLETE
Rubroboletus satanas
Location: Central and southern Europe
Size: Cap is up to 12 in (30 cm) wide

The poisonous satan's bolete has pores (small holes) rather than gills on the underside of its cap. This fungus partners with the roots of oak and beech trees to provide them with water and nutrients, while it gets sugars from the trees.

The devil's tooth mushroom's fruit body oozes **red droplets** that look like blood.

The largest known fruit body belongs to a polypore fungus in China and **weighs up to 1,100 lb (500 kg).**

167

BRIGHT MUSHROOM
Roridomyces phyllostachydis
Location: Northeast India
Size: Less than 1.2 in (3 cm) tall

Scientists have only recently discovered the bright mushroom, a fungus that feeds on dead bamboo. Its fruit bodies appear in the wet season. Although it is tiny and not brightly colored, its stem (but not its cap) glows green in the dark. The light might attract insects that help spread its spores.

VIOLET CORAL
Clavaria zollingeri
Location: Widespread
Size: Up to 4 in (10 cm) tall

Coral fungi are so named because their fruit bodies resemble corals in the sea. This rare species is found in grasslands and woodlands, where it feeds on dead leaves.

WOOD EAR
Auricularia auricula-judae
Location: Widespread
Size: Up to 3.5 in (9 cm) wide

The wood ear's fruit bodies feel like jelly and often look like ears. They turn hard, thin, and crispy when they dry out. If rain makes them wet, they sometimes start making spores again. Wood ear was once common on elder trees but now usually grows on beech trees, possibly because of climate change.

BIRCH POLYPORE
Fomitopsis betulina
Location: Asia, Europe, North America
Size: About 2.4 in (6 cm) deep, up to 12 in (30 cm) wide

Found on birch trees, this fungus causes the tree's trunk to rot. In the past, its dried fruit bodies were used as tinder to light fires. A piece of birch polypore was found on Ötzi the Iceman, a 5,300-year-old body found buried in a glacier in the Italian Alps. He may have used it as a medicine.

COBALT CRUST
Terana caerulea
Location: Widespread in warm climates
Size: 0.04 in (1 mm) thick

The dark blue fruit body of this fungus grows on the underside of fallen logs and branches in damp forests. It feels velvety or waxy when damp, but brittle and crusty when dry.

OCTOPUS STINKHORN
Clathrus archeri
Location: Australia, New Zealand, southern Africa, introduced into Europe and North America
Size: Arms can be up to 4 in (10 cm) long

With 4–8 arms erupting from an egglike structure, the fruit body of this species resembles an octopus. When mature, the fungus smells like rotting meat, which attracts flies that spread its sticky spores.

CORAL TOOTH
Hericium coralloides
Location: Northern hemisphere
Size: Up to 10 in (25 cm) wide

This rare but spectacular species grows on tree trunks and rotten logs. Spores are produced by hundreds of small spines that hang from every part of the fruit body like icicles.

Bioluminescence

Like fireflies and many marine organisms, some fungi glow in the dark, including southern Australia's ghost fungus (*Omphalotus nidiformis*), seen here.

This glowing is called foxfire or bioluminescence. In some species, just the fruit bodies glow, but in others, the mycelium or even the whole fungus is bioluminescent. Only mushroom-producing fungi that live in decaying wood have this unusual ability. It may be an accidental byproduct of the chemical process the fungi use to break down wood.

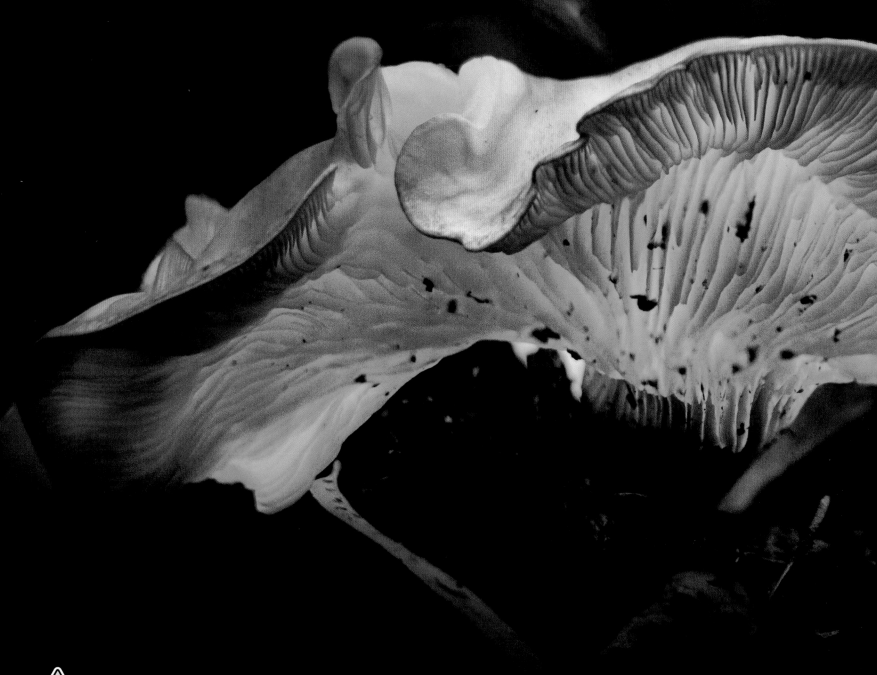

170 the fungus kingdom ○ **SPREADING SPORES**

The hat-thrower fungus can throw its spore
packets at speeds of up to **56 mph (90 kph)**.

Flattened cap
The top of a mushroom is called a cap. The cap
of the fly agaric mushroom (seen here) is domed
when young but becomes flat as it matures.

Mushroom spores
After mating, many fungi produce
spores in fruit bodies. There are lots of
different types of fruit bodies, including
mushrooms, the shelflike brackets on
trees, and puffballs. In a mushroom,
spores are made on gills—flaps of tissue
that hang on the underside of the cap.

Stipe
The mushroom's
stipe (stalk) holds
the cap above the
ground so that
spores can be
blown away by
air currents.

Spreading spores

**Most plants spread by seeds, but fungi spread by spores.
A fungus spore is a microscopic cell wrapped in a protective
wall and contains nutrients to help a new mycelium grow.**

Most spores have a thin wall, sometimes containing a dark pigment
(melanin) that acts as a sunblock. Some spores have a smooth surface,
while others are bumpy. Some spores spread in water, but most simply
drift in the air. The chance that a spore will land in an ideal place to
grow is very small, but each mushroom makes more than a billion
spores, ensuring some will survive. To improve the odds, some fungi
encourage animals to spread their spores.

Spore dispersal
Just as plants
have many ways
of spreading seeds,
fungi use a range of
techniques to launch
and disperse their
microscopic offspring.

Puffballs
If anything falls on a puffball, its
fruit body puffs out a powdery
mass of spores. Take care not to
inhale spores from a puffball.

Stinkhorns
The smell of rotting meat attracts
flies to stinkhorns. Their spores
stick to the insects and are spread
when they fly elsewhere.

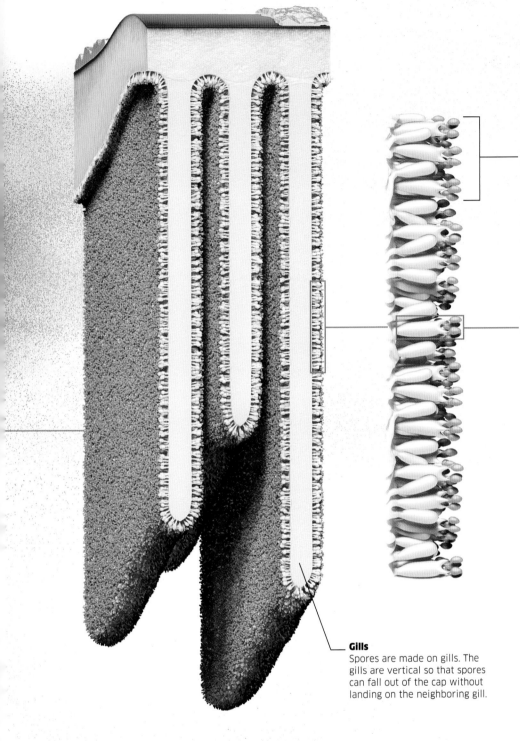

Basidia
Tiny structures called basidia cover
the gills. Inside each basidium, two cell
nuclei—one from each of the fungus's
parents—join. The genes are mixed
and the combined nucleus divides
to produce four nuclei, each of which
goes into a spore.

ONE BASIDIUM

Spores
Each basidium usually
makes four spores. These
spores are shot into the
gaps between the gills.

Gills
Spores are made on gills. The
gills are vertical so that spores
can fall out of the cap without
landing on the neighboring gill.

Asexual spores

Many fungi can produce spores without mating first.
The spores are produced asexually, which means
their genes are identical to the parent's genes. In
some fungi, such as the mold *Penicillium*, chains
of spores are made on stalks.

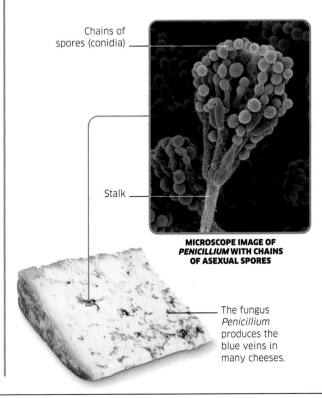

Chains of
spores (conidia)

Stalk

**MICROSCOPE IMAGE OF
PENICILLIUM WITH CHAINS
OF ASEXUAL SPORES**

The fungus
Penicillium
produces the
blue veins in
many cheeses.

Bird's nest fungi
The spores of these fungi are clumped
together in packages of cup-shaped fruit
bodies that look like nests. When rain hits
the "nest," the spore packages shoot out.

Cannonball fungus
This mushroom's tiny, cup-shaped fruit body holds
a single ball-shaped spore package. When the fruit
body is ripe, its lining pops out, firing the spore
package up to 20 ft (6 m) away.

Puffballs

The fruit bodies of puffballs get their name from the way they spread their spores.

Unlike mushrooms that have gills under the caps, puffballs make their spores inside a hollow ball. When the spores are mature, a small hole forms in the top. All it takes is a raindrop, a falling twig, or the slightest touch from a passing animal to force out a cloud of airborne spores. The largest species—the giant puffball—can produce 1 trillion spores. Take care not to breathe in the cloud of spores from a puffball as it can be harmful.

174 the fungus kingdom ○ **PLANT PARTNERS**

The sleepy grass plant of North America has endophytes that **make horses sleep** if they eat it.

Plant partners

Most plants would be unable to absorb the water and nutrients they need from soil without the help of fungi that live on and inside their roots.

Around 85 percent of plant species form close partnerships with soil fungi. These partnerships are called mycorrhizas, from the Greek words *mykes*, meaning fungus, and *rhiza*, meaning root. The two partners help each other. The plant gets water and mineral nutrients from the soil more easily, and the fungus gets sugars made by the plant through photosynthesis.

Tree mycorrhizas

Nearly all trees have mycorrhizas of one type or another. One of the main types is called an ectomycorrhiza (*ecto* means outside). The fungus in an ectomycorrhiza covers the tree's tiny root tips in layers of hyphae like socks. Hyphae also spread out into the soil beyond the roots, extending their reach, and some hyphae grow into the roots (but not into the plant's cells).

Mycorrhiza on root tip

Ectomycorrhizas of pine trees form short, Y-shaped root tips. These roots branch differently from roots without fungi and live longer.

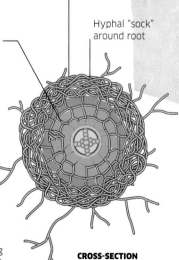

Ectomycorrhiza

Hyphae in roots

Hyphae grow into the roots and form a network around the root cells. This is where the fungus swaps water and nutrients from the soil for sugars from the plant.

Hyphae between root cells

Hyphal "sock" around root

Hypha spreading outside root

CROSS-SECTION OF ROOT

Fruit bodies
We only see mycorrhizal fungi when they produce fruit bodies such as mushrooms. Some of the fungus species that form mycorrhizas with pine trees are shown here.

Lurid bolete

Penny bun

One teaspoon of soil contains **several hundred feet** of fungal hyphae.

175

Pine tree

Saffron milkcap

Pine bolete

Death cap

Endophytes
All plants, including this bilberry shrub, have tiny fungi called endophytes inside their leaves, stems, and roots. Some endophytes provide benefits, but others are waiting for a chance to kill the plant or for the plant to die naturally so that the fungus can digest the remains.

Hyphae in soil
Hyphae spread out from the tree roots into the surrounding soil. There, they take up water and nutrients.

Wood-wide web

Each tree has lots of mycorrhizas. Some are formed by different species of fungus, while others are different individuals of the same fungus species. All their hyphae together form a huge web that sometimes connects roots on the same tree and on different trees. This fungal network is called the wood-wide web. Sugars, nutrients, and water may sometimes be transferred through this network from one tree or sapling to another.

Cheats and copycats

The close partnerships that form between fungi and plants don't always provide equal benefits. Sometimes one partner cheats the other.

Plant roots and soil fungi form close partnerships called mycorrhizas. These usually help both partners, as the roots get extra water and mineral nutrients from the fungus while the fungus gets food made by the plant. However, some plants and fungi cheat by living as parasites— they steal from their partner and give nothing in return. Another tactic used by nature's cheats is to mimic other species. Plants and fungi both do this, using fake flowers, fake mushrooms, and even fake insect eggs to trick animals into helping them.

GHOST PLANTS

The ghost plant is a waxy white color because it has no chlorophyll (the green pigment that plants use to capture sunlight) and doesn't photosynthesize. Instead of making its own food, it steals it. Its roots form a partnership with a mycorrhizal fungus that grows into the roots of trees. The ghost plant gets its sugars from the tree through the fungal mycelium but gives nothing back in return.

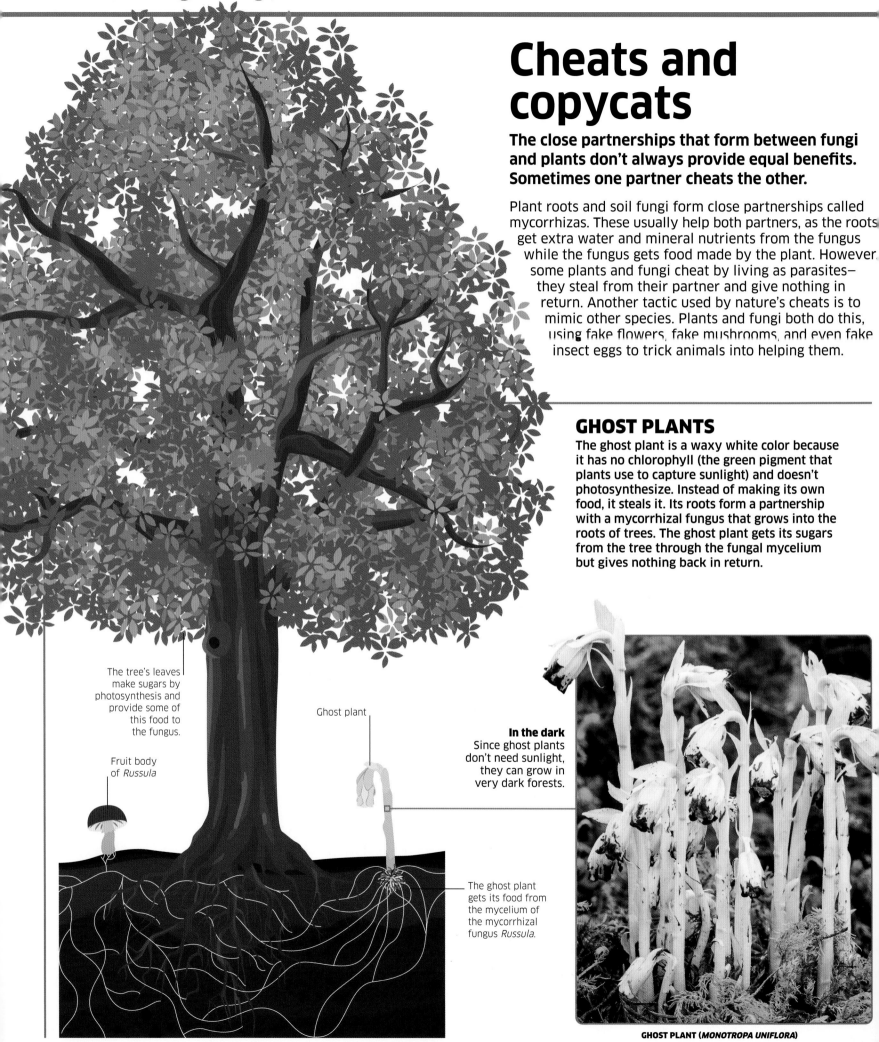

The tree's leaves make sugars by photosynthesis and provide some of this food to the fungus.

Fruit body of *Russula*

Ghost plant

In the dark
Since ghost plants don't need sunlight, they can grow in very dark forests.

The ghost plant gets its food from the mycelium of the mycorrhizal fungus *Russula*.

GHOST PLANT (*MONOTROPA UNIFLORA*)

More than 400 plant species can't photosynthesize and instead **steal food from fungi**.

Fungi that mimic termite eggs are called **cuckoo fungi** because cuckoos use the same trick of laying their eggs in other birds' nests.

177

PARASITIC ORCHIDS

Orchids have tiny seeds, with hardly any stored food. They can't germinate or grow without a fungus partner. Fungi such as *Trametes* and *Marasmius* give orchids water, nutrients, and even sugars. When orchids are fully grown, most have green leaves and can make sugars by photosynthesis. They then share this food with the fungus. But more than 200 orchid species can't photosynthesize at all. They are parasites fed entirely by the fungus.

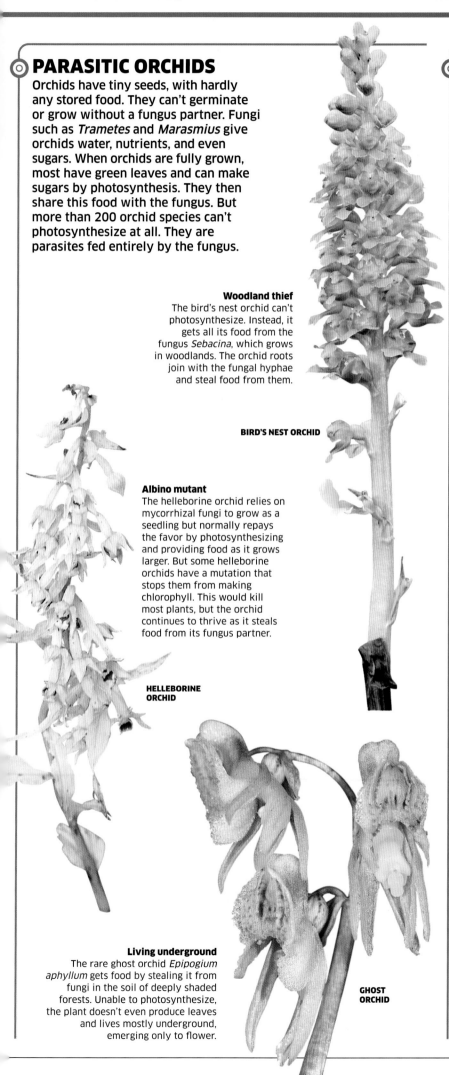

Woodland thief

The bird's nest orchid can't photosynthesize. Instead, it gets all its food from the fungus *Sebacina*, which grows in woodlands. The orchid roots join with the fungal hyphae and steal food from them.

BIRD'S NEST ORCHID

Albino mutant

The helleborine orchid relies on mycorrhizal fungi to grow as a seedling but normally repays the favor by photosynthesizing and providing food as it grows larger. But some helleborine orchids have a mutation that stops them from making chlorophyll. This would kill most plants, but the orchid continues to thrive as it steals food from its fungus partner.

HELLEBORINE ORCHID

Living underground

The rare ghost orchid *Epipogium aphyllum* gets food by stealing it from fungi in the soil of deeply shaded forests. Unable to photosynthesize, the plant doesn't even produce leaves and lives mostly underground, emerging only to flower.

GHOST ORCHID

COPYCATS

Deception is common in nature. Many insects mimic the bright yellow and black stripes of wasps to scare off predators, and some caterpillars mimic bird droppings to avoid being eaten. Plants and fungi use mimicry, too. The victim of deception is usually an animal that is tricked into helping the copycat complete its life cycle.

DRACULA ORCHID

Fake mushroom at the center of the flower

Fake mushrooms

The flowers of dracula orchids mimic mushrooms that grow in cloud forests and even have a similar smell. The trickery attracts insects that normally lay eggs in mushrooms and thereby helps pollinate the orchid.

Fake buttercups

A parasitic fungus called mustard flower rust infects the rockcress plant. It makes the plant produce clusters of bright yellow leaves that look and smell like buttercups, attracting insects in search of nectar. The fungus makes its reproductive structures inside these fake flowers, and the insects help spread the fungal spores.

Fake eggs

The fungus *Athelia termitophila* makes small fungal balls that feel and smell like termite eggs. Termites carry them into their nurseries and look after them. Sometimes, hyphae grow out of the fake eggs and begin feeding on the real ones.

ATHELIA TERMITOPHILA

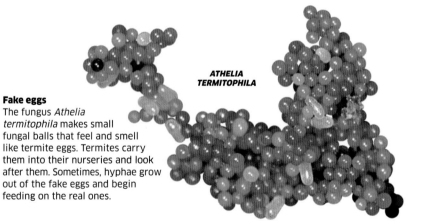

Real flower

Fake flower formed by the fungus

Fake grass flowers

The fungus *Fusarium xyrophilum* is a parasite on yellow eye grasses. It stops the plant from making flowers. Fungal hyphae then make a structure that looks like a flower, but it makes fungal spores instead of pollen or nectar. The spores are spread by visiting insects.

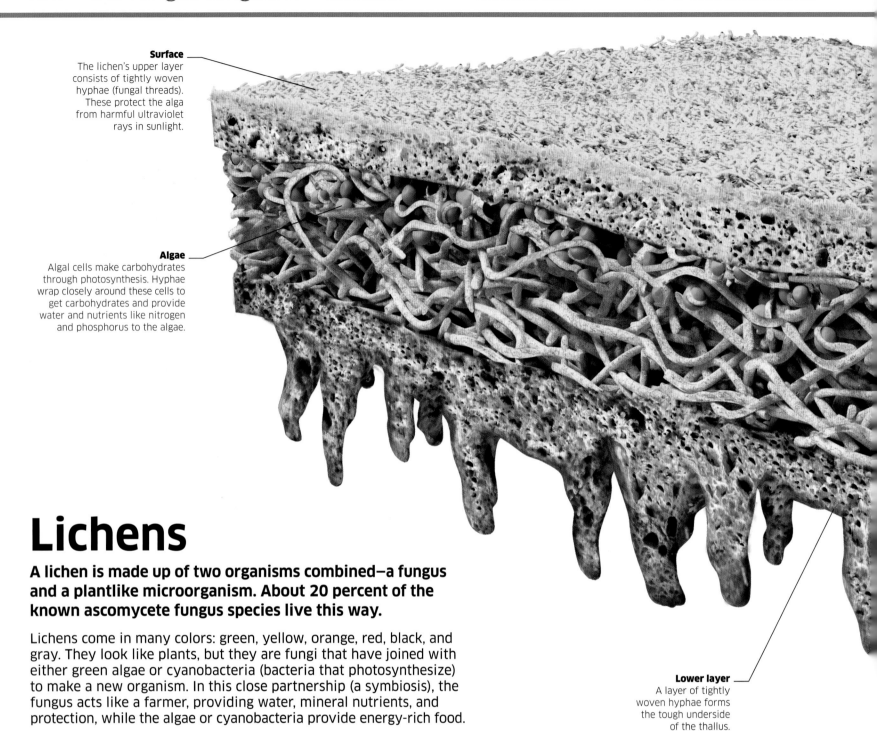

Surface
The lichen's upper layer consists of tightly woven hyphae (fungal threads). These protect the alga from harmful ultraviolet rays in sunlight.

Algae
Algal cells make carbohydrates through photosynthesis. Hyphae wrap closely around these cells to get carbohydrates and provide water and nutrients like nitrogen and phosphorus to the algae.

Lower layer
A layer of tightly woven hyphae forms the tough underside of the thallus.

Lichens

A lichen is made up of two organisms combined—a fungus and a plantlike microorganism. About 20 percent of the known ascomycete fungus species live this way.

Lichens come in many colors: green, yellow, orange, red, black, and gray. They look like plants, but they are fungi that have joined with either green algae or cyanobacteria (bacteria that photosynthesize) to make a new organism. In this close partnership (a symbiosis), the fungus acts like a farmer, providing water, mineral nutrients, and protection, while the algae or cyanobacteria provide energy-rich food.

Types of lichen
Lichen species have different shapes: leafy (foliose), powdery (leprose), crusty (crustose), or branching (fruticose). Around 20,000 fungi species form lichens. Most are ascomycete fungi, but a few are basidiomycete fungi that produce mushrooms when they are ready to make spores.

Leprose
These are the simplest lichens and look powdery. A common example is dust lichen, which grows on rocks and tree trunks.

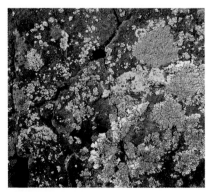

Crustose
The most common type of lichen, crustose lichens form crusts that stick tightly to objects.

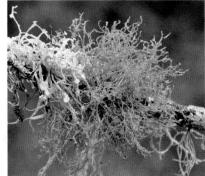

Fruticose
These lichens are made of tough, branching strands. They stand upright, form tufts, or dangle from trees.

Reindeer can **sniff out carpets of lichen** through a layer of snow more than 3 ft (1 m) deep.

179

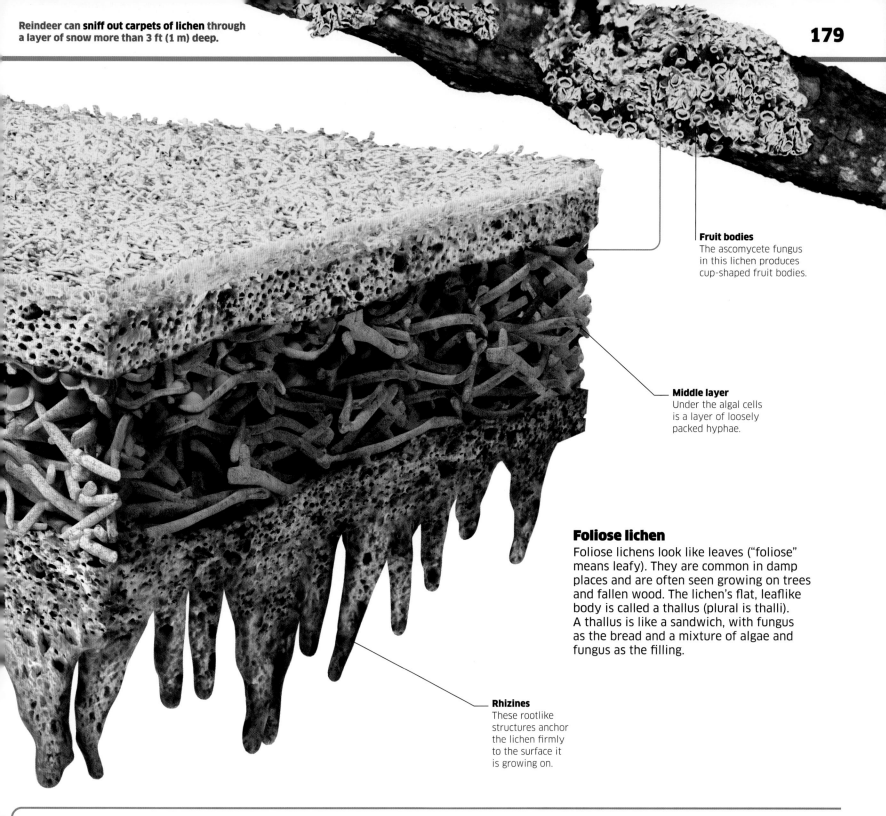

Fruit bodies
The ascomycete fungus in this lichen produces cup-shaped fruit bodies.

Middle layer
Under the algal cells is a layer of loosely packed hyphae.

Foliose lichen

Foliose lichens look like leaves ("foliose" means leafy). They are common in damp places and are often seen growing on trees and fallen wood. The lichen's flat, leaflike body is called a thallus (plural is thalli). A thallus is like a sandwich, with fungus as the bread and a mixture of algae and fungus as the filling.

Rhizines
These rootlike structures anchor the lichen firmly to the surface it is growing on.

Survivors

Lichens grow slowly— often less than 0.04 in (1 mm) in a year. However, they can live in harsh environments where nothing else survives, from bare rock to hot deserts, the Arctic, and Antarctica—and everywhere in between.

Bare rock
Some lichens can colonize bare rock. They secrete acids that slowly break down the rock, releasing minerals.

Desert lichen
The fruticose cape hair lichen flourishes on the parched soil of Africa's Namib Desert— one of the world's driest places.

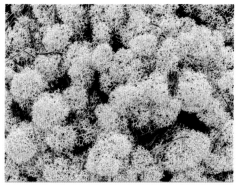

Reindeer lichen
The lichen *Cladonia rangiferina* (also called reindeer lichen) forms a lush carpet more than 6 in (15 cm) deep in the Arctic tundra, providing the main winter food for reindeer.

Rotters and recyclers

Without fungi, we would be buried under heaps of dead stuff and poop. Along with invertebrates and bacteria, fungi break down dead organic matter and recycle the nutrients in it.

All organisms make waste. Dead leaves and rotten branches fall off plants all the time. Animals scatter droppings wherever they go and shed fur, hair, feathers, and skin. Eventually, they die. Thanks to fungi, nutrients don't stay locked up in all this waste material for long. By growing into dead organic matter and digesting it from within, fungi recycle the nutrients and fertilize soil, helping new plants grow.

Dung fungi

Some fungi have evolved to live on dung. Sheep droppings already contain fungal spores before they hit the ground. The spores germinate, hyphae grow out to feed on the droppings, and fruit bodies form. The first fruit bodies to appear are often those of the hat-thrower fungus, which uses explosive force to disperse its spores. Doing this ensures they land on fresh grass that another sheep is likely to swallow.

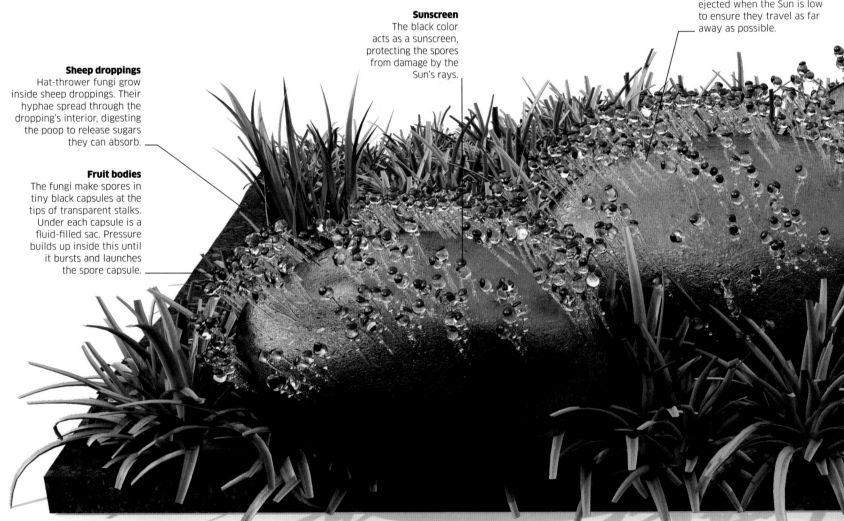

Sensing light
The fruit bodies are light-sensitive and bend to face the Sun. Spore capsules are ejected when the Sun is low to ensure they travel as far away as possible.

Sunscreen
The black color acts as a sunscreen, protecting the spores from damage by the Sun's rays.

Sheep droppings
Hat-thrower fungi grow inside sheep droppings. Their hyphae spread through the dropping's interior, digesting the poop to release sugars they can absorb.

Fruit bodies
The fungi make spores in tiny black capsules at the tips of transparent stalks. Under each capsule is a fluid-filled sac. Pressure builds up inside this until it bursts and launches the spore capsule.

Life cycle of dung fungi

To complete its life cycle, the hat-thrower fungus must ensure its spores are swallowed by animals. However, animals don't like eating grass that's covered with poop or near poop. So the fungus fires its spores as far away as it can. The sticky spore packages cling to blades of grass, waiting to be swallowed by grazing animals.

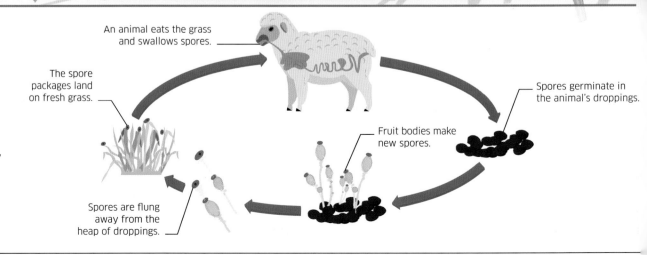

An animal eats the grass and swallows spores.

The spore packages land on fresh grass.

Spores germinate in the animal's droppings.

Fruit bodies make new spores.

Spores are flung away from the heap of droppings.

A hat-thrower fungus spore capsule contains up to **90,000 spores**.

More than **55 billion tons of carbon are recycled** by fungi worldwide every year.

181

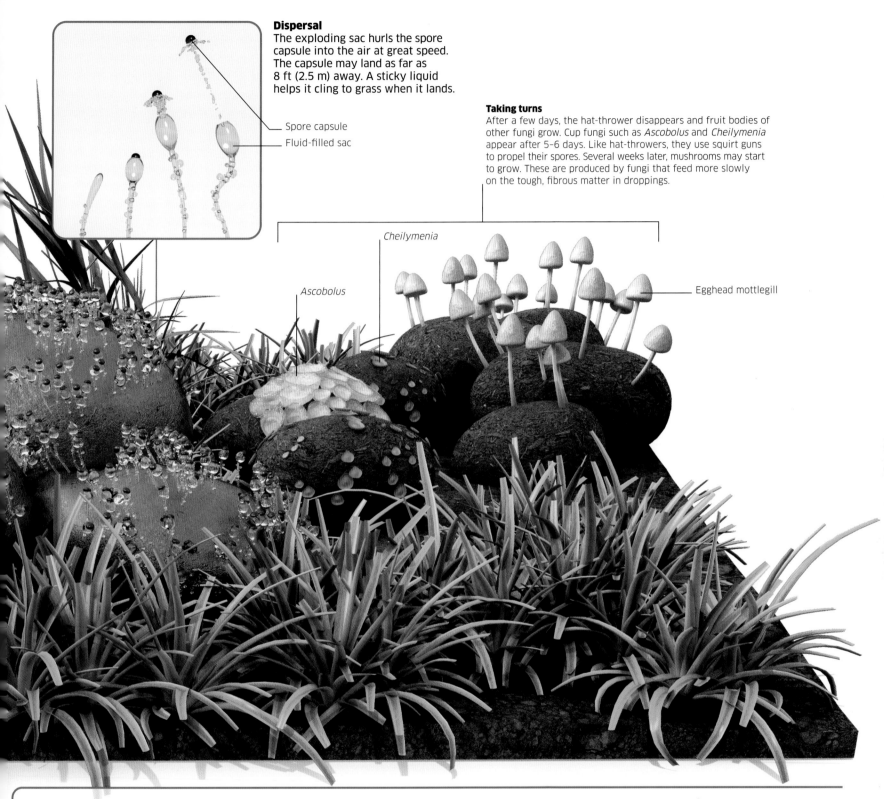

Dispersal
The exploding sac hurls the spore capsule into the air at great speed. The capsule may land as far as 8 ft (2.5 m) away. A sticky liquid helps it cling to grass when it lands.

Spore capsule

Fluid-filled sac

Taking turns
After a few days, the hat-thrower disappears and fruit bodies of other fungi grow. Cup fungi such as *Ascobolus* and *Cheilymenia* appear after 5–6 days. Like hat-throwers, they use squirt guns to propel their spores. Several weeks later, mushrooms may start to grow. These are produced by fungi that feed more slowly on the tough, fibrous matter in droppings.

Cheilymenia

Ascobolus

Egghead mottlegill

Moldy food
Most fresh food has fungal spores on its surface even before it reaches our kitchens. In moist, warm conditions, the fungi start to digest the food, reducing appetizing treats to mush. Some food fungi, including *Aspergillus*, *Penicillium*, and *Fusarium*, make toxic chemicals, so always avoid food that has mold growing on it.

Mold appears after a week or so.

The strawberries collapse as the soft flesh is consumed.

FRESH STRAWBERRIES

10 DAYS OLD

12 DAYS OLD

Making compost
Gardeners use fungi to help recycle waste matter such as leaves, weeds, and uneaten vegetables and fruit. Fungi and other organisms digest the heap of waste over several months, transforming it into a crumbly black material called compost. This is rich in nutrients that plants need. If you handle compost, take care not to breathe in dust as it may contain harmful fungal spores.

182 the fungus kingdom ○ **FUNGUS WARS**

The most common result of a **battle between two fungi** is a draw, with neither fungus gaining territory from the other.

Piggyback fungi

Some fungi make their fruit bodies on those of other fungi. Often, they are parasites of the fungus they are growing on.

Bonnet mold

The bonnet mold fungus grows from the cap of bonnet fungi. Bonnet mold is related to bread mold, with masses of tiny spores packed into small black capsules on the end of fine threads.

Mushrooms on mushrooms

Piggyback boletes produce mushrooms that sprout from the much larger earthball fungi.

Powdery piggyback

The powdery piggyback mushroom grows on the larger and much darker blackening brittlegill. As the name suggests, blackening brittlegills start off light-colored but turn dark with age.

Fungus wars

Wherever a fungus grows, there will be other fungi and bacteria, too. They compete for the sources of food available, sometimes with deadly consequences.

Fungi use a range of different strategies to win the battle for food. Some produce huge numbers of spores to ensure they arrive first. They then grow into the food quickly before other fungi arrive, and leave— by making fruit bodies and spores—just as new arrivals begin to compete with them. Fungi that arrive later are often aggressive fighters. Those that win get the territory and the food.

Defensive walls

Fungi that grow in wood sometimes surround their territory with walls of dense fungal tissue to protect them from neighbors. These walls appear as dark lines in the wood.

Fighting fungi

Fungi battle for territory whether they are growing in a rotting log, in soil, or in any other source of food. They do this by releasing chemicals that kill or slow down their opponents. They can also change the acidity of the environment to suit themselves. Different fungi have different fighting abilities. While some are good attackers, others are good defenders. Some are good at both, and a few are good at neither.

The **chemical weapons** produced by the fungus *Penicillium* are used by people as drugs to kill bacteria.

183

Space invader
The mycelium of this white-rot fungus is spreading to the right and invading the territory of a sulfur tuft fungus. Some fungi, like these, arrive by growing through soil.

Sulfur tuft mushrooms
The sulfur tuft fungus is a common sight in woodlands. It grows in rotting logs and tree stumps and produces yellow mushrooms that are poisonous. Its spores can spread to wood.

Sulfur tuft mycelium

Under the bark
Wood decay fungi often spread in the space between rotting bark and the harder wood underneath.

Chemical warfare
Some fungi can kill opponents without even touching them. They do this by releasing toxic chemicals.

Mycoparasites
Some fungi are mycoparasites, which means they are parasites that feed on other living fungi. In some cases, the mycoparasitic fungus's hyphae coil tightly around the victim's hyphae. In other cases, the parasite grows inside its prey.

Parasitic fungus coiling tightly around another fungus

Victim's hypha

Hypha of parasitic fungus penetrating host

Hypha of host

Plant killers

Fungi live on all parts of plants, often doing little harm and even helping the plant. However, some fungi are parasites on plants or even kill a part (or all) of their host so they can feed on its dead remains.

Plants have many defenses to protect themselves from deadly fungi. Solid barriers like bark, waxy layers on leaves, and thick cell walls make it hard for fungi to get in. If a fungus does get through, plants switch to defensive chemicals. However, these don't always work, and symptoms of a disease may appear. There might be wartlike swellings, black spots, red spots, mold, wilting shoots, or soggy stems that turn to mush and die. These diseases are well known to gardeners and farmers and can wipe out whole crops.

Gardeners' enemies

Plants can get lots of different fungal diseases, but not usually all at the same time. Some fungi infect just small areas, while others harm the whole plant. Some kill quickly and feast on the dead plant. Others keep the victim alive for a long time and act like a parasite, stealing food and making the plant weak.

Anthracnose
Dark, sunken patches on strawberries are caused by the fungus *Colletotrichum*, which can also damage leaves and stems. The fungus can survive in soil for months and spreads to new plants when heavy rain splashes soil onto them.

Fusarium wilt
The *Fusarium* fungus gets in through roots and grows upward, preventing the plant from getting enough water. The whole plant may die. The fungus then feeds on the dead tissue.

Botrytis mold
The fungus *Botrytis cinerea* gets into plants through wounds. Its gray, fluffy mycelium rots soft fruits such as strawberries, causing crop losses worth billions every year.

Chocolate spot
This disease of bean plants is caused by *Botrytis fabae* and *Botrytis cinerea*. Brown spots appear in spring, then spread to cover whole leaves. Bean pods are ruined and the beans inside turn black.

Mildew
This white fungus grows on the surface of leaves. It pokes hyphae into leaf cells to feed but doesn't kill the plant. However, it can block a lot of sunlight, which weakens the plant.

Damping off disease
This disease makes the stems and roots of seedlings soggy and rotten, killing them. It is caused by fungi such as *Rhizoctonia*, which survive in soil as spores.

The beans have all turned black.

The *Colletotrichum* fungus can survive on fava bean seeds for **two years**.

50 percent of ash trees in Europe have been killed by the fungus *Hymenoscyphus fraxineus*.

185

Rust
Fava bean rust is caused by the fungus *Uromyces viciae-fabae*, which produces small brown spots on the leaves of bean plants in summer. It doesn't kill the leaves, but the fungus is a parasite and takes a lot of food from the plant.

Corn smut
Corn smut is caused by the fungus *Ustilago maydis*. It's also called "devil's corn" because it looks horrible and damages crops. However, in Mexico, the deformed tissue caused by the fungus is known as *huitlacoche* and is eaten. It is said to be delicious.

Ear rot
The fungus *Gibberella zeae* infects the silky strands at the top of a corn ear, then spreads down to cover the whole ear with a pinkish-red mycelium. It can ruin crops and produces toxins that are harmful if eaten.

Save our bananas
Most of the bananas we eat come from a seedless variety of the plant called the Cavendish. Cavendish bananas were bred to resist the *Fusarium* fungus, which nearly wiped out the world's banana crops in the 1950s. For a while, this worked well, but a new variety of *Fusarium* that attacks Cavendish banana plants has now evolved. It is especially deadly because all Cavendish bananas are genetically identical plants grown from cuttings.

BANANA PLANT AFFECTED BY *FUSARIUM*

Green islands
When leaves take on their fall colors, there are sometimes still patches of bright green on them. This is where a parasitic fungus is keeping the plant cells alive longer so that the fungus can carry on getting food from it.

Animal killers

Some fungi attack animals and grow in their bodies, causing disease and death. A few types have killed so many animals that they have put whole species at risk.

Many fungi are highly nutritious, and animals—from insects and worms to mice and people—eat them. However, fungi feed on animals, too. Some fungi consume dead parts of animals such as skin, hair, and nails. Others attack living tissue and feed on it, causing fungal diseases. And some fungi go even further, trapping microscopic animals, then killing and eating them.

⊙ EGG DESTROYERS

Sea turtles lay their eggs in pits on sandy beaches, then go back to the sea. Heated by the Sun, the sand keeps the eggs warm until the baby turtles are ready to hatch. However, warm, damp sand is also ideal for the *Fusarium* fungus, which can infect and kill the eggs. Sea turtles are already rare, so the fungus poses a major threat to their survival.

GREEN TURTLE LAYING EGGS

***FUSARIUM* SPORE**

⊙ WHITE-NOSE DISEASE

Many bats spend winters hibernating in caves, where it is cool but rarely freezing, which is also ideal for the fungus *Pseudogymnoascus destructans*. This fungus causes white-nose disease—it spreads through the bat's skin, turning the nose white. Affected bats wake up more frequently, causing them to use up their fat reserves and starve before spring arrives.

Little brown bats
Infected *Myotis* bats develop white noses as the fungus spreads around the snout. Ears and wings often turn white, too.

⊙ CORAL KILLERS

Coral reefs, which are home to about a quarter of all marine species, are being damaged by global warming. The problem has worsened due to the fungus *Aspergillus sydowii*. This species has been found in Caribbean seawater since the 1990s. It infects corals called sea fans. Colored blotches appear on the infected corals, which may then die.

CORAL DAMAGED BY *ASPERGILLUS* FUNGUS

⊙ CARNIVOROUS FUNGI

Fungi living in soils that are low in nutrients sometimes get extra food by trapping microscopic worms called nematodes. More than 300 fungus species capture nematodes or feed on their eggs. They use a range of different tricks and traps to ensnare their tiny wriggling victims.

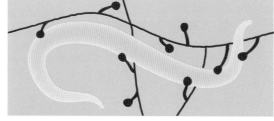

Lethal lollipops
The simplest traps are just sticky pegs that grow from hyphae. When a nematode touches one of these lethal lollipops, it gets stuck. A hypha grows from the knob into the nematode and eats it from the inside.

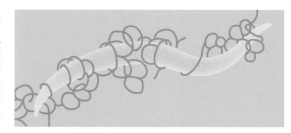

Caught in a net
Some fungi, such as *Arthrobotrys oligospora*, trap nematodes in a tangled net of sticky loops. The fungi then grow into the trapped worms.

Up to **90 amphibian species** have become extinct because of fungi.

Chytrid spores are **less than 0.0002 in** (five thousandths of a millimeter) wide.

187

DISAPPEARING FROGS

Since the 1980s, frogs and other amphibians have been falling in number all over the world. There are several causes, including loss of habitat, pollution, and invasive species. However, the number-one killer is a disease caused by chytrids—fungi that live in water. Chytrids have been spread by traders shipping exotic pets from one country to another. They have caused some species of amphibians to go extinct.

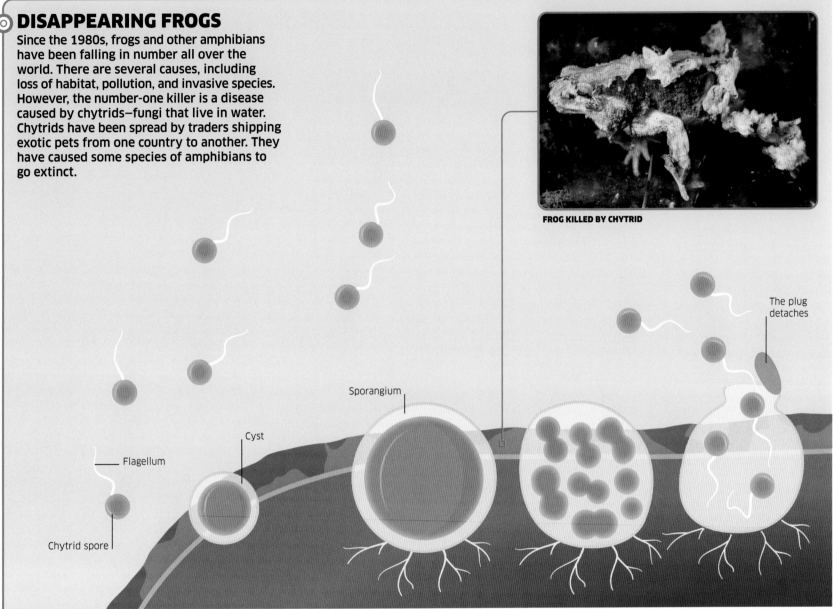

FROG KILLED BY CHYTRID

The plug detaches

Sporangium

Cyst

Flagellum

Chytrid spore

1 Swimming spore
A chytrid spore is microscopic—too tiny to be seen by the naked eye. It swims through water in search of a frog by beating a kind of tail called a flagellum.

2 Burrowing in
When the spore finds a suitable frog, it sticks to it and burrows into its skin. The spore absorbs its flagellum and forms a rounded structure called a cyst.

3 Growing
Rootlike hyphae grow into the frog's skin cells, allowing the chytrid to feed and grow. It develops into a larger structure called a sporangium.

4 New spores form
As the sporangium matures, its cells divide to produce new spores.

5 Spores released
Finally, a plug at the top of the sporangium detaches, allowing the spores to swim away and infect more frogs.

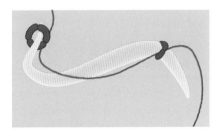

Shrinking noose
The *Arthrobotrys dactyloides* fungus catches prey in a noose made of three cells arranged in a ring. When a nematode wriggles through and touches the trap, the three cells swell with water and the noose tightens.

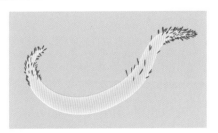

Sticky spores
Instead of making worm traps, fungi such as *Drechmeria coniospora* produce spores that stick to nematodes, then grow inside them.

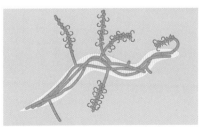

On the hook
Spores of the fungus *Harposporium anguillulae* have hooks that stick in nematodes' throats when eaten. When the hyphae have devoured the worm's insides, they burst out of its body and release new spores.

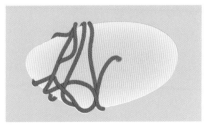

Egg parasites
The fungus *Amylostereum areolatum* grows on the outside of nematode eggs, then burrows inside to feed on the nematode's developing body.

The zombie-making fungus *Cordyceps* inspired the smash-hit Playstation game *The Last of Us*.

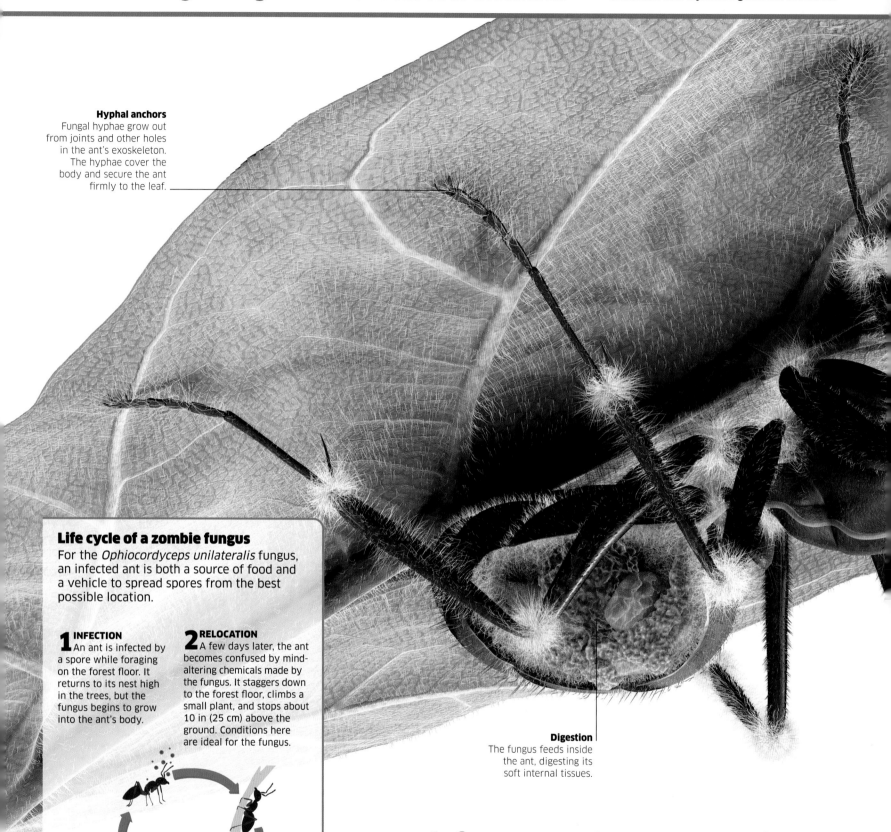

Hyphal anchors
Fungal hyphae grow out from joints and other holes in the ant's exoskeleton. The hyphae cover the body and secure the ant firmly to the leaf.

Digestion
The fungus feeds inside the ant, digesting its soft internal tissues.

Life cycle of a zombie fungus

For the *Ophiocordyceps unilateralis* fungus, an infected ant is both a source of food and a vehicle to spread spores from the best possible location.

1 INFECTION
An ant is infected by a spore while foraging on the forest floor. It returns to its nest high in the trees, but the fungus begins to grow into the ant's body.

2 RELOCATION
A few days later, the ant becomes confused by mind-altering chemicals made by the fungus. It staggers down to the forest floor, climbs a small plant, and stops about 10 in (25 cm) above the ground. Conditions here are ideal for the fungus.

4 SPREADING SPORES
The fungus grows over the ant and secures its jaws and feet to the leaf. A fruit body with a long stalk erupts from the ant's body and releases spores, infecting new ants.

3 LOSING CONTROL
Its mind controlled by the fungus, the ant bites into a leaf and its jaws lock shut. Then it dies.

Zombies and mummies

Deadly fungi that turn their hosts into mindless zombies might sound like the stuff of horror films, but many species do exactly this. Their usual victims are small animals such as insects.

More than a thousand different kinds of fungi are insect killers. The fungus starts out as a spore and grows through a chink in the insect's exoskeleton before spreading through its body, either as single cells (yeasts) or as hyphae. Then the fungus eats the insect alive, eventually killing it and releasing more spores to infect more insects. To ensure those spores find suitable hosts, some fungi take control of the victim's mind and body and make it travel to the perfect spot for spreading spores.

Insect-killing fungi have been used to **kill pests on crops** to reduce the use of chemical pesticides.

When **cicadas infected by killer fungi** try to mate, they pass fungal spores to their partners.

189

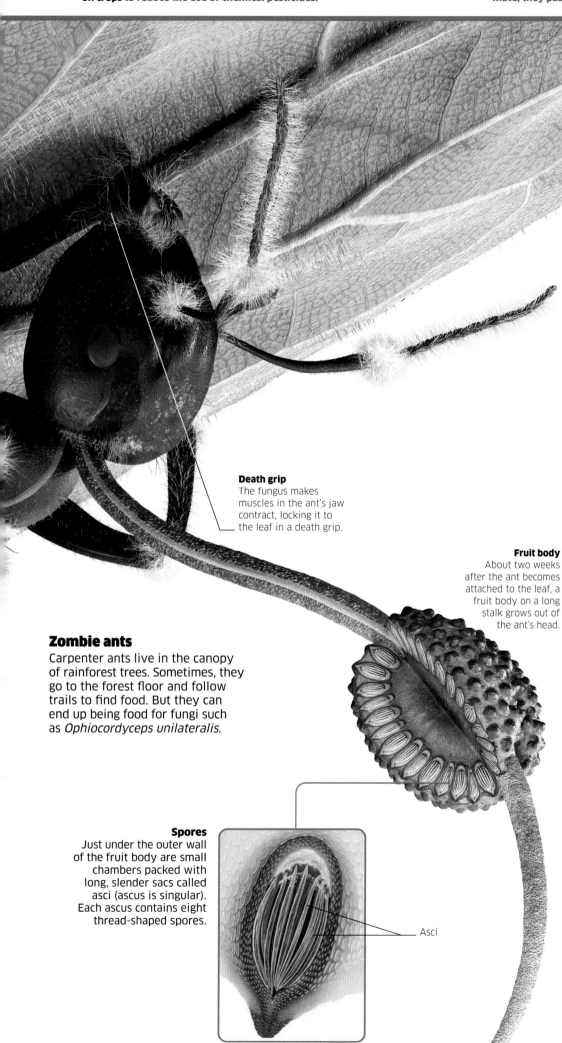

Death grip
The fungus makes muscles in the ant's jaw contract, locking it to the leaf in a death grip.

Fruit body
About two weeks after the ant becomes attached to the leaf, a fruit body on a long stalk grows out of the ant's head.

Zombie ants

Carpenter ants live in the canopy of rainforest trees. Sometimes, they go to the forest floor and follow trails to find food. But they can end up being food for fungi such as *Ophiocordyceps unilateralis*.

Spores
Just under the outer wall of the fruit body are small chambers packed with long, slender sacs called asci (ascus is singular). Each ascus contains eight thread-shaped spores.

Asci

Rocket launchers

Strongwellsea fungi eat living *Helina* flies from the inside. Then the fungus makes one or two holes on the fly's abdomen and shoots out spores like rockets from a plane. Spores are shot out for several days before the fly dies.

Cicada killers

Periodical cicadas spend most of their lives underground, sucking sap from plant roots. Every 13 or 17 years, all the adults crawl out together to mate, but the fungus *Massospora cicadina* is waiting for them. It grows inside their rear ends, which rot and fall off.

Mummified moths

Some fungi, such as *Cordyceps*, mummify their victims, growing around them in a shroud of fungal material. The fungus feeds on the corpse until it is ready to produce spores. It makes the infected moths move to higher ground before they die so that the spores spread to a larger area.

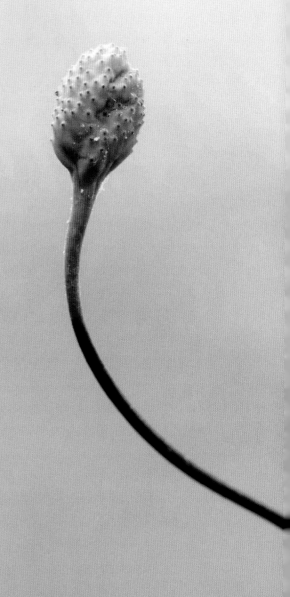

Eaten alive

This dead weevil in the Amazon Rainforest was a victim of *Ophiocordyceps*. The fungus takes control of insects, kills them, and makes fruit bodies that stick out of their corpses to infect new prey.

Ophiocordyceps is one of many fungus species that thrive in the Amazon Rainforest, along with around 60,000 insect species; 40,000 plant species; and more than 1,000 bird species. The warm, damp climate and the huge diversity of food sources are ideal for fungi. Most rainforest species have probably not even been discovered yet.

ERGOT
Claviceps purpurea
Location: On cereal crops such as wheat
When: Spring to early fall

Ergot is a fungus that grows on the seedheads of grasses and can poison cereal crops. It was a major problem in medieval Europe, when flour infected with ergot sometimes poisoned entire villages. The toxins made people tremble and twist in pain and caused hallucinations.

BROWN ROLL RIM
Paxillus involutus
Location: Under birch and other broadleaved trees
When: Summer and fall

This very common fungus is a partner with tree roots. It is extremely poisonous to humans and other animals and can be deadly. There is no known antidote.

ANGEL'S WINGS
Pleurocybella porrigens
Location: Well-decayed wood on the forest floor
When: Summer and fall

This wood-decay fungus grows on conifer tree stumps and produces fruit bodies with wavy caps that look like oyster mushrooms. It can cause brain damage and death in some people.

⚠ Poisonous fungi

Picking mushrooms might sound like a fun hobby, but edible and poisonous mushrooms can be very difficult to tell apart. Mushrooms found growing in the wild should not be eaten.

Many fungi produce poisonous chemicals called toxins. Some toxins make us feel unwell, but others can be deadly—even in small amounts. Eating toxic mushrooms often leads to vomiting, which helps your body get rid of the dangerous substance. However, if toxins get into the bloodstream, they can do serious damage to internal organs such as the liver and kidneys. For some fungal toxins, there is no known antidote.

The fruit bodies of angel's wings look like edible oyster mushrooms.

YELLOW STAINER
Agaricus xanthodermus
Location: Grassland
When: Late spring to winter

Yellow stainer mushrooms cause many poisonings, as they are often mistaken for edible field mushrooms. Eating them causes stomach cramps, vomiting, and diarrhea, but people usually get better.

A bright yellow color appears when the fungus is cut or bruised.

In the USA, around **7,500 cases of mushroom poisoning** are reported every year.

193

FUNERAL BELL
Galerina marginata

Location: Woodland
When: Summer and fall

This small, deadly fungus is widespread and commonly found on rotting wood and wood chips. It contains a toxin called alpha-amanitin, which causes vomiting, stomachache, difficulty in breathing, and liver damage. Severe cases can be fatal.

DEATH CAP
Amanita phalloides

Location: Deciduous woodland
When: Summer and fall

Death caps are the world's deadliest mushrooms. When young, they look like edible puffballs, but eating as little as half a death cap can kill you, thanks to high levels of alpha-amanitin, the same toxin found in funeral bell mushrooms.

The cap can be white, yellowish, or brownish green.

ASPERGILLUS
Aspergillus

Location: Grows as mold on food
When: All year round

If foods such as corn (maize), beans, peanuts, rice, sunflower seeds, or wheat are not dry enough when stored, fungi can grow in them. *Aspergillus* fungi make chemicals called aflatoxins, which can cause stunted growth in children, potentially fatal liver damage, and cancer. Most countries have strict rules to prevent aflatoxins from forming in food.

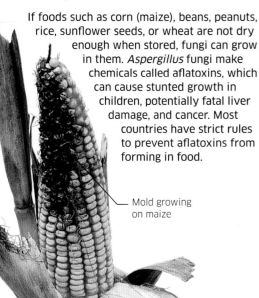

Mold growing on maize

BLACK MOLD
Cladosprium, Alternaria, and *Stachybotrys* species

Location: Damp spots indoors
When: All year round

Homes that aren't properly heated and ventilated can become damp, which causes black mold to grow on walls and ceilings. When spores released by black molds are breathed in, they can cause allergic reactions such as asthma, or other ill effects.

PANTHER CAP
Amanita pantherina

Location: Woodland
When: Summer and fall

The panther cap fungus partners with plant roots, especially those of beech and oak trees. It produces several different toxins and causes a range of physical and mental effects if eaten. These can include vomiting, diarrhea, heavy sweating, hallucinations, convulsions, and sometimes even death.

Domed cap
The brown cap with creamy white warts is domed but flattens as the mushroom matures.

DESTROYING ANGEL
Amanita virosa

Location: Deciduous woodland
When: Summer and fall

This deadly mushroom is a close relative of the death cap. It can be mistaken for a puffball when young and an edible field mushroom when larger, though it grows in woodland rather than grassland. It is very toxic and damages the liver and kidneys.

Giant mushrooms

The *Termitomyces* fungi that live in termite mounds produce the world's largest edible mushrooms. These grow by termite mounds in the rainy season and are sometimes sold at the roadside as a delicacy. However, there are also poisonous mushrooms that look like *Termitomyces*, so remember, don't pick or eat wild mushrooms.

Leafcutter ants

Foraging leafcutter ants snip leaves into pieces and carry these to their nest. Here, smaller ants clip and crush them to make pellets and add fungal hyphae. The fungus digests the leaves and produces special hyphae that feed the ants.

Ambrosia beetles

The larvae of ambrosia beetles live in dead or dying trees. They can't digest wood, but they can digest the ambrosia fungi that line the tunnels. When the larvae turn into adults, they fly to new trees and carry fungi with them in special pouches.

Chimney
Hot, stale air from the termite colony rises to leave the mound through a tall central chimney.

Inside a termite mound

The grasslands of tropical Africa are dotted with towering mounds of mud built by termites. These insect skyscrapers provide air conditioning to create the perfect climate for the fungi deep inside.

Ventilation tunnel
Fresh air is drawn in at ground level by the flow of air rising through the chimney.

Nursery
Larvae are tended in the nursery.

Extra chambers
These chambers may be used for storage or raising young, depending on need.

Queen
The queen termite lays all the colony's eggs in the queen cell.

The caps of *Termitomyces titanicus* mushrooms can reach **3 ft (1 m)** wide.

At up to **26 ft (8 m)** tall, termite mounds are the **tallest structures built by animals** other than humans.

195

Climate control
Termites continually maintain their chimneys and ventilation shafts to control the climate inside the colony. Daytime temperatures can soar to 104°F (40°C) in tropical Africa, but the temperature inside the fungus garden stays a steady 84–88°F (29–31°C). The air stays humid and waste carbon dioxide is flushed out.

Mud walls
Termites construct their mounds one mouthful at a time, using mud, saliva, and droppings.

A pangolin digs the mound for termites— its favorite food.

Farmers or servants?

From termites and ants to beetles, many insects have teamed up with fungi to turn inedible plant matter into nutritious food.

Animals can't make the digestive enzymes needed to break down cellulose—the fibrous substance found in all plant cell walls. However, fungi can break down cellulose. Millions of years ago, termites and other insects formed partnerships with fungi to turn indigestible plant material into food. Termites collect all kinds of plant debris, eat it, and put their undigested droppings in a "fungus garden." The fungi finish digesting the slimy poop and turn it into edible food pellets that feed the termites. Some people call this the first form of agriculture, with termites as the farmers. Another point of view is that the fungi have made servants of the termites. Either way, both partners benefit.

1 Foragers
Worker termites leave the mound through tunnels. They search for bits of wood and other plant fragments and bring them back underground.

2 Fungus garden
Smaller workers eat the plant bits found by foragers but don't fully digest them. They add their droppings to the fungus garden. A fungus called *Termitomyces* digests the poop.

4 Food pellets
The fungus produces small white pellets of food that the termites eat.

3 Weeding
Worker termites tend the fungus garden and weed out any foreign fungi that shouldn't be growing there.

Habitat creators

When fungi break down dead plant and animal matter, they change its make-up and create habitats for many other organisms.

Trees such as oak provide shelter and food to all sorts of animals, from caterpillars to squirrels and songbirds. Forks in branches and nooks and crannies in the bark create tiny homes for insects and other small animals. Fungi create even more. They digest dead wood and soften it, making it easier to burrow into. They make tiny openings that insects can wriggle into, and large hollows that birds can nest in. And many wood-decay fungi make nutritious food for animals from insects to deer.

Rare beauties
Some fungi are found only on large pieces of wood in ancient forests. *Hericium coralloides*, for instance, grows only on dead broadleaved trees. Its beautiful fruit bodies have earned it various common names, including coral tooth fungus and comb tooth.

Rare uglies
The rare oak polypore is found only on oak trees that are several hundred years old. There are only 500 sites with this fungus worldwide. The world stronghold is a former royal hunting forest at Windsor, UK.

Pond life
Water beetles, frogs, and hoverflies breed in pools that form where wood has rotted away.

Cardinal beetles
Fungi growing on bark are eaten by cardinal beetles, wood awl flies, and false ladybugs.

Bracket fungi
Bracket fungi are breeding grounds for beetles.

Fungus gnats
Mushrooms and other fruit bodies are food for slugs and fungus gnats.

Trees with **rotten, hollow centers** grow extra
roots that feed on their own decaying insides.

Deathwatch beetles are so named because they make tapping
sounds in the timbers of old houses in the dead of night.

197

Squirrel dreys
Forks provide support for
birds' nests and squirrel dreys.

Barn owl
High cavities are ideal for
barn owl roosts, stiletto
flies, cardinal click beetles,
and darkling beetles.

Stag beetles
Spongy wood produced by
white-rot fungi attracts lesser
stag beetles, rhinoceros beetles,
and comb-horn crane flies.

Woodpeckers
Woodpeckers search for
soft, rotting wood that's
easier to drill into. They
spread fungal spores
when they travel from
one tree to another.

Lion's mane fungus

Woodboring beetles
A hanging, broken branch makes a good
egg-laying site for woodboring beetles.

Damaged bark
Bark damaged by deer lets
in white-rot fungi, stag
beetles, comb-horn crane
flies, and hoverflies.

Hornet nests
Dry holes left by rot are
good for birds' nests, bat
roosts, and hornet nests.

Hollows
Hollows at the base where wood
has rotted provide premade
burrows for mammals such
as weasels and pine martens.

Decomposer fungi break down
dead plant parts on and in the soil.

Weasel kits
in burrow

What fungi make for us

In our everyday lives, we see fungi making food moldy or rotting the timber in our homes or garden fences. But fungi can be incredibly useful, too.

We couldn't live without fungi. As well as playing an essential role as recyclers in natural ecosystems, fungi are used by people to manufacture everything from food and fuel to medicines, building materials, packaging, and even clothing.

LIFE-SAVING MEDICINE

In the natural world, fungi compete with each other and with microorganisms such as bacteria. Some fungi kill bacteria by making chemicals called antibiotics. When these germ-destroying substances were discovered, they were used to create new medicines.

Antibiotics
While studying a bacterium called *Staphylococcus*, Scottish microbiologist Alexander Fleming noticed that it died if a kind of mold (*Penicillium rubens*) grew on the same dishes as the bacteria. This was because the mold had produced a bacteria-killing substance called an antibiotic. Today, we use antibiotics as drugs to cure bacterial diseases and make surgery safer.

Fleming at work
Alexander Fleming discovered penicillin by accident in 1928. It has been called a wonder drug because it has saved so many lives. It is still the world's most used antibiotic.

Penicillium mold growing on a Petri dish

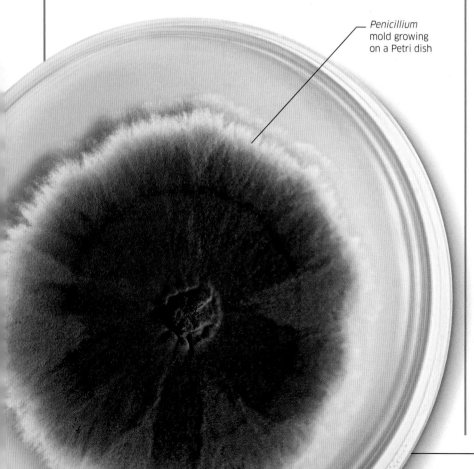

FOOD AND DRINK
Even if you don't like edible mushrooms, you probably eat or drink products made from fungi every day.

Edible mushrooms
People have been cultivating and eating mushrooms since 600 CE. The most popular cultivated fungi are shiitake mushrooms from Southeast Asia and button mushrooms, which are sold throughout Europe and North America.

Portobello mushroom

Button mushroom

Shiitake mushroom

Oyster mushroom

Bread
Bread rises when it bakes because the dough contains tiny bubbles of carbon dioxide made by yeast, a single-celled fungus. People have been using yeast for thousands of years to make bread, beer, and wine.

Soy sauce
This salty sauce was invented more than 2,000 years ago in China. It is made by fermenting a mix of soybeans, wheat, and salty water with the fungus *Aspergillus oryzae*.

Meat substitutes
The fungus *Fusarium venenatum*, originally found in English soil, is used to make meat substitutes for burgers, sausages, and other foods. Fed with sugar, the fungus is grown in huge vats. The high-protein mycelium is then processed to give it a meatlike texture.

Tempeh
The Indonesian food tempeh is made by adding the fungus *Rhizopus oryzae* to boiled soybeans and leaving them to ferment. The fungus binds the beans into a nutritious, savory cake.

Blue cheese
Legend has it that a French shepherd once left his lunch in a cave, returned to find it moldy, but ate it anyway—and the famous blue cheese Roquefort was born. Today, there are many blue cheeses. Most of them get their distinctive color and flavor from *Penicillium* fungi.

Canned drinks
Canned drinks get their refreshing flavor from citric acid, which is manufactured in huge vats using the fungus *Aspergillus niger*.

About **20 years have been added** to the average human lifespan by antibiotics.

Mushroom pickers often use **dogs and pigs** to sniff out expensive fungi called truffles in the ground.

199

MYCELIUM BRICKS

Materials such as concrete, cement, and plastic are harmful to the environment. Eco-friendly alternatives are needed, and fungal mycelium might be the answer. Mycelium bricks are made by putting farm waste from crops into brick-shaped molds, then adding fungi that feed on the waste and grow to fill the space. The same technique can be used to make insulation boards and packaging materials or even to grow a whole house from a hollow framework packed with plant waste.

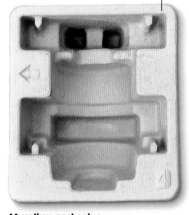

Containers made from fungal mycelium are biodegradable, unlike plastic packaging.

Mycelium packaging
This environmentally safe packaging is a green alternative to styrofoam.

The Hy-fi building
In 2014, this cluster of circular towers, more than 39 ft (12 m) tall, was built in New York City as an art installation to promote sustainable architecture. The towers consisted of 10,000 bricks made from fungal mycelium grown in waste straw. Three months later, the biodegradable building was demolished and turned into compost.

Mycelium bricks

WEARABLE FUNGI

People have long used lichens and fungus fruit bodies to dye clothes or make leather substitutes. Today, fashion designers are turning to fungi to find sustainable alternatives to synthetic fabrics or materials made from animals.

Fungus leather
The horse's hoof fungus grows on tree trunks. It was traditionally used in North America and eastern Europe to make a soft, spongy material like felt or leather. This is called amadou and can be made into hats, bags, and other items.

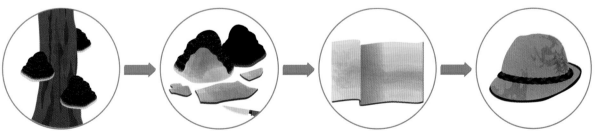

1 GATHERING
The fruit bodies of the horse's hoof are cut from tree trunks.

2 CUTTING THE CRUST
The tough outer crust of the fruit body is first scraped off.

3 BEATING
The soft inner tissue of the fruit body is beaten to make a flat sheet.

4 MAKING ACCESSORIES
The material is then boiled in salty water and stretched into sheets, ready to be made into clothes or accessories.

Fungus dyes
Dyes are extracted from lichens and fungus fruit bodies by simmering them in water for a few hours or by soaking them in ammonia water for much longer. The "dyer's polypore" fungus produces dyes of yellow, deep green, orange, and russet red depending on the chemical used to extract it. Other fungi yield a single color, often like the leaves of trees in fall.

Glossary

ACHENE
A dry, one-seeded fruit. All plants in the buttercup family have achenes.

ALGA
(Plural algae) A plantlike, usually water-dwelling organism, such as a seaweed, that contains the green pigment chlorophyll.

AMADOU
A spongy substance from certain fungi used as a leathery material or to light fires.

ANGIOSPERM
A plant that reproduces by growing flowers, fruits, and seeds.

ANTHER
The part of a flower that produces pollen (male sex cells).

ANTHOCYANINS
Plant pigments responsible for red, blue, and purple colors in leaves and flowers.

ANTIBIOTIC
A medicine that kills or limits the spread of harmful bacteria in humans or other animals.

APICAL
At the tip of a stem or branch; usually refers to a bud or flower.

ASEXUAL
The production of offspring by a single parent.

AUXIN
A plant hormone that controls the way shoots and roots grow, such as in response to light or gravity.

BARK
The tough outer skin of a tree or shrub.

BASAL
At the bottom, or base, of a plant or part of a plant.

BIODEGRADABLE
Able to decay naturally in the environment.

BIOLUMINESCENCE
Production of light by a living thing.

BIOME
A major division of the living world, such as tropical rainforest, desert, or temperate grassland. Each biome has its own distinctive climate, vegetation, and animal life.

BUD
An undeveloped shoot or flower on a plant.

BULB
A shortened underground plant stem with fleshy leaves or leaf bases that store food.

BUOYANCY
The upward force on an object in a liquid, caused by the fluid pressure underneath it.

CAMBIUM
A layer of plant tissue capable of producing the new cells that increase the girth of stems and roots.

CANOPY
The top layer of vegetation in a forest.

CAPITULUM
(Plural capitula) A group of flowers on a stem that together look like a single flower. An example is a sunflower.

CAPSAICIN
A chemical in chili peppers that causes a burning sensation in the mouth or on skin.

CARBOHYDRATE
An energy-rich substance made by plants and found in most foods. Carbohydrates include sugars, which taste sweet, and starch.

CAROTENE
A substance in plants and fungi that gives them a yellow, red, or orange color. Carrots and chanterelle mushrooms contain carotene.

CARPEL
The female reproductive organ in a flower.

CATKIN
A long cluster of male or female flowers produced by some trees, usually pollinated by the wind.

CELL
A tiny unit of living matter. Cells are the building blocks of all living things, apart from viruses.

CELLULOSE
A tough, fibrous carbohydrate found in all plants. It is the main substance in the walls of plant cells.

CENSER
A seed pod that develops openings as it dries out. The seeds are dispersed when wind shakes the pod.

CHLOROPHYLL
The green chemical that gives plants their color. Chlorophyll traps the sunlight energy that plants use to make their food.

CHLOROPLAST
A microscopic green structure that contains chlorophyll and is found in plant cells. Photosynthesis takes place in chloroplasts.

CLIMBER
A plant that grows upward by attaching itself to other plants or objects such as walls.

COLONY
A number of related living things that live closely together.

CONE
A conifer's reproductive structure. Male and female cones usually grow separately.

CONIFER
A plant that reproduces by making cones. Most conifers are evergreen trees or shrubs.

CORAL
A small sea animal that catches food with stinging tentacles. Many corals live in large colonies on coral reefs.

COTYLEDONS
Food-storing leaves in seeds, also known as seed leaves. Cotyledons are the first leaves to appear when seeds germinate.

CULTIVATED
Grown in farms or gardens.

CYANOBACTERIA
Bacteria that make food by photosynthesis; also known as blue-green algae.

CYTOKININ
A plant hormone involved in cell growth in plant roots and shoots.

DECIDUOUS
A deciduous plant sheds its leaves in a cold or dry season.

DECOMPOSER
A living thing that obtains food by breaking down the remains of other living things. Many fungi are decomposers.

DEFORESTATION
The removal of forests by felling or burning.

DEVELOPMENT
The formation of more complex physical structures as a living thing matures.

DICOTYLEDON
A flowering plant that produces two seed leaves (cotyledons) when it first starts to grow.

DIGESTION
The process of breaking down food into chemicals that cells can absorb. In most animals, digestion takes place in a tube that runs through the body.

DNA (deoxyribonucleic acid)
The chemical that carries all the information needed to build a living thing and keep it alive. DNA is passed from one generation to the next when living things reproduce.

DORMANT
In an inactive state. Many plants become dormant in the winter or in times of drought, remaining alive but shutting down to save energy.

ECOSYSTEM
A community of living things and their environment. An ecosystem can be anything from a puddle to a vast forest.

EGG CELL (ovum)
A female sex cell. When an egg cell fuses with a male sex cell (sperm), a new individual is produced.

ELAIOSOME
A fat-rich structure attached to a seed to attract ants, which then disperse the seed.

EMBRYO
The early stage of development of an animal or plant. The embryo of a flowering plant forms inside a seed.

ENDANGERED
At risk of extinction.

ENDOSPERM
A store of food in a seed. The endosperm fuels a seedling's early growth.

ENVIRONMENT
A living thing's surroundings. The environment includes nonliving matter, such as air and water, as well as other living things.

ENZYME
A molecule, usually a protein, that accelerates a chemical reaction in a living thing.

EPIDERMIS
The outer, protective layer of cells of a plant.

EPIPHYTE
A plant that grows on another plant for support without taking nutrients from it.

EQUATOR
An imaginary line that encircles the Earth halfway between the poles. The climate at the equator is hot because the Sun is almost directly overhead at midday.

EROSION
The wearing away of soil, rock, or land by the sea, rivers, or weather.

EVAPORATION
The change of a liquid into a gas as it warms up. Water evaporates into the air when warmed by the Sun.

EVERGREEN
An evergreen plant keeps its leaves throughout the year.

EVOLUTION
The gradual change in a species over many generations.

EXTINCTION
The permanent disappearance of a species.

FERTILIZATION
The joining of a male sex cell and female sex cell, leading to the formation of an embryo.

FIBONACCI SEQUENCE
A sequence of numbers in which each number equals the previous two numbers added together.

FLAGELLUM
(Plural flagella) A long, hairlike structure attached to a cell and used for movement.

FOOD CHAIN
A series of living things through which food passes—for instance, from a plant to a herbivore and then a carnivore.

FOOD WEB
A collection of connected food chains.

FOSSIL
The remains or trace of a living thing preserved in rock.

FROND
The divided leaf of a fern or a palm.

FRUIT
A ripened ovary that contains a flower's seeds. Some fruits have a juicy, edible wall to attract animals.

FRUIT BODY
The spore-making part of a fungus. Mushrooms are fruit bodies.

GAMETOPHYTE
A stage in the life cycle of plants that produces gametes (sex cells). All plants have a life cycle that alternates between two stages: a gametophyte and a sporophyte.

GENE
The basic unit of heredity. Genes are passed from parents to offspring and determine each living thing's characteristics. Most genes are made of DNA.

GEOTROPISM
The response of plants to gravity. For example, a plant shoot growing upward (against gravity) shows negative geotropism.

GERMINATION
The start of growth in a seed or spore.

GRAZE
To eat vegetation, usually grass or other low-growing plants.

GREENHOUSE EFFECT
The trapping of heat by gases such as carbon dioxide in Earth's atmosphere.

GRUB
An immature beetle, wasp, or bee.

GYMNOSPERM
A plant that produces seeds but not flowers. Most gymnosperms are trees that make seeds in cones, such as conifers.

HABITAT
Natural home of a plant or animal, such as a forest or meadow.

HEMIPARASITE
A parasitic plant that has green leaves and can photosynthesize. An example is mistletoe.

HEMISPHERE
One of the halves of Earth created by an imaginary division along the equator. This divides Earth into the northern and southern hemispheres.

HERBIVORE
An animal that eats only plant food.

HERMAPHRODITE
A living thing that has both male and female reproductive organs, such as an earthworm.

HESPERIDIUM
A fruit with a thick, leathery rind, such as a lemon or orange.

HIBERNATION
A resting state like very deep sleep that occurs in some animals in winter.

HOLOPARASITE
A parasitic plant with no leaves that is totally dependent on its host for food.

HORMONE
A signaling molecule produced by a multicellular organism that travels to another part of the organism to change how it functions or behaves.

HOST
An organism that a parasite lives on or inside and feeds on.

HYBRID
The offspring of parents from two different species.

HYDROTROPISM
A change in the growth of a plant in response to water. Roots, for example, grow toward water. (They are positively hydrotropic.)

HYPHA
(Plural hyphae) A very fine thread, or filament, of a fungus.

INFLORESCENCE
A group of flowers on a single stem.

INSULATION
Reduction of heat loss by a layer of air-trapping material, such as hairs.

KEYSTONE SPECIES
A species that plays an important role in an ecosystem and whose removal would alter or endanger the entire ecosystem.

KINGDOM
The highest category into which living things are classified. Examples of kingdoms include the animal kingdom, the plant kingdom, and the fungus kingdom.

LARVA
A young animal that develops into an adult by a complete change in body shape (metamorphosis). A grub is the larva of an insect such as a beetle.

LICHEN
A plantlike partnership between a fungus and a green alga or cyanobacterium.

LIFE CYCLE
The pattern of changes that occurs in each generation of a species.

MEIOSIS
A form of cell division that halves the number of genes in cell nuclei.

MEMBRANE
A thin barrier that separates a cell from its surroundings.

MERISTEM
Plant tissue made up of dividing cells that have the potential to create any part of a plant, including roots, stems, and leaves.

MESOPHYLL
The soft, inner tissue of a leaf between the upper epidermis and lower epidermis.

MICRON
Also called a micrometer, one-millionth of a meter.

MICROORGANISM
A living thing that can be seen only by using a microscope, such as a bacterium.

MICROSCOPIC
A term for something that is very small and can be seen only through a microscope.

MIGRATION
A journey by an animal to a new habitat. Many birds migrate each year between their summer and winter homes.

MINERAL
An inorganic chemical that living things need.

MITOCHONDRION
An organelle found inside the cells of plants, animals, and fungi that is involved in energy production.

MOLD
A fungus that does not produce large fruit bodies. Molds often have green, blue, or black mycelia and spores.

MOLECULE
A chemical unit made of two or more atoms linked together. Nearly all matter is made of molecules.

MONOCOTYLEDON
A plant whose seeds have a single cotyledon (seed leaf). The leaves of a monocotyledon, or monocot, usually have parallel veins.

MUSHROOM
A fungus fruit body that has a cap, stalk, and usually gills.

MUTATION
A sudden change in a gene or group of genes. Mutations may be harmful, but some bring accidental benefits.

MUTUALISM
A close relationship between two species in which both partners benefit.

MYCELIUM
(Plural mycelia) The main body of most fungi, formed from a branching network of hyphae.

MYCOPARASITE
A fungus that lives in or on another fungus and obtains its food from it.

MYCORRHIZA
A partnership between a fungal mycelium and plant roots. Most plants have mycorrhizas.

NECTARY
A gland that secretes a sugary liquid called nectar. Nectaries in flowers attract pollinators such as bees.

NITROGEN FIXATION
The conversion of nitrogen gas from air into a chemical that living things can absorb. Nitrogen is a vital part of all proteins.

NUCLEUS
The control center of a cell. A cell's genes are stored in the nucleus as DNA molecules.

NUTRIENT
Any material taken in by a living thing to sustain life.

ORGANELLE
A tiny structure inside a cell that has a specific function.

ORGANISM
A living thing.

OVARY
An organ in a female animal that produces egg cells, or the part of a flower that contains ovules.

OVULE
The part of a flower that develops into a seed after pollination. Each ovule contains an egg cell.

OXYGEN
A gas that makes up 21 percent of the atmosphere. Most plants generate oxygen from photosynthesis, and living things breathe in the oxygen during respiration.

PALISADE CELL
A type of cell found in a layer under the top surface of a leaf. Palisade cells are important in photosynthesis and contain large numbers of chloroplasts.

PALMATE
Shaped like an open hand with fingers extended. Some leaves are described as palmate.

PARASITE
A living thing that lives on or inside the body of another species, called a host.

PETAL
A leaflike part of a flower that is often large and colorful to attract pollinating animals.

PHLOEM
A system of microscopic pipelines that carry sugars and other nutrients around a plant.

PHOTOSYNTHESIS
The process by which a plant uses the energy in sunlight to create food for itself from water in the soil and carbon dioxide in the air.

PHOTOTROPISM
The response of plants to light. For example, shoots grow toward light (positive phototropism).

PHYTOPLANKTON
Plantlike microorganisms that live in the oceans and fresh water.

PIGMENT
A colored chemical.

PLANKTON
Tiny organisms that float in water.

PNEUMATOPHORE
A root that grows up out of swampy soil and helps a plant obtain oxygen from the air.

POLLEN
A dustlike substance produced by the male parts of flowers. Pollen grains contain male sex cells.

POLLINATION
The transfer of pollen from the male part of a flower to the female part of a flower. Pollination is essential for sexual reproduction in flowers.

POLYMER
A large molecule made from many identical units joined together.

PREY
An animal that is killed and eaten by another animal.

PROBOSCIS
A long, flexible snout or mouthpart. Butterflies and moths use a proboscis to suck nectar from flowers.

PROTEIN
A substance made by all cells that is essential for life. There are millions of different proteins. Some control chemical processes in cells, while others are used as building materials. Spider webs, muscles, and hair are made of protein.

PROTIST
A single-celled organism that has a cell nucleus. Protists make up one of the kingdoms of life.

RECYCLE
To use something again or make it into something new.

REGENERATION
The regrowth of a missing part of an animal or plant.

REPRODUCTION
The production of offspring.

RESPIRATION
A chemical process in cells that involves the release of energy from food molecules.

RHIZOME
A stem that grows horizontally in the ground.

RHIZOMORPH
A stringlike structure formed from the mycelium of a fungus.

RODENT
A mammal with sharp incisor teeth used for gnawing. Rats, mice, and squirrels are all rodents.

SAMARA
A dry, one-seeded fruit with a wing that aids dispersal by wind. Maple trees produce samaras.

SAP
A liquid that transports nutrients in plants.

SAPLING
A young tree.

SCHIZOCARP
A dry, papery fruit that breaks up into single-seeded parts.

SEED
A reproductive structure containing a plant embryo and a food store.

SEPAL
An outer flap that protects a flower bud. Most sepals are green, but some flowers have big, colorful sepals that look like petals.

SEX CELL
A special cell that is involved in sexual reproduction.

SEXUAL REPRODUCTION
Production of offspring by two parents.

SPECIES
A group of living things that can breed together in the wild.

SPERM
A male sex cell.

SPORANGIUM
(Plural sporangia) A structure that produces spores.

SPORE
A cell produced by a fungus or plant that can grow into a new individual.

SPOROPHYTE
A stage in the life cycle of plants that produces spores. All plants have a life cycle that alternates between two stages: a gametophyte and a sporophyte.

STAMEN
A male reproductive organ in a flower. A stamen consists of an anther and a stalk called a filament.

STEM CELLS
Cells that can develop into other types of cells.

STIGMA
The pollen-collecting tip of the female reproductive organ in a flower.

STOMA
(Plural stomata) A microscopic pore in the surface of a leaf.

SUCCULENT
A plant that stores water in thickened, fleshy leaves or stems. Cacti are succulents.

SYMBIOSIS
A close relationship between two types of organisms. A symbiotic relationship that benefits both partners is described as mutualistic.

TAPROOT
A large, main root growing straight down.

TENDRIL
A threadlike growth on the tip of a leaf that is used by climbing plants to hold on to a support.

TEPAL
An outer part of a flower that is not clearly a petal or a sepal.

THALLUS
A leaflike structure in liverworts and lichens or a ball-shaped structure in some fungi.

THYLAKOID
A flattened sac within a chloroplast. Molecules of chlorophyll, the light-capturing pigment used in photosynthesis, are found on the surface of thylakoids.

TOXIN
A poisonous substance.

TRANSPIRATION
The loss of water vapor from a plant through evaporation.

TROPISM
The growth of part of a plant toward or away from light, gravity, or water.

TRUFFLE
The underground fruit body of some types of fungus.

TUBER
An underground food storage organ formed from a swollen stem or root. Potatoes are tubers.

TUNDRA
Cold, treeless areas of land in Earth's polar regions.

VACUOLE
A fluid-filled sac inside a cell. Plant cells typically contain a single large vacuole that helps keep plant tissues firm.

VARIEGATED LEAF
A leaf with different-colored areas due to lack of chlorophyll in some cells.

VASCULAR PLANT
A plant that has transport vessels to carry food and nutrients around it.

VESICLE
A small, fluid-filled sac inside a cell, smaller than a vacuole.

VINE
A plant that climbs other plants or trails along the ground.

WARREN
A network of rabbit burrows.

XYLEM
A plant tissue made up of tubelike cells that carry water. Wood consists of xylem cells.

YEAST
A microscopic, single-celled fungus. People use yeast to make beer and wine.

Index

Acknowledgments

Dorling Kindersley would like to thank the following people for their help with making the book: Duur Aanen, Ali Ashby, Peter Crittenden, Jordan Cuff, Peter Mortimer, Meike Piepenbring, and Tom Rhy-Bishop for their help on content in the Fungus Kingdom chapter; Sam Atkinson, Sreshtha Bhattacharya, Virien Chopra, Upamanyu Das, Aman Kumar, Steve Setford, and Amanda Wyatt for editorial assistance; Tory Gordon-Harris, Clare Joyce, and Naomi Murray for help with scamps; Steve Crozier for picture retouching; Jaypal Chauhan for DTP assistance; Subhashree Bharati and Simon Mumford for cartographic assistance; Saloni Singh for the jacket; Katie John for proofreading; and Helen Peters for the index.

Smithsonian Enterprises:
Matthew Fleming, Smithsonian Gardens Horticulturist;
Avery Naughton, Licensing Coordinator, Licensed Publishing;
Paige Towler, Editorial Lead, Licensed Publishing;
Jill Corcoran, Senior Director, Licensed Publishing;
Brigid Ferraro, Vice President, Business Development and Licensing;
Carol LeBlanc, President

Special thanks to Kealy Gordon

The publisher would like to thank the following for their kind permission to reproduce their photographs:

(Key: a-above; b-below/bottom; c-centre; f-far; l-left; r-right; t-top)

123RF.com: fotoplanner 12cra (tree), hmalny 13cra (DIOECIOUS), microgen 86clb (Mangrove), Sura Nualpradid 113tr, olegdudko 83tr, Vassiliy Prikhodko 95clb, schan 53bc, Pavel Timofeev / scorpp 133cla, Oksana Tkachuk 134tc, utima 83clb, Gert-Jan van Vliet 8c, 26tr; **Alamy Stock Photo:** agefotostock / J M Barres 178bc, 185tc, Keith Allen 26l, Sally Anderson 167tr, Anka Agency International / Anka Petrovic 140tl, Auk Archive 43cra, Eyal Bartov 94bc, BIOSPHOTO / Bruno Mathieu 193br, David Massemin / Biosphoto 26bl, Denis Bringard / Biosphoto 85cr, Franco Banfi / Biosphoto 32clb, Frank Deschandol & Philippe Sabine / Biosphoto 190-191, Michel Loup / Biosphoto 32tr, Gerry Bishop 54-55, Sabena Jane Blackbird 159br, blickwinkel / F. Fox 15cla, 15bl, blickwinkel / F. Hecker 108tc, 196cb, blickwinkel / Franz 140bl, blickwinkel / H. Bellmann / F. Hecker 33cb, blickwinkel / Hecker 197crb, blickwinkel / Jagel 21bc (cone), blickwinkel / McPHOTO / HRM 136tl, blickwinkel / McPHOTO / MAS 75ca, M & J Bloomfield 107ca, Maksym Bondarchuk 24cl (tree), Charcrit Boonsom 147tc, Botanic World 24cl, Steffen Hauser / botanikfoto 31bl, 151bc, Botany vision 28br, Mark Bourdillon 25br, John Bracegirdle 107bc, Buiten-Beeld / Michel Geven 150clb, Stuart Burford 141crb (Bonnet), John Burnham 155cl, Nigel Cattlin 51br, 129c, 185tl, 192tl, CharlinX USA Collection 11cl, Helmut Corneli 25tl, Zoltn Csipke 117crb, DanitaDelimont.com 148bc, Andrew Darrington 192br, David Tipling Photo Library 105crb, Barry Davis 137tc, Igor Dibrovin 155br, Faris Fitriano 193bl, David Fleetham 115cb, Florapix 149cb, Flowerphotos 30cr, Corey Ford 21fbr, Tim Gainey 21bl, 22bl, Bob Gibbons 116tr, Andreas Harbarth 25c, Frank Hecker 33tr, 108ca, Rieger Bertrand / Hemis.fr 41br, Robert Henno 126cla, Brian Hird (Wildflowers) 87cr, Michael Holloway 25tr, Oliver Thompson-Holmes 159bc (Dung), Image Source / Gregory S. Paulson 122cl, imageBROKER / Adelheid Nothegger 23cr, imageBROKER / Christian Htter 27cr, imageBROKER / Fabian von Poser 194cla, imageBROKER / Farina Grassmann 166c, imageBROKER / FB-Rose

149br, imageBROKER / Guenter Fischer 99crb, 177tc, imageBROKER / Hans Lang 192tr, imageBROKER / Juergen & Christine Sohns 137br, imageBROKER / Stefan Huwiler 116clb, Barbara Jean 178br, Mark A. Johnson 94br, Don Johnston 94clb, Dominic Jones 21fbl, Juniors Bildarchiv / R30 85br, Juniors Bildarchiv GmbH / juniors@wildlife / Maier, R. 30br, Juniors Bildarchiv GmbH / Schulz, H. 167bc, Olga Khomyakova 10r, Henri Koskinen 167c, 182bl, Lev Kropotov 20r, Nurlan Kulcha 87crb, H Lansdown 106cl, Henrik Larsson 21c, Ken Leslie 22cra, Iophius 127cra, Wanda Lotus 75br, Johnny Madsen 117tr, mauritius images GmbH / David & Micha Sheldon 17c, mauritius images GmbH / Gabi Wolf 182cla, John McKenna 136bl, migstock 148br, MigstockRF 91clb (Potato), Ch'ien Lee / Minden Pictures 124bl, Mark Moffett / Minden Pictures 119cra, 194bl, 195bc, Mitsuhiko Imamori / Minden Pictures 194br, Norbert Wu / Minden Pictures 115br, Paul Bertner / Minden Pictures 195cra, Piotr Naskrecki / Minden Pictures 120clb (Ant), Sean Crane / Minden Pictures 117tc, Sumio Harada / Minden Pictures 197tr, Ben Molyneux 24bl, Monkey Biscuit 146ca, Dawn Monrose 129bl, Graham Moon 155tc, William Mullins 77tc, Nature Picture Library / Alex Hyde 69bc (Beetle), 150br, Nature Picture Library / Chris Mattison 27bc, 28l, 91crb, Nature Picture Library / Kim Taylor 194clb, Nature Picture Library / Nick Upton 15crb, Roberto Nistri 29bc, Panther Media GmbH / emer 150bl, Shaun Pascoe 112bl, Stefano Paterna 129clb, Alberto Perer 111ca, Picture Partners 17clb, 134br (Plant), Morley Read 120cl, REDA &CO srl / Paroli Galperti 148tr, robertharding / Tony Waltham 130cr, 149tr, Gina Rodgers 118-119, Manfred Ruckszio 8cl, 22tl, Elsa dos Santos 73cb, Nigel Sawyer 22bc, Science History Images 198ca, Science History Images / Photo Researchers 49cra, Alfio Scisetti 23br, 140r, Andy Selinger 147bc, Adrian Sherratt 141crb (Naga Viper), Martin Shields 129br, Hakan Soderholm 171bc, Vincius Souza 120bl, Matthew Taylor 82ca, tbkmedia.de 17cl, Erich Teister 31bc, The Picture Art Collection 61tc, P Tomlins 149bc, Universal Images Group North America LLC / DeAgostini / C. Dani 21bc, Universal Images Group North America LLC / Medicimage 129clb (Wolfsbane), Greg Vaughn 176br, Deborah Vernon 84cla, Valery Voennyy 24cla, Dimitrios Volovotsis 193tr, Jon G. Fuller / VWPics 99ca, WaterFrame_fba 33cra, Kuki Waterstone 87cra, Tony Watson 155tr, Chris Howes / Wild Places Photography 179bc, Robert McGouey / Wildlife 104bc, Ray Wilson 17cr, Robert Wyatt 27l, Zoonar / Manfred Ruckszio 141bc, Zoonar / Tarabalu 155tc (Cauliflower), 193cra; **Bill Anderson:** 138-139; **Avalon:** Luca Invernizzi Tettoni 30bc; **Steve Axford:** 166cl, 167c; **Jacobus J Boomsma:** 195bl; **Depositphotos Inc:** Ale-ks 69br; **Dorling Kindersley:** Chris Gibson 144br, Paolo Mazzei 197cra, Ruth Jenkinson / RGB Research Limited 39ca, 39cb, 39br, 39bc (Iron), Frank Greenaway / Royal Botanic Gardens, Kew 144bl; **Dr. Ernesto Weil, Dept. Marine Sciences, U. of Puerto Rico:** 186cr; **Dreamstime.com:** Aga7ta 106cra, Alexan24 91c, John Anderson 11tr, Andreusk 13cra (Grass), 24cra (Grass), 24clb, 136crb, Anest 16cla, Arttrongphap8 141bl, Paul Atkinson 137cl, Atman 24cra, Aviahuismanphotography 123cb, Dmytro Balkhovitin 13cra (grapes), Bat09mar 144clb, Arpan Bhatia 86bl, Thomas Biegalski 13cra (Maple), Karen Black 75bc, Maciej Bledowski 147bl, Maksym Bondarchuk 136cr, Olga Bosharova 87cb, Marc Bruxelle 53br, Buriy 13cra (Marigold), Oksana Byelikova 108bl, Cameramannz 95br, Wagner Campelo 33cla, Carmentianya 127cb, Cathywithers 75cla, Przemyslaw Ceglarek 193c, Chabkc 195crb, Jean Paul Chassenet 72bc, Chernetskaya 83cb, 132clb (avocado), Jim Cumming 105bc, Cynoclub 151tr, Denicamp 104tc, Design56 83c, Nadiia Diachenko 56clb, Dndavis 28bc, Dndavis 69bl, Le Thuy Do 13cra (pine), Domnitsky 132crb, Dtvphoto 23bl, Jinying Du 113br, Alena Dudaeva 13cb, Oleg Dudko 56cla, Catherine Eckert 184bl, 184clb, Elenarostunova 25cra, Empire331 155ca

(Exidia), Flynt 90br, Sergey Frolov 24crb, Peter Hermes Furian 24bl (Beechnuts), 39bl, Brian Glowacki 94cr, Elena Grishina 90c, Helga11 20crb, Jeffrey Holcombe 12ca, 107bl, Artem Honchariuk 134br, Hotshotsworldwide 98tc, Irinaroibu 12cra, Jdmfoto 106cra (acorns), Jessicahyde 155ca, Juliengrondin 95br (tree), Sirirak Kaewgorn 31br, Venus Kaewyoo 13cra (foxglove), Kagab4 151cla, Evgeny Karandaev 141cra, Katerynabibro 83cr (raspberry), Kato000008 111cb, Khaofofa 136bc, Sergey Kichigin 170bc, Tomasz Klejdysz 196clb (fungus), Kateryna Kon 186cra, Alexandr Kornienko 145br, Yuriy Kovtun 116cb, Kpalimski 95crb (tree), Lev Kropotov 144cra, Ksena2009 13bc (wheat), Ksushsh 38cb, Anna Kucherova 133cb, Vera Kudareva 179bc (rock), Tamara Kulikova 22br, 24ca, Nikolai Kurzenko 167cr, Lcswart 31ca, Lenazajchikova 90tr, Lianem 147cra, Luckydoor 13cla, Robyn Mackenzie 143tr, Paul Maguire 56c, Mahira 82cra, Lyudmila Makhova 184cb, Martingraf 104crb, Matauw 79crb, Jim Mcdowall 150bc, Mursalin . 185crb, Nanthm 198crb (Juice), Natador 11cr (mushrooms), Nbvf 140cla, Carlos Neto 136br, Inga Nielsen / Inganielsen 111bl, Npdotcom 148c, Nurmahidah - 99bc, Febrika Nurmalasari 12ca (funaria), Okemppainen 179br, Iuliia Panova 199cla, Iuliia Panova 146bl, Nipaporn Panyacharoen 144crb, Paulpaladin 141crb (Chilli), Simona Pavan 151clb, Tomas Pavelka 39bc, Martin Pelanek 196ca, Edward Phillips 95cb, Phive2015 198ca (Bread), Photodynamx 158clb, Anna Kucherova / Photomaru 144bc, Jay Pierstorff 103cra, Karunakaran Parameswaran Pillai 140clb, Cornelia Pithart 52bl, Pixura 133clb, Pnwnature 178bc (Crustose), Pawel Potemkowski 13cra (Hazel), Pproman 12cb (moss), Ppy2010ha 198crb, Glenn Price 141crb (Jolokia), Frans Rombout 28br, 82bc, 134ca, Manfred Ruckszio 15bc, Ghassan Safi 135bl, Saletomic 83cla, Galina Samoylovich 164tr, Elena Schweitzer 132cr, 132cb, Alfio Scisetti 22bl (Peas), 30cl, 145cl, Seawaters 140ca, Victoria Shibut 12cb, Serhiy Shullye 135c, Benjamin Simeneta 135cl, Olya Solodenko 29br, Sommaiphoto 13bl, Spaxia 83ca, Srekap 104tr, Bidouze St¥_phane 94bl (Forest), Anton Starikov 82bl, 141bc (Cumin), Andreea Stefan 140bc, Strixcode 133clb (Cola), suriya silsaksom khunaspix@yahoo.co.th 148-149b, Viroj Suttisima 132cr (Sugarcane), Abdelmoumen Taoutaou 184ca, Maxim Tatarinov 141br, Thawats 69bc, Thecrossroads 133ca, Tissiana 11cl (Algae), Jamlong Tunkaew 135br, Valentyn75 132crb (oil), Serg_velusceac 21tr, Vily6075 151br, Joao Virissimo 141crb, Vasiliy Vishnevskiy 106bl, Ostancov Vladislav 15tc, Volodymyrkrasyuk 141cra, Han Van Vonno 135r, Jrgen Wackenhut 31cl, Christian Weinktz 166-167c, Willypd 155cr, Wirestock 133bc, Wojphoto 31r, Bjrn Wylezich 39cb, Yuryz 185br, Zayacksz 128tr, Zerbor 144c, Zerbor 13cra; **Jørgen Eilenberg:** Jørgen Eilenberg 189tr; **First Nature:** Elaine Hagget, Coedpoeth, N. Wales 177cl; **Food and Agriculture Organization of the United Nations:** FAOSTAT. All Land Use Data, 2019. Latest update: 2019. Accessed: 2023 Hannah Ritchie and Max Roser, November 2019 / Our World in Data | https://ourworldindata.org/ 133cr, FAOSTAT. World production of crops by commodity group. Latest update: 2020. Accessed: 2023. https://doi.org/10.4060/cb1329en-fig21 133tr; **Getty Images:** Cavan Images 20l, Eskay Lim / EyeEm 82crb, Robert Kneschke / EyeEm 150tl, imageBROKER / Joachim Moebes Claudino 145cr, imageBROKER / Peter Giovannini 32-33b, ds3ann / Imazins 145tr, Moment / ak_phuong 151ca, Moment / MirageC 83br, Moment / Pakin Songmor 129ca, Darrell Gulin / Photodisc 29bl, Stone / Ed Reschke 16br, Stone / Rosemary Calvert 82br, Andia / Universal Images Group 109tc; **Getty Images / iStock:** ALEAIMAGE 133cla (Cocoa), Khalid Alhelali 94br (Dessert), ArendTrent 113cra, Petar Belobrajdic 168-169, CathyDoi 95crb, CathyKeifer 123cra, Czgur 129cla (Chilli), designsstock 83cr, Devonyu 199crb, DigiTrees

8cr, 24tr, domnicky 198cb (Cheese), E+ / JohnGollop 198cra, E+ / Ron and Patty Thomas 102cla, E+ / Schroptschop 146cla, E+ / slobo 83bl, E+ / Yoela 132br, frank600 11cr, Iamraffnovais 91clb, Pannarai Nak-im 33br, Jaap2 170br, Chidanand M. 24br, magicflute002 12br, Marccophoto 133cb (field), marekuliasz 94bl, Ivan Marjanovic 116bl, MortenChr 196bl, myshkovsky 82cb, proxyminder 118cra, robynmac 198cra (Mushrooms), Elizabeth M. Ruggiero 94ca, Cristi Savin 185cra, schulzie 159bc, studiocasper 133ca (coffee), Tanja_G 154tr, visual7 141cr, wwing 79cra; **Kenneth Wurdack:** 177bc; **The Met Office:** UK © British Crown copyright 107tr; **Michael D. Guiry, seaweed.ie:** 15cra; **naturepl.com:** Ross Hoddinott / 2020VISION 107cla, Neil Anderson 107cra, Sylvain Cordier 186tr, Adrian Davies 182cl, Paul Harcourt Davies 27tc, 177bc (Orchid), Georgette Douwma 114bl, Juergen Freund 116cla, Alex Hyde 70-71, 115tc, 172-173, Chien Lee 100-101, Thomas Marent 177tr, Chris Mattison 126bl, Chris O'Reilly 17tr, Andy Sands 109bl, Warwick Sloss 112clb, Nick Upton 192bl, Staffan Widstrand / Wild Wonders of China 75bl; **Dr. Scot Nelson:** www.flickr.com / photos / scotnelson / 15521494223 / in / photostream 184cra; **Photos © 2022 Kenji Matsuura:** 177crb; **Photo Scala, Florence:** Digital Image 2021 © MOMA, New York / Kris Graves 199t; **Science Image, CSIRO:** Dr Alex Hyatt, CSIRO Livestock Industries' Australian Animal Health Laboratory (AAHL) 155clb; **Science Photo Library:** Biophoto Associates 43cra, Dr Jeremy Burgess 90cb, 128cr, 150cra, Dennis Kunkel Microscopy 46clb, Eye Of Science 123ca, Frank Fox 12clb, Frank Fox 18-19, Steve Gschmeissner 14tl, 14bl, 14cra, Gerd Guenther 120clb, Tommaso Guicciardini 146bc, Lewis Houghton 198bl, Steve Lowry 124cla, Merlintuttle.org 117tr (Bat), Dennis Kunkel Microscopy 171crb, Marek Mis 129tr, Mona Lisa Production / Thierry Berrod 112cl, Andy Sands / Nature Picture Library 156-157, Emanuele Biggi / Nature Picture Library 187tr, Lawrence Naylor 114clb, Susumu Nishinaga 66tr, Martin Oeggerli 118cl, Power And Syred 14br, 123tl, 129cla, Dr Morley Read 189crb, Bjorn Rorslett 66bc, 66bc (Silverweed), Viktor Sykora 137bl, Us Fisheries And Wildlife Service / Ryan Von Linden, New York Department Of Environmental Conservation 186cl, Dr Keith Wheeler 43cr, Paul Whitehill 23t; **Shutterstock:** Setiani Antari 134bc, Yuriy Bartenev 16tr, Jon Benedictus 193cl, Gerry Bishop 189cr, BridgetSpencerPhoto 84cla (Bird), Chutima Chaimratana 141tc, CKHatten 154-155b, COLOA Studio 134cr, conscarsch 26-27b, Ethan Daniels 86clb, Denys.Kutsevalov 98c, Fotofermer 198crb (Can), Petr Ganaj 13bc, Petr Ganaj 104clb, guentermanaus 27br, Bess Hamitii 108cb, hvoya 91br, juerginho 29tr, Henri Koskinen 171bl, Marina Lohrbach 13cra (ficus), Dusan Matousek 167br, mbarredo 99tc, John Navajo 166bl, perfectloop 198cb, Supee Purato 34-35, Peter Rockstroh 149tl, Vitalina Rybakova 137cr, scubaluna 111tl, SIM ONE 11cla, Spalnic 198cra (Sauce), Akepong Srichaichana 141cra, Super Prin 118tr, susanto art 13crb, Tristan Tan 29cb, Pond Thananat 13cra (Cherry), Vadvenn 129tl, Tom Viggars 90cl, weinkoetz 196clb, Mike Workman 166cb; **TurboSquid:** 3d_molier International 1, 2-3, 122-123, 124-125, 160-161 (branch), asag3D 4-5, 162-163, macrox 98-99c, NiceModels 72-73, 200, Tornado Studio 158-159, 160-161; **U.S. Geological Survey:** Debra A. Willard 79br; **Ian R. Walker:** 177c; **Our World in Data | https://ourworldindata.org/:** Hannah Ritchie and Max Roser, November 2019 133cr; **WorldClimate (www.worldclimate.com):** 98bl

All other images © Dorling Kindersley

DK WHAT WILL YOU DISCOVER NEXT?

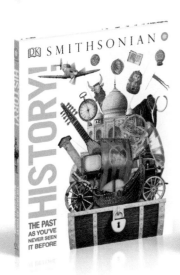   

DK For the curious